本成果受"北京高校高精尖学科项目（中国语言文学）"支持，特此致谢！

韵律语法研究

Studies in Prosodic Grammar

第九辑
Volume 9

主编　冯胜利　马秋武

北京语言大学出版社
BEIJING LANGUAGE AND CULTURE
UNIVERSITY PRESS

《韵律语法研究》

Studies in Prosodic Grammar

主 办 北京语言大学
Sponsor: Beijing Language and Culture University

承 办 北京语言大学语言科学院章黄学术理论研究所
Editorial Office: Institute of Zhang-Huang Academic Theories, Faculty of Linguistic Sciences, Beijing Language and Culture University

编委会（Editorial Board）

目　录

CONTENTS

Word Stress and the Music of Mandarin Morphology

Christoph Harbsmeier (何莫邪)

Abstract: This paper provides a detailed account of early Western systematic studies of word stress in Chinese, from late Qing times onwards. The modern technical literature is vast. Professional summaries are many, and this paper can only provide a critical survey of a few selected modern works on word stress in Mandarin Chinese that is influential in the West. The paper informally defines and illustrates a number of general rules that appear to govern the placement of stress in Mandarin Chinese. Since stress varies not only between dialects of Mandarin, but also between speakers of the same dialect, it is suggested that on-line MANDARIN AUDIO IDIOLECT DICTIONARY (MAID) may come in usefully as a basis for the objective quantified study of the stress systems in extensive spontaneous speech from at least one pristine Beijing dialect of Chinese. The impact of conversational context on word stress is left open, since the material in MAID consists of monologues.

Keywords: stress; word stress; morphology; history of sinology; Chinese linguistics

"For studies of isolated words, such as minimal pairs of noun versus verb, a desk dictionary or a researcher's own intuitions may be sufficient (Hyman, 1977: 85)."[1] For languages like Mandarin Chinese such expectations are not met: none of the published Chinese-Chinese or Chinese-English desk dictionaries distinguish between pairs of noun versus verb like bǎwò' (把握) "to grasp" and bǎ'wò (把握) "a grasp" in the way that all desk dictionaries of English distinguish between *condu'ct* and *co'nduct*. My claim in this paper is that the difference is not between the languages English and Chinese but between the lexicographers of English and of Chinese. At least since the *Royal Dictionary Abridged* published in 1700, word stress-accent has tended to be indicated in monolingual English dictionaries. *Condu'ct* and *co'nduct* have not tended to be confused in the lexicography of English. The latest *Modern Chinese Dictionary* (《现代汉语词典 Xiàndài Hànyǔ Cídiǎn》) still treats bǎwò' "to grasp" and bǎ'wò "a grasp" as exactly homophonous. In that desk dictionary *par excellence* 不行 bùxí'ng "it is not OK" is treated as exactly homophonous with bù'xíng (步行) "go on foot". Remarkably, the situation is the same for all the many dozens of other dictionaries of Mandarin Chinese that I own or have seen.[2]

Mandarin Chinese, based on Peking pronunciation, has been called a stress-prominent language ever since the 19th century, as we shall see below. But the most useful reference grammar of modern Chinese that I know is *Modern Chinese Descriptive Grammar* (《现代汉语描写语法 Xiàndài Hànyǔ Miáoxiě Yǔfǎ》) (2010) edited by Zhang Bin. Unfortunately, the book deals in commendable detail with morphology, but it has nothing to say about the matter of predictable word-stress in morphology which is my concern in this paper. *A Comprehensive Grammar of the Chinese Language* (《汉语语法长编 Hànyǔ Yǔfǎ ChángBiān》) by Shi Yuzhi has a chapter on "phonetics", but

---

[1] Hyman also finds no dominant stress placement in Mandarin. "In the following cases either I or Ruhlen (R) were not able to ascertain any dominant stress placement. …: Chinese: Mandarin (tone).", see "On the Nature of Linguistic Stress", in Larry Hyman ed., *Studies in Stress and Accent,* Los Angeles: University of Southern California Press, 1977, p. 67. I have found this paper uniquely useful for its admirable general range, clarity and theoretical economy of analysis.
[2] In the essay below, I shall mainly present some not often discussed evidence published in the West. Chinese contributions have been expertly surveyed for example in the work of Feng (2016). See also the helpful bibliography Třísková (2020).

this important, thoughtful and wonderfully detailed work basically has nothing to say about the role of stress in Chinese.

My chosen way of marking stress may offend many scholars since it is customary to attach stress to the whole syllable in all current notations. But whereas it is common in general linguistics to take the syllable as the typical stress-bearing unit (Hyman, 1985), I find that stress – like tone – typically resides in the main vowel of a syllable, so that in liǎ'ojiě the main vowel /a/ bears both the tone and the stress: the tonal contour I find is overwhelmingly realized over /a/ and not over /i/ or /o/. Therefore I find it is natural to add the stress-marker after the main vowel in all cases.

1. Some Notes on Stress in the History of Sinology

Before entering a detailed discussion of the facts of stress in Mandarin, it may be useful to survey briefly some features of recent history of the analysis of stress in Mandarin handbooks and dictionaries of the world.

1.1   Early Foreign Scholars (1890–1920)

The prominence of stress in Peking Mandarin Chinese has been recognized by a number of scholars since the 19th century Sanskrit scholar and sinologist Arendt (1894). Three of his books pay persistent careful attention to stress throughout, and they are replete with original observations based on extensive fieldwork in Northern China. Seidel (1901) pays special attention to stress, and not surprisingly Bernhard Karlgren was not the kind of linguist to overlook the central theoretical as well as pedagogical importance of the system of stress in Peking Mandarin. (Karlgren, 1918)

1.2   Early Chinese Scholars

1.2.1   Fang Chaoying and the Stress-assigned Textbook

Among Chinese educationalists none less than the redoubtable Fang Chaoying (房兆楹 Fáng Zhàoyíng) (1908–1985) was the leading advocate of crucial importance of stress-assignment even in elementary teaching of Chinese. Together with Charles F.

Hockett (1916–2000), he published a textbook that assigned stress patterns wherever possible to all words. (Hockett & Fang, 1944) His summary on stress is of considerable value because we have (and I have listened to) extensive tapes of the speaker on whom Hockett's observations will most probably have been based:

"The stress-contour of a mesosegment consists of varying degrees of prominence (produced largely by volume, but partly by length and speed) of its constituent microsegments…The most prominent microsegment in a mesosegment bears loud stress (/'/ before the microsegment). The remaining microsegments bear quiet stress (/,/), or else no stress at all (unmarked; "zero stress" if that terminology is preferred). In addition, in macrosegments bearing certain intonations (e.g., /./), it is necessary to specify one of the loud stresses in the macrosegment as the nuclear stress, the stressed element at which the intonation turns. The nuclear stress is often, but not always, the last loud stress in the macrosegment. Since its location is not predictable, nuclear stress must be recognized as phonemically distinct from loud stress. No separate symbol is here provided, however, because none of the forms cited require distinctive marking of the nuclear stress in contrast to loud stresses. Finally, in some cases one finds an extra-loud contrastive stress (/"/) instead of a loud stress; further intonational analysis may eliminate this as a separate stress-level."(Hockett, 1947)

1.2.2　Fred Wang Fangyu and His Dictionary with Stress Registered

Fred Wang Fangyu (王方宇Wáng Fāngyǔ) (1913–1997) compiled the War Department edition of the *Dictionary of Spoken Chinese* (Wang, 1966), of which I have the unpublished 1945 edition which carefully registers stress wherever possible. As a matter of principle, this textbook provides no characters, except at one point in the introduction where the following phrase is quoted in classical Chinese. "Speech is the voice of the heart; writing serves to record words" (言为心声，文以记言 Yán wéi xīnshēng, wén yǐ jì yán). The first part of this is proverbially famous, but the very important second part I have yet to find in Pre-Tang literature.

Fred Wang Fangyu paid a visit to Oslo to support my efforts there in paying proper attention to stress in the teaching of Chinese. And in Oslo he told the moving story of how Yale University Press insisted on cutting out all his stress markings from the War

Department dictionary to produce the public edition of the *Dictionary of Spoken Chinese* to conform with universal lexicographic practice of disregarding the regular stress-patterns in Mandarin Chinese.

1.2.3   Chao Yuanren and His Deplorable Practice on Stress

"Most Chinese dialects have a rhythm similar to that of French, in which syllables succeed one another in a flat-footed fashion, except for enclitic particles. Mandarin, on the other hand, is one of the few Chinese dialects which is a mixture of French rhythm and English rhythm." (Chao, 1948/1961: 26)

In his justly famous *Grammar of Spoken Chinese*, Chao (1968: 37–38) writes:

"Some writers (for example, Hockett Peip Phon, 256) set up a medium degree of stress between the normal and the weak. For instance:

(1) *Jeh bush   ,kuu'gua, yee bush   tyan.gua, jiow sh i-joong   'tyan ,gua.*

　　Zhè bù shì kǔguā,   yě bù shì tiánguā, jiù shì yī zhǒng tiánguā.

　　（这不是苦瓜，也不是甜瓜，就是一种甜瓜。）

'This is not bitter-melon (Momordica charantia), nor sweetmelon (Cumumis melon), it's just a kind of sweet melon', where apparently the second *tyan* has normal stress and the second *gua*, though less stressed, is not completely neutral and weak...My treatment of such cases is to regard *'tyan, gua* 'sweet melon' as having contrasting stress: *"tyan 'gua*. Since stress is relative, putting a contrasting stress is often physically equivalent to putting an average normal stress on the syllable to be contrasting-stressed and reducing the degree of other normal stresses," "...another reason for not recognizing a phonemic medium stress is the difficulty of obtaining agreement among native speakers of Peiping in a significant proportion of cases tested, as against the occurrence of the neutral tone, on which there is a good degree of agreement."

Chao Yuanren's skepticism is based on passionately careful observation. And as Chao Yuanren always focuses on the essence of all questions of stress in Mandarin, namely the question whether – and exactly where – stress is phonemic and systemic or not. Stress in Modern Standard Chinese is highly context-sensitive. Contrastive stress will affect word stress throughout. But this is true of all languages I know of and it does not affect the question of stress in the citation form of words.

By far the majority of Chinese and Western dictionaries follow Chao Yuanren's deplorable practice. However, Wang Fangyu's *Dictionary of Spoken Chinese* (War Department) (1945), Oshanin (1952), Isaenko (1957), Kuraishi (1963), Oshanin (1983–1984) and Švarný (1998–2000) systematically indicate stress patterns, and it is very interesting indeed to see how often they do differ among each other on the question where exactly the stress is in a given word. Even between the two versions of the *Dictionary of Spoken Chinese* there are many interesting differences. (For our purposes the War Department version of 1945 is superior because it distinguishes words without a distinction in stress between the constituent syllables from those words which have standard second syllable stress.) This does tend to support Chao Yuanren's skepticism. At the very least we must conclude that there is no rigid and pervasive grammatical regime on stress in Chinese. Chao (1968: 360) does generalize: "From the rules of relative stress, it follows that a compound has the main stress on the last non-neutral syllable." This is certainly a useful observation, but the facts are more complex and much more interesting than suggested here.

1.3 Current Scholars

1.3.1 Lyu Shuxiang and *Qingzhongyin*

Lyu Shuxiang conducts a stimulating survey of some rules for "light and heavy pronunciation" (or *qingzhongyin*) in verbal compounds along the following lines:

1. The specification of the direction after a verb is unstressed, for example: fàngxià (放下), dàishàng (戴上), shājìnqù (杀进去), fàngchūqù (放出去), sònghuí (送回), lākāi (拉开).

2. Transitive verbs with non-pronominal objects have light readings.

3. In constructions like mǎibudào/mǎidedào (买不到 / 买得到), the main verb is unstressed and the stress is on the final dào (到).

4. When negated by méi (没) in contrastive contexts as in Xiěle bàntiān méi xiě chūlái (写了半天没写出来), the lái (来) is obligatorily stressed, but lái (来) is not stressed in differently contrastive contexts such as Wǒ xiǎng xiě kěshì méi xiě chūlái (我想写可是没写出来) where stress has to be on xiě (写).

These observations have been an important inspiration for the present work on stress patterns as presented below. (Lyu, 1980: 38–41)

Any respectable dictionary of English would need to indicate stress in the pronunciation of words, and so will any respectable dictionary of German or Russian. It is remarkable that among the many thousands of dictionaries of Standard Chinese published in the People's Republic of China, including those in Hong Kong SAR and Taiwan Province, not a single dictionary indicates stress (or indeed the pronunciation of words using the International Phonetic Alphabet).

It is instructive to observe the progress in Chinese linguistics as it manifests itself in teaching material on Mandarin Chinese. Observing local dictionaries and local teaching material one might well conclude that Peking Mandarin Chinese has ceased to be a stress-prominent language. Stress was clearly found to play a highly significant role by a linguist like Bernhard Karlgren, and it has become noticed and then defocused in more recent teaching material for Mandarin Chinese.

The variety of phonetic realizations of a syllable under different conditions comes out nicely in the pronunciation of 子 zǐ in the following:

1. 鱼子 yúzǐ

   "roe"; lengthened elaborate stress (on the head of the construction)

2. 妻子 qīzǐ

   "wife and children"; full tonal pronunciation

3. 老子 Lǎozǐ

   "proper name: 老子 Lǎozǐ"; weak tonal pronunciation

4. 孩子 háizi

   reduced atonal pronunciation close to "ze" with a very short "e"

5. 妻子 qīzi

   modern suffixed noun: wife; regular atonal pronunciation, close to "z" with very little of a vowel following it

1.3.2   Monique Hoa and Peking Accentuation

Monique Hoa's monograph on accentuation in Peking speech from 1983 makes an entirely original contribution to the study of stress in that she makes it very clear how assignment of stress in sentences depends on antecedent determination of immediate constituent structure, and that stress inscribes itself on the syntactic tree, as it were. Thus in Zhōngguó rén (中国人) the stress within the word Zhōngguó (中国) is on a separate level of immediate constituent analysis. In this way she enables one to assign stress at different levels in one and the same tree structure. I have learnt a great deal from her in the first chapter of my *Modern Chinese Analytic Syntax*, vol. 1 (Harbsmeier, 1992). Monique Hoa's remarkable book contains the best survey on pre-1980 literature on stress in Mandarin Chinese that I have seen. Since the book is in French, it is disregarded everywhere by Chinese linguists. As is the extensive Russian literature, mainly by students of the inimitable and unforgettable Professor Nikolay A. Speshnev of St Petersburg who spent much of his life bringing to life the delicacies of the rhythm and prosody of his second mother tongue, Peking Chinese.

1.3.3   Stress Assignment Problems Raised by Lin Yen-Hwei

Lin (2007: 222) sets out her account of stress in Chinese by stating: "SC is a tone language and English is a stress language."[①] She goes on: "However, when each syllable in a word as a full tone as in most words in SC, it is not clear which syllable is stressed." (2007: 224) The problems around stress assignment in Standard Chinese are also surveyed in Chen (2000) and particularly in Duanmu (2000/2007: 129–157) and later articles. All of these linguists emphasize the controversial nature of stress assignment in Chinese. None of these three authors set their starting point on an extensive study of those minimal pairs distinguished by stress patterns only on the basis of an appropriate basic corpus. For the question of stress is no longer a matter of abstract typology (Is Chinese a stress language or not), nor of phonological analysis and phonetic description only. To the extent that we can identify minimal pairs distinguished by stress only, the question of stress becomes a crucial part of the systematic semantics of lexicography and even of the grammar of the language.

The main Modern Chinese grammars and dictionaries written in English have this in common, namely, they very systematically disregard all matters of stress.

---

① "SC" is "Standard Chinese" in Lin (2007).

1.3.4   Duanmu San and Nonhead Stress Rule

On a much higher theoretical level of analysis than that aspired to in this essay, Duanmu San has raised fundamental issues of linguistic analysis around stress in Mandarin that appear to be of great interest to theoretical linguists.

At one point Duanmu (2000) proposes a general rule for assigning compound and phrasal stress, as follows:

Nonhead Stress Rule

In the syntactic structure [X XP] (or [XP X]), where X is the syntactic head and XP the syntactic nonhead, XP should be stressed.

This is a useful rule and we shall see in detail below to what extent it covers the observed facts of Peking Mandarin.[①]

2. MAID: Mandarin Audio Idiolect Dictionary

Word stress differs widely across the varieties of the Mandarin Chinese language. Discussing stress in Mandarin quite generally, disregarding these profound differences between the dialects of Mandarin is in my opinion deeply disingenuous. Stress-wise Peking Mandarin, Nanjing Mandarin, and Taiwan Mandarin should not be discussed under one system, even though there turn out to be more commonalities than sometimes suggested.

Even within today's current Peking Mandarin, there is again a noticeable variety owing to the local non-Mandarin dialect background of the immigrant majority in the population.

One would like to test one's observations on stress in Peking Mandarin NOT on self-observation by speakers of Mandarin so much as on the objectively measured phonetic analysis of the natural and spontaneous linguistic practice of such native speakers of the Peking dialect little affected by other dialect substrata in the family or

---

① Compare, for example, hǎoré'n "good person" versus huà'irén "evil person". Moreover, as we shall see the problems of lexical stress versus stress-in-context are considerable in Mandarin.

social background.[①] Having texts read out for one by such speakers does not produce the pristine evidence that one is ideally looking for.

Ideally, one would like to take as one's starting point the systematic analysis of a large and maximally diverse spontaneously produced free corpus of an idiolect by such a local-based speaker of Peking Mandarin. Preferably with video documentation of the typical gestural repertoire that plays an important part in any dialect.

Unfortunately, we do not have any such extensive video corpus. What we do have, and what I have made available on-line, is the Mandarin Audio Idiolect Dictionary (**MAID**). The crucial contribution of this database is the provision of objective quantifiable measurability of stress and prosody of Mandarin Chinese words and idiomatic expressions. Stress judgments are often contested. MAID was conceived to allow us to move from subjective impression concerning stress to systematic quantified measurement and analysis.

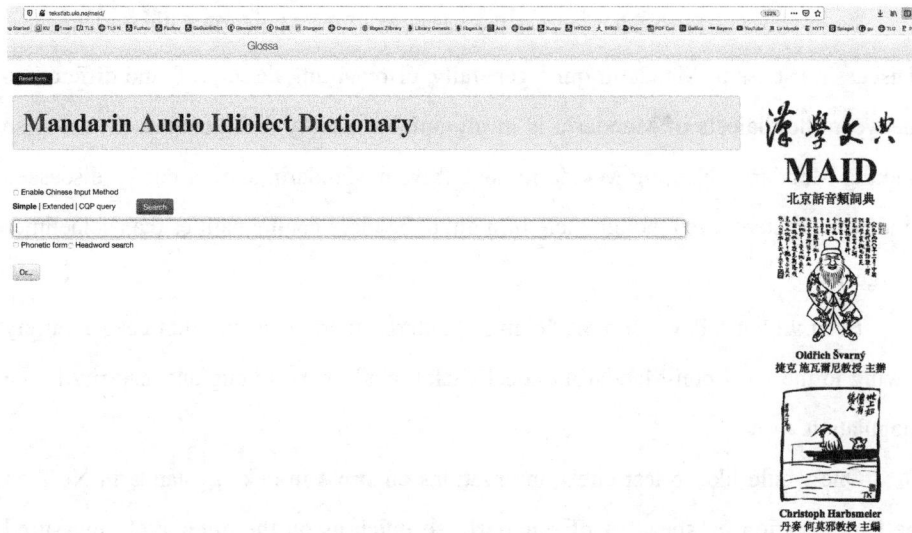

Graphic 1　MAID website

---

① For the important historical influence of the language of the Manchu bannermen of Peking in the formation of Mandarin, see the excellent survey in Elisabeth Kaske, *The Politics of Language in Chinese Education, 1895–1919*, (Sinica Leidensia 82), Leiden: Brill Academic Publishers, 2007, particularly pp. 69ff.

On any word or any idiom, one can consult the visualization of the phonetic contours of their pronunciation as follows:

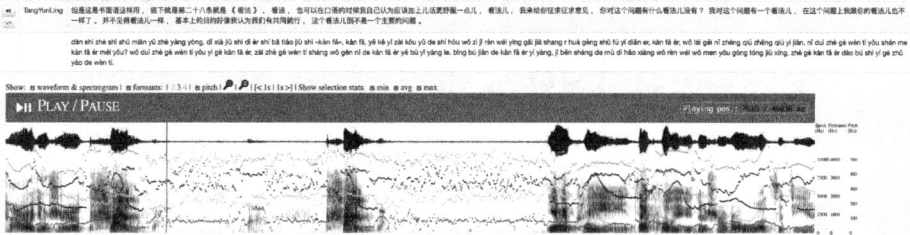

Graphic 2   Phonetic contours of kànfǎr

For example, one finds that the native speaker feels kànfǎ'r (看法儿) is more natural than kànfǎ (看法). And we can investigate how far her objective practice is in accordance with her subjective self-observation. One can investigate a wide range of pronunciations of kànfǎ (看法) to see how, in different contexts, tones and stress of this word are actually realized by her, and how much that realization varies across different contexts. One can look up all occurrences of kànfǎ (看法) in the database to make up one's mind to what extent the idiolect speaker actually lives up to the rules she imagines she is following.

We can also observe to what extent what comes to her mind as the main meanings of a word, and the most natural pronunciations of that word, and how her intuitions differs from the standard for Mandarin Chinese that came to be laid down in *Modern Chinese Dictionary* (《现代汉语词典 Xiàndài Hànyǔ Cídiǎn》).

Unfortunately, the vocabulary covered by this database is very far from complete. Only some 60,000 words are defined and thus available for detailed phonetic study in the corpus. For kànfǎ (看法) one can conveniently study all the transcribed uses in the database as follows:

Reset form
Found 386 matches
Enable Chinese Input Method
Simple | Extended | CQP query
Search
看法
Phonetic form Headword search
Or...
Sort
Statistics
Page 1 of 26 pages
TangYunLing 这也行， 就是这种话， 是吧。 有的时候那个酒话是有用的， 为什么呢？ 因为有一些个人比如说没有这个勇气平常说出一些什么来。 平常比如说对一些什么样的现象不满意， 或者对什么人有什么样的 看法。
zhe4 ye3 xing2， jiu4 shi4 zhe4 zhong3 hua4， shi4 ba。 you3 de shi2 hou4 na4 ge4 jiu3 hua4 shi4 you3 yong4 de， wei4 shen2 me ne？ yin1 wei4 you3 yi1 xie1 ge4 ren2 bi3 ru2 shuo1 mei2 you3 zhe4 ge4 yong3 qi4 ping2 chang2 shuo1 chu1 yi1 xie1 shen2 me lai2。 ping2 chang2 bi3 ru2 shuo1 dui4 yi1 xie1 shen2 me yang4 de xian4 xiang4 bu4 man3 yi4， huo4 zhe3 dui4 shen2 me ren2 you3 shen2 me yang4 de kan4 fa3。
TangYunLing 特别是对领导有什么 看法， 认为他哪方面不对， 想说出来， 可是没有这个勇气是吧， 但是喝醉酒以后什么都说， 嘻嘻哈哈的， 你他妈的怎么怎么着， 你原来是怎么怎么着， 就都给他揭露出来， 这个酒话有的时候可信的。
te4 bie2 shi4 dui4 ling3 dao3 you3 shen2 me kan4 fa3， ren4 wei2 ta1 na3 fang1 mian4 bu2 dui4， xiang3 shuo1 chu1 lai2， ke3 shi4 mei2 you3 zhe4 ge4 yong3 qi4 shi4 ba， dan4 shi4 he1 zuì， he1 zui4 jiu3 yi3 hou4 shen2 me shuo1， xi1 xi1 ha1 ha1 de， ni3 ta1 ma1 de zen3 me zen3 me zhao1， ni3 yuan2 lai2 shi4 zen3 me zen3 me zhao1， jiu4 dou1 gei3 ta1 jie1 lu4 chu1 lai2， zhe4 ge4 jiu3 hua4 you3 de shi2 hou4 ke3 xin4 de。
TangYunLing 由于借这个， 平常有那么一句话叫借酒撒疯， 就是借这个酒的劲儿， 撒出疯来， 疯就是好像神经不正常似的， 其实有的时候说酒话是有用的， 能够听得出来这个人真正思想或者是真正 看法。
you2 yu2 jie4 zhe4 ge4， ping2 chang2 you3 na4 me yi1 ju4 hua4 jiao4 jie4 jiu3 sa1 feng1， jiu4 shi4 jie4 zhe4 ge4 jiu3 de jin4 r， sa1 chu1 feng1 lai2， feng1 jiu4 shi4 hao3 xiang4 shen2 jing1 bu4 zheng4 chang2 shi4 de， qi2 shi2 you3 de shi2 hou4 shuo1 jiu3 hua4 shi4 you3 yong4 de， neng2 gou4 ting1 de2 chu1 lai2 zhe4 ge4 ren2 zhen1 zheng4 si1 xiang3 huo4 zhe3 shi4 zhen1 zheng4 kan4 fa3。
TangYunLing 你怎么现在， 你怎么今天来了？ 我问你。 你怎么来了？ 或者说这都是旧话了， 你提那些旧话干什么？ 那时候我对你没有正确的 看法 是吧。 那都是旧话了， 算了吧， 把那些旧话就是撇在一边， 不提了， 也可以， 是过去的， 过去说的。
ni3 zen3 me xian4 zai4， ni3 zen3 me jin1 tian1 lai2 le？ wo3 wen4 ni3。 ni3 zen3 me lai2 le？ huo4 zhe3 shuo1 zhe4 dou1 shi4 jiu4 hua4 le， ni3 ti2 nei4 xie1 jiu4 hua4 gan4 shen2 me？ na4 shi2 hou wo3 dui4 ni3 mei2 you3 zheng4 que4 de kan4 fa3 shi4 ba。 na4 dou1 shi4 jiu4 hua4 le， suan4 le ba， ba3 nei4 xie1 jiu4 hua4 jiu4 shi4 pie1 zai4 yi1 bian1， bu4 ti2 le， ye3 ke3 yi3， shi4 guo4 qu4 de， guo4 qu4 shuo1 de。
TangYunLing 因为普通就说早了， 我早就对他怎么， 我很早以前就已经怎么怎么样， 很早以前就怎么怎么样， 是吧， 我久已对某某人， 我久已对这个问题有什么什么样的 看法， 不是现在对这个问题有什么样看法儿， 早就已经有了， 这个意思。
yin1 wei4 pu3 tong1 jiu4 shuo1 zao3 le， wo3 zao3 jiu4 dui4 ta1 zen3 me， wo3 hen3 zao3 yi3 qian2 jiu4 yi3 jing1 zen3 me zen3 me yang4， hen3 zao3 yi3 qian2 jiu4 zen3 me zen3 me yang4， shi4 ba， wo3 jiu3 yi3 dui4 mou3 mou3 ren2， wo3 jiu3 yi3 dui4 zhe4 ge4 wen4 ti2 you3 shen2 me shen2 me yang4 de kan4 fa3， bu2 shi4 xian4 zai4 dui4 zhe4 ge4 wen4 ti2 you3 shen2 me yang4 kan4 fa3 er2， zao3 jiu4 yi3 jing1 you3 le， zhe4 ge4 yi4 si1。

Graphic 3 Transcribed uses of kànfǎ

One does NOT have to rely on the transcription to identify the places where er-ization [or érhuà (儿化)] is or is not present: one can listen to all the cases where our specialists in China have no er-ization and see to what extent they have negligent.[①]

Even in the case of idiom [or chéngyǔ (成语)] one finds predictable prosodies and stress patterns. And in MAID the prosodies and stress patterns of thousands of these may studied and documented in quantified detail. One may look for counterexamples for the generalizations one is interested in. And one can evaluate the prominence of the features one finds, as well as the contextual conditions under which these features are neutralized. And one will not be referring to one's subjective impressions of these phenomena. One can refer painlessly to visualized phonetic analysis of what is going on in any occurrence of a use of the idiom one is interested in.

Here as everywhere issues of stress assignment are never simple in Chinese. Even the quite separate matter of de-stressing and the confident assignment of the zero tone [or light tone, neutralized tone, qīngshēng (轻声)], on which there is an extensive literature, is far from uncontroversial and needs empirical confirmation in corpora.[②] MAID provides a tool where the study of stress, destressing, and other features of the pronunciation of Mandarin become available for fairly objective investigation. In addition, one may get subjective perceptions of each item by Madame Tang Yunling, a bannerman [or qírén (旗人)] who grew up in a eight banners milieu in Peking.

It is my claim that progress in the study of stress in Mandarin Chinese can be made on the basis of a comparison between well-circumscribed and extensive idiolect corpora like MAID. Corpora that are not spontaneous and involve many different speakers with different dialect interferences of all sorts have their obvious interest, because they represent what we are most likely to encounter. However, they are too complex to allow

---

① I have personally found that most of the er-ization on these tapes I first notice when I listen to a passage for the fourth time, but that Professor Meng Zong, a Manchu [or qírén (旗人)] from Peking the Academy of Sciences, immediately hears many of them clearly that I never get to recognize at all. One recognizes more in things gets attuned to them. The task is to get more attuned to details of stress and prosody in Chinese words and phrases.

② Even stress in French, which is supposed to be on the final syllable of words, turns out to be an extremely complex matter to sort out convincingly.

truly systematic analysis.

I believe it remains crucial to recognize that Ferdinand de Saussure was profoundly mistaken when he assumed that languages as a whole constituted *systèmes d'opposition*. In fact the strict systematicity he rightly set out to discover, applies not even to dialects or subdialects. Strictly speaking, it only applies to an idiolect, if ever it applies to anything real. Dialects arise from sufficiently wide overlap between different individual linguistic systems. To the ancient Greeks there were only dialects, *dialektoi*. A language, to the Greeks, was merely a privileged dialect. The Athenian dialect does not become for them any less of a *dialektos*, and more of a language – Greek – by becoming the privileged medium of literary composition among writers of Greek. Essentially, Greek is the dialect of Athens, nothing more.

For example, the basic principle of tone-sandhi according to which in a sequence of two fourth tones the first tone changes significantly does not apply when the first fourth tone is stressed. Thus, as we shall see below, the rule applies to bujian (不见) but never ever to bujian (部件). This proves straightforwardly that stress is an integral part of the Chinese phonological system. No one can learn to pronounce these words with the correct tones unless he recognizes stress and takes stress into account when deciding on the realization of the tonal pattern in these words.

3. Minimal Pairs

The following English words will be found to have two "readings" in different word classes, and stress is distinctive in all cases, though not always in the same way, for example:

(3) *abstract*　　*convict*　　*insult*　　*refit*

　　compound　　*digest*　　*misprint*　　*refund*

　　compress　　*discard*　　*perfume*　　*regress*

　　conduct　　*discount*　　*permit*　　*reject*

　　confine　　*escort*　　*pervert*　　*segment*

　　conflict　　*export*　　*present*　　*survey*

conscript	*extract*	*produce*	*suspect*
consort	*ferment*	*progress*	*torment*
construct	*import*	*protest*	*transfer*
contest	*impress*	*rebel*	*transform*
contrast	*incline*	*record*	*transplant*
convert	*increase*	*refill*	*transport*

Any dictionary of English, good or bad, will tend to take account of hundreds such minimal pairs for English. And in some cases there are predictable vowel changes as for example in *con'duct* versus *conduct'*. We shall see that the situation is interestingly similar in Mandarin Chinese. A dictionary of the English language that would disregard the difference between the pronunciation of the verb *conduct* and the different word, the noun *conduct* would be justly dismissed as unprofessional. A dictionary of Chinese that disregards the difference between the pronunciation of the verb bǎ'wò (把握), and that of the different word, the noun bǎwò' (把握), is to be similarly deplored as scandalously unprofessional.

In fact, it can be easily demonstrated that Modern Peking Mandarin Chinese has an even larger number than English of such minimal pairs distinguished by stress contour. An even larger number of Chinese words written different characters, and consisting of different morphemes, is regularly distinguished in pronunciation by their different stress patterns only.

Two problems have made lexicographic progress on this so difficult in the case of Chinese. One problem is that since in articulatory terms basic frequency and pattern of changing frequency are taken up by the Chinese tonal system, stress cannot simply be expressed by high frequency, and in terms of audial perception, pitch cannot simply function as an indicator of stress. However, it is primarily greater duration of the stressed syllable that plays a role, and in addition the "exaggeration" or hyper-specification of the physical contours of the tone of a syllable that is stressed, loudness apparently playing a much lesser role in the articulation of stress in Chinese.

The other more serious problem is that stress in Chinese is so often variable according to context. Even a lexically toneless Chinese syllable can receive a tone in a variety of contexts: a lexical qī'ngshēng (轻声) will in various contexts (e.g. when one is trying to make clear what character it is written with) be pronounced with its etymological tone. But in ordinary circumstances qī'ngshēng will certainly not be pronounced with stress on the second syllable as qīngshē'ng. In fact, the latter pronunciation makes the word almost unrecognisable in ordinary discourse, except when there is contrastive "logical" stress which is irrelevant to our purposes.

I give an example of the variability of stress in contrastive contexts which I come across in a television programme from 2007, as I am reading as I read these lines:

(4) 曹操会（yò'ngrén）用人

是因为他会（shí'rén）识人

也就是因为他会（kò'nrén）看人。

他（kànré'n）看人可以达到入木三分的程度。（易中天）

In the contrastive context of the first three lines Yi Zhongtian (易中天) has stress on the verb and not on the object, thus breaking the general rule to be discussed below that non-pronominal objects receive more stress than the verb of which they are the object. But the rules of stress in Chinese do invite just this kind of contrastive stress in more contexts than the rules of stress in English. Stress is more flexible in Chinese than it is in English. As we shall see, this does not mean that stress is absent in Chinese: when there is no contrastive meaning, Yi Zhongtian naturally reverts to the default stress pattern. Examples like this are many. They show that the concepts of stress are quite different in Chinese and in English. Stress is not the same thing in different languages. The word stress system as well as prosody deserves close attention, and especially the latter has received close attention from many scholars, including notably Oldřich Švarný (Prague), Meng Zong (Peking), Nikolay Speshnev (St Petersburg), and our friend and beneactor Feng Shengli. My analyses are deeply indebted to the work of these scholars. Oldrich Švarný has devoted his entire life to the study of prosody in Chinese. And the unforgettable Nikolay Speshnev has trained generations of Russian students in the mysteries of stress and prosody in modern Chinese.

In the first part of this section I shall illustrate how stress is semantically distinctive by presenting a selective series of minimal pairs in which a difference in stress marks a difference in meaning. In the second part I shall demonstrate that stress is not only semantically distinctive but also very often grammatically predictable by presenting a selective series of rules governing stress in Peking Mandarin Chinese, with illustrations.

3.1 Stress Minimal Pairs Overview

To begin with, I shall consider a short series of minimal pairs which illustrate the crucial importance for stress for comprehension of what people say in Modern Standard Chinese. It will be seen that as far as I can I am avoiding phonetic and phonological terminological technicalities. But at this point it may be worth pointing out that stress patterns are suprasegmental morphemes in the sense that they are explicit markers of clear lexical distinctions in the language. And one must hasten to add that the phonetic realisation of these suprasegmental stress morphemes in modern Chinese is often much less indisputably prominent and stable across dialects than the realisation of stress distinctions is in English.[1]

We have è'rshíjǐ (二十几) which has to mean "twenty-odd" versus èrshíjǐ' (二十几) "how many more than twenty?" The two phrases can never be synonymous. Nor are they ever homophonous. But Standard Pinyin transcription is inadequate to distinguish between them. Again, we have "Táng Yún <u>shénme</u>?" (唐云什么？) "Tang Yun what?" versus "<u>Táng Yún</u> shénme?" (唐云什么？) "Tang Yun – something-or-other." We have tā jiāli hái yǒu shénme rén ma? (他家里还有什么人吗？) "Is there anyone else in his family?" versus tā jiāli hái yǒu <u>shénme</u> rén? (他家里还有什么人？) "Who else is there in his family?" We have yǒ'urén (有人) "some people" versus yǒu ré'n (有人). "There is someone there; there are people there" and there is no doubt that yǒ'urén (友人) "friend" could never be pronounced yǒuré'n. We also have fè'ihuà (废话) "nonsense" versus fèi-huà' (费话) "talk a lot, make too many words" which may be said to involve a very short discontinuity of pronunciation between the verb and its stressed object, just as in the pair jiè'kǒu (借口) "pretext" versus jiè-kǒ'u (戒口) "observe a diet".

---

[1] The realization of stress in French raises immense systematic problems and demonstrates the well-known fact that "stress on a syllable" is not at all the same in all languages. The present paper is not concerned with such cross-linguistic comparisons.

Clear-cut cases like this are surprisingly common, but they are not typical for the complex situation concerning stress which is also common – in other contexts – in Modern Standard Chinese.

Stress assigned in this little primer always relates to an expression under the interpretation as indicated in the translation provided. The stress markings try to keep as close as possible to an indication of what is perceived as the most representative and typical stress pattern in a normal citation form of the word or expression under that interpretation. Contrastive stress within a larger pragmatic context as well as any contextually conditioned deviation from the normal citation form of the stress pattern has to be disregarded.

Moreover, what I indicate in this primer is just one stress pattern that has emerged as common and natural in Peking Standard Chinese speech. Listing up variants, where applicable, is impracticable and would have led too far for our purposes. Disregarding stress, for this reason, would have been a profound mistake. The contrastive pairs below are designed to illustrate the systematic importance of word stress in Modern Standard Chinese. By way of an introduction I concentrate on binomes. These present an interesting special problem in Modern Standard Chinese.

The distribution of the completely unstressed zero tone is relatively clear much of the time, even for speakers of southern varieties of Standard Chinese, and it is even recognised in many current dictionaries of the Chinese language:

(5) dì'xià' 地下 EARTH UNDER "underground"

　　dìxia· 地下 EARTH UNDER "on the ground"

Learning Chinese is, among other things, learning to distinguish between pairs like these. Here is another example:

(6) xiàluò' 下落 DOWN FALL "fall"

　　xiàluo· 下落 DOWN FALL "whereabouts"

In many cases the contrast is between a verb-object construction in which both the verb and the object receive stress contrasting with another construction where the second syllable receives no tone. At this point we do not take sides on the controversial issue whether such verb-object constructions must count as morphological or as syntactic. In either case it must be noted that there often is a slight pause in the verb-object construction whereas there never is a pause between a tonal and a subsequent atonal syllable.

(7) xià' chǎ'ng 下场 GO-DOWN FIELD "make an appearance"

xiàcha · ng 下场 DOWN FIELD   "ending"

The recognition of the distinctive zero tone is necessary for the explanation of this sort of very common minimal contrast. This is why good dictionaries of Standard Modern Chinese will indicate zero stress where it clearly applies, in order to distinguish the following:

(8) yào-shì' 要事 IMPORTANT MATTER "important matter"

yà'oshi· 要是 WANT BE   "if"

(9) cúnzà'i 存在 EXIST BE-IN   "exist"

cú'nza · i 存在 DEPOSIT BE-IN   "deposit in (e.g. money in a bank)"

There is no need to go into details about these phenomena relating to zero stress. Consider a series of minimal pairs where non-zero secondary initial stress is important:

(10) bùdùi' > búduì' 不对 NOT CORRECT "incorrect"

bù'duì'   部队 PART COLUMN "army"

When one has contrastive stress on bù (不), tone sandhi can still be retained, and a standard form of contrastive stress could be represented like this: búduì' (不对) "That is NOT right!" But the crucial observation is that in bù'duì' (部队) tone sandhi is grammatically excluded. In other words, as we shall see in more detail below, in order to explain tone sandhi in Chinese, it is necessary to refer to stress pattern. Stress is an integral part of the grammar. Similar observations apply, for example, to the following three minimal pairs.

(11) bùjià'n > bújià'n 不见 NOT APPEAR "disappear"

bù'jiàn   部件 PART ITEM   "components"

There is no doubt that the realisation of a fourth tone in front of another fourth tone changes. It is a simplification to write the changed fourth tone as a second tone. As we shall see below, the issue is that tone sandhi applies only on unstressed fourth tones.

(12) bùlià'*o* > búlià'o　不料　NOT FORESEE　　　"unexpectedly"

　　　bù'liào　　　　　布料　CLOTH MATERIAL　"cloth"

Consider:

(13) bùfè'n > búfè'n　不忿　"refuse to submit"

　　　bù'fè'n or bùfè'n 部分　"part"

We need to know whether the pronunciation búfè'n is acceptable at all for 部分, as in all cases with stress on the second syllable. But when the stress is on the first syllable, there is no doubt that tone sandhi does not occur.

Our dictionaries, e.g. the *ABC Dictionary* gives us the following as two separate meanings of the same word/expression involving two consecutive fourth tones, whereas in fact these are two words differing by stress, of which the first does not admit tone sandhi:

(14) ài'wù　　　　爱物　　　*n.* "a cherished object"

　　　ài wù'　　　　爱物　　　*v.* "love all creatures"

Compare:

(15) fèi'wù 废物 "good-for-nothing"

which is even read fèi'wu with a toneless unstressed second syllable.

Even without any sandhi impact, the pattern is the same for the following pair which shows that what is involved is a general rule on stress rather than idiomatic and idiosyncratic stress patterning:

(16) à'irén　爱人 "lover; spouse"

　　　ài-ré'n　爱人 "love others"

Importantly, the tendency for the first of two fourth tones to come to sound like a second tone is not in fact limited to bù (不) where we have not a tendency but a strict rule. Thus whereas in Taiwan the following may even be found pronounced with a double peak, Northern Mandarin tends to allow for a clear modification of the first of the the fourth tones in cases like the following:

(17) pàshì' > páshì'　怕事 "fear trouble"

　　　pà-fù' > páfù'　　怕妇 "be afraid of one's wife"

　　　jù-nè'i > júnè'i　惧内 "be afraid of one's wife"

However, in all these matters, Chao Yuanren's general observation remains valid here as everywhere else: stress pattern distinctions are less markedly stable in Mandarin Chinese than in many other languages with stress. The stress régime in Chinese is less tight in Chinese than in English.

One notes that tone sandhi is not allowed in any of the following:

(18) dò'ngwù   动物   "animal"

     shì'wù   事物   "thing; object"

     zuò'wù   作物   "literary composition"

     huò'wù   货物   "goods;commodity; merchandise"

     yà'owù   药物   "medicines; pharmaceuticals; medicaments"

     kuà'ngwù   矿物   "mineral"

     guài'wù or guàiwu   怪物   "monster; freak"

     yì'shù   艺术   "art"

     zhà'nshù   战术   "military tactics"

     jì'shù   技术   "technology"

     suà'nshù   算术   "arithmetic"

     dò'nglì   动力   "impetus" (Kuraishi)

     dià'nlì   电力   "electricity"

     dà'lì'   大力   "with great force"

     qì'lì   气力   "energy"

     xì'ngzhì   兴致   "enthusiastic"

     gè'xìng   个性   "character"

     pà'ixìng   派性   "factionalism"

     tè'xìng   特性   "special feature" (Kuraishi)

     dà'olù   道路   "way" (Kuraishi)

     dì'dào   地道   "tunnel" (not to be confused with dìdao
                                        "thorough; well-done")

     chì'dào   赤道   "equator"

Moreover, dà'dào (大道) "main road" is never pronounced with a reduced fourth tone in dà, almost a little like dá'dào (达到) "reach". Tone sandhi does not apply to stressed syllables. The rule is everywhere that tone sandhi applies only to unstressed fourth tones before another fourth tone. Since this rule applies to all varieties of Chinese with tone sandhi, this must mean that all dialects with tone sandhi recognise stress. We need to try to find a dialect or a variety of Chinese in which nè'ibù (内部) "restricted" has tone sandhi changing the pronunciation of the first syllable.

Similarly for tone sandhi with two consecutive third tones: we need to see whether there is any variety of Chinese with this kind of sandhi where the first of two consecutive third tones is changed according to sandhi rules when in fact it is stressed.

Consider this neat case of lexically unstressed but not atonal initial negation bù (不):

(19) bù'xíng 步行 STEP WALK "walk by foot"

　　 bùxí'ng 不行 NOT BE OK "it is not OK"

The pattern is regular, since we predictably also have:

(20) bù'chū 步出 STEP LEAVE "walk off"

　　 bùchū' 不出 NOT LEAVE "not leave"

Predictably, we do have zǒ'uchū (走出) "walk out". But as far as the minimal pair is concerned, but one might object that the second form is much more colloquial than the first in both pairs: we still do not have two equally colloquial forms that contrast with respect to stress only. Similar observations apply to the following, to varying degrees:

(21) bù'gōng	步弓	STEP BOW	"(rare:) measuring instrument for measuring fields"
bùgō'ng	不公	NOT JUST	"unjust"
(22) bù'zú	部族	PART TRIBE	"tribe"
bùzú'	不足	NOT SUFFICIENT	"literary: insufficient"
(23) bù'fá	步伐	STEP ATTACK	"pace"
bùfá'	不乏	NOT LACK	"literary: have no shortage of"
(24) bù'fǎ	步法	STEP METHOD	"footwork, dancing mode"
bùfǎ'	不法	NOT LAW	"unlawful"

There seems to be a general rule that the negative prefix bù (不) does not receive the main stress, except in the case of "contrastive stress" or "logical stress".

Some minimal pairs may, of course, be disputable, because the words involved are not sufficiently current:

(25) xīn-lí'ng　心灵　MIND SPIRIT　"quick-witted" cf. 心灵手巧

　　 xī'nlíng　心灵　MIND SPIRIT　"spirit"

Many minimal pairs have no grammatical contrast as in the following case where both members are nouns:

(26) cá'iwù'　财务　"manager of financial affairs"

　　 cá'iwù　财物　"property, belongings"

Sometimes syntactic and morphological constructions are distinguished not so much through pauses between words but through stress patterns:

(27) cá'inéng　　　　才能　"ability"

　　 cái né'ng　　　　才能　"only then be able"

(28) lǎ'oshì' or lǎoshì'　老式 OLD SHAPE　　　　"old-fashioned"

　　 lǎ'oshì' or lǎoshì'　老事 OLD MATTER　　　"well-known fact"

　　 lǎ'oshì or lǎ'oshi　老是 OLD BE　　　　　"always"

(29) cá'i-shì'　　　　 财势 "wealth and influence"

　　 cáishì'　　　　　 才是 "then that will be all right"

　　 cá'ishì or cá'ishi　才是 "only then is it..."

Less convincing in some superficial ways but theoretically quite interesting are cases where the characters are different, and/or where one of the members of the minimal pair is relatively rare by comparison with the other:

(30) cá'i-xué'　才学　"ability and learning"

　　 cái xué'　才学　"have just learned"

The point is that one would simply not be understood if one mispronounced the first of these expressions with heavy emphasis on the first syllable; and that even someone who has never heard the second word, can guess what it means and will certainly pronounce it with stress on the first syllable, and probably with less stress on the second syllable.

(31) fē'nbié　　分别　"distinguish"

　　　fē'nbié'　　分别　"to leave, part with" (Tang Junling)

(32) fē'nghuǒ　　烽火　"signal fire; flames of war"

　　　fēng huǒ'　　封火　"bank up fire (in an oven, to reduce the intensity)"

The quasi-suffix -shǒu (手) tends to retain its tone, although it loses the primary stress on the last syllable which is so common in Modern Standard Chinese:

(33) zhù'-shǒ"u　　住手　STOP HAND　　　"desist, stop"

　　　zhù'shǒu　　助手　HELP HAND　　　"helper"

(34) xià'-shǒ"u　　下手　PUT-DOWN HAND　"start"

　　　xià'shǒu　　下手　UNDER HAND　　　"helper, aide; next player in card games"

(35) shà'ng-shǒ'u　上手　"to start with"

　　　shà'ngshǒu　　上手　"leading practitioner"

When shǒu (手) is without stress, this is a regular feature of the use of this word as a suffix.

Cases of this sort are not rare, and some more will be introduced below. We may have a distinctive slight pause between these two syllables, so that one might want to argue that this pause and not the stress contrast is what makes the difference.

There is no pause in the following, where the directional suffix -dào (到) receives secondary stress whereas the noun head dào (道) has to receive the main stress except when contrastive stress interferes with the lexical stress pattern:

(36) pǎ'odào　　跑到　RUN REACH　"run to"

　　　pǎodà'o　　跑道　RUN WAY　　"runway for aircraft; running-track"

　　　[But note that we have zhōngyú pǎodà'ole· (终于跑到了) "in the end he got there".]

Verb/noun contrasts are sometimes marked through stress contrasts:

(37) bǎwò'　把握　GRASP GRIP　"have a grip on"

　　　bǎ'wò　把握　GRASP GRIP　"assurance, confidence" [yǒu bǎ'wò (有把握) "have a grasp on")

There are those who deny contrasts like these, but when tested by our "exaggeration tests" very few seem indifferent to the distinction. Thus one must distinguish carefully between the distinctions people make and the distinctions they think they make.

The words are not homophonous: the noun is marked by first-syllable stress as derived from the verb with the final stress, just as in *permi't* versus *pe'rmit* and many of the examples I opened this chapter with. Certain varieties of Chinese neutralize this contrast, perhaps. And even within the speech of a single speaker the distinction may under certain circumstances be neutralized.

Many verb-object constructions give rise to minimal pairs that work in generally predictable ways:

(38) guà'i-ré'n (or guài ré'n)　怪人 BLAME MAN　　"blame others"

　　 guà'irén or guà'iren　　怪人 STRANGE MAN　"strange person"

(39) péi-kè'　　陪客 ACCOMPANY GUEST　"accompany a guest"

　　 pé'ikè　　陪客 ACCOMPANY GUEST　"accompanying guest"

(40) shà'ng-zuò'　上座 GO-UP SEAT　　　"take a seat"

　　 shà'ngzuò　　上座 TOP SEAT　　　　"seat of honour; your honour"

(41) dǒng-shì'　懂事 UNDERSTAND MATTER "be knowledgeable"

　　 dǒ'ngshì　董事 SUPERVISE MATTER　"member (of board of directors)"

(42) jiàn-ré'n　　见人 SEE PERSON　　　"meet other people"

　　 jià'nrén　　贱人 VULGAR PERSON　"slut"

(43) gēnjiǎ'o　　　跟脚 FOLLOW FOOT　"follow closely after someone"

　　 gē'njiǎo/gēnjia·o 根脚 BASIS FOOT　　"solid base" gē'njiǎor (根脚儿)

In the case of verbal constructions ending in the semi-suffix -lái (来) there is already regularly reduced stress on the second syllable so that the grammaticalized form may contrastively receive stress on the second syllable:

(44) kà'n[-]lái　看来 LOOK COME　"come to see"

　　 cf. 他是看来了 "He has come to see [it]"

　　 kànlá'i　　看来 LOOK COME　"apparently"

Sometimes stress distinguishes adnominal verbs (noun-modifying verbs) from other verbs:

(45) shuōmí'ng　说明　TALK CLEAR　"explain"

　　 shuō'míng　说明　TALK CLEAR　"explanation; explanatory"

　　 (cf. shuōmí'ng kē'xué 说明科学 "explain science"

　　 vs. shuō'ming kē'xué 说明科学 "explanatory science")

(46) yìngyò'ng　应用　RESPOND USE　"apply"

　　 yì'ngyòng　应用　RESPOND USE　"application; applied"

　　 (cf. yìngyò'ng kē'xué 应用科学 "apply science in practice"

　　 vs. yì'ngyòng kē'xué 应用科学 "applied science")

Sometimes the contrast marked is that between an ungrammaticalized form and a more grammaticalized form (see our chapter on grammaticalization):

(47) kàndà'o > kándào　看到　LOOK REACH　"catch sight of"

　　 kà'ndào　看到　LOOK REACH　"turning one's attention to, going over to"

(48) tó'u-shuǐ'　投水　CAST WATER　"cast oneself into the water"

　　 tó'ushuǐ　头水　HEAD WATER　"best quality"

The noun jiā (家) "home" often receives full stress whereas the quasi-suffix -jiā (家) has reduced stress:

(49) dào-jiā'　到家　REACH HOME　"reach a very high level"

　　 dà'ojiā　道家　WAY SCHOOL　"Taoism"

　　 [cf. also dà'o-jiā'/dào-jiā' (到家) REACH HOME "reach home"]

(50) dà'zhǐ' (or dà'-zhǐ')　大旨　BIG MEANING　"main meaning"

　　 dà'zhǐ　大指　BIG FINGER　"thumb"

(51) shē'ng ré'n　生人　LIVE PERSON　"person born in a (certain) place"

　　 shē'ngrén　生人　STRANGE PERSON　"stranger"

In a good number of cases, it is still hard to think of clear reasons for stress contrasts at this stage:

(52) fā'jué　发觉　EMIT FEEL　"become aware"

　　 fājué'　发掘　EMIT DIG-OUT　"unearth"

(53) xíng-shì'   行事 ACT MATTER   "carry out a task"

    xí'ngshì (or: xí'ngshì') 形势 FORM SITUATION "appearance or condition
                                                                    of things"

Even when old-fashioned ways of speaking are involved, stress patterns can appear
fairly clear, even when one:

(54) yú'-mí"n   愚民 STUPID PEOPLE   "treat people as stupid, make the
                                             people stupid"

    yú'mín   渔民 FISHER PEOPLE   "fisherman"

(55) yóushuǐ'   游水 WANDER WATER   "swim"

    yó'ushuǐ   油水 OIL WATER   "profit"

We need to investigate whether Peking speakers make a difference as predicted
between yú'mí'n and yú'-mí'n, or indeed between:

(56) shē'n-shǒ'u 伸手 STRETCH-OUT HAND "stretch out hand"

    shē'nshǒu   身手 BODY HAND   "ability"

These last four pairs, and the many similar ones, are problematic and deserve close
empirical study: when asked to make explicit the difference in meaning between the
two different meanings, do speakers of Peking Modern Standard Chinese bring this out
through a pause (which in ordinary contexts is usually neutralized) or do they not?

The distinctions perhaps get a little clearer when there is a difference in stress:

(57) jiè'-kuǎ'n   借款 BORROW AMOUNT "make debts"

    jiè'kuǎn   借款 BORROW AMOUNT "debt incurred"

(58) cú'n-kuǎ'n 存款 DEPOSIT MONEY   "deposit money"

    cú'nkuǎn   存款 DEPOSIT MONEY   "financial deposit"

But do Peking speakers clearly recognize all these distinctions? Clearly, in some
contexts these distinctions are neutralized. These conditions of neutralization of stress
patterns need close empirical investigation.

3.2   Regular and Predictable Stress Patterns

In búduà'n (不断) "incessantly" the tone sandhi on the first syllable demonstrates
that bù is unstressed and hence accessible to tone sandhi leading to its getting something

like the second tone which it retains even under "logical" contrastive stress. There is a general rule in modern Chinese that the negative bù (不) is unstressed in compound words. We can thus predict the stress in constructions like bùxí'ng (不行) "is not OK" and in many hundreds of expressions like it. When the second syllable is in the fourth falling tone, a stressed preceding fourth tone never undergoes sandhi to sound like a second tone. Thus we have bù'duì (部队) which can never come to sound anything remotely like búduì' (不对) with its stress on the second syllable and its either toneless or unstressed first syllable. Moreover, none of these rules depend on any decision on our part on the question of wordhood of such constructions: there is no clear distinction in Chinese between English *un-* and *not*.

Let us look first at some regularities in the stress pattern in Chinese verbs. It turns out that one single rule may serve to explain many of these regular stress patterns: In a binome that consists of a head plus a non-head, the non-head will tend to be stressed, if anything is stressed at all.

1. Prepositions (or more correctly: co-verbs) and grammaticalized elements are generally unstressed.

(59) zhù'zài　住在　"live in"

　　　fà'ngzài　放在　"place in"

　　　liú'zài　留在　"leave in"

　　　cá'ngzài　藏在　"hide in"

Note also the full verb followed by a preposition, as in zà'iyú (在于) "consist in".

2. More generally, compound words with recurrent semi-affixes or other recurrent elements have stress on the non-recurrent element.

The stress pattern of Hà'nyǔ (汉语), Fǎ'yǔ (法语), Yǐ'ngyǔ (英语) does not have to be learnt any more than that of Zhō'ngguó (中国), Fǎ'guó (法国), Yǐ'ngguó (英国), or indeed of gō'ngrén (工人) "worker", kè'rén (客人) "guest", bì'ngrén (病人) "sick person". (What has to be learned are the exceptions that do exist, like hǎoré'n (好人) "fine person" versus huà'irén (坏人): we have no explanation for this deviation of the rule so far. Note also hǎoqiú' (好球) "good ball!", which is equally inexplicable by the regularities we have so far established.)

The stress patterns of hó'nghuā (红花) "safflower" does not have to be learnt because there are so many kinds of huā (花) "flowers".

For convenience, I just list some further series to illustrate the pervasiveness of the phenomenon. In all these series the stress is regularly on the non-recurrent element, and the unstressed element may even lose its tone in rapid speech:

(60) zǎ'oshàng   早上   wǎ'nshàng   晚上   mǎ'shàng   马上

zhuō'zishàng 桌子上   yǐ'zishàng   椅子上   wū'dǐng-shàng 屋顶上

(61) jī'ntiān   今天   mí'ngtiān   明天   hò'utiān   后天

(62) yī'yuè   一月   è'ryuè   二月   sā'nyuè   三月

(63) xīngqīyī'   星期一   xīngqiè'r   星期二   xīngqīsān   星期三

(64) lǐbàiyī'   礼拜一   lǐbàiè'r   礼拜二   lǐbàisā'n   礼拜三

(65) yīdì'ng   一定   yīdiǎ'n   一点   yīgò'ng   一共

yīqǐ'   一起   yīliá'n   一连

(66) yīhuì'r (sic!) 一会儿   yīkuà'ir   一块儿

(note the elision of the final [i] in pronunciation)

(67) dà'nhuà   淡化   è'huà   恶化   fǔ'huà   腐化   xū'huà   虚化

(68) chē'fū   车夫   "chauffeur"

mǎ'fū   马夫   "groom"

yú'fū   渔夫   "fisherman"

(69) shuǐ'shǒu 水手   "mariner"

né'ngshǒu 能手   "capable person"

gā'oshǒu   高手   "advanced expert"

(70) mù'jiàng   木匠   "carpenter"

pí'jiàng   皮匠   "cobbler"

tiě'jiàng   铁匠   "blacksmith"

(71) gǔ'dài   古代   "ancient"

jì'ndài   近代   "modern"

dā'ngdài   当代   "present-day"

xià'ndài   现代   "present-age"

(72) zuò'jiā   作家   "author"

zhuā'njiā   专家   "specialist"

huà'jiā   画家   "painter"

(73) kē'xué   科学   "science"

Hà'nxué   汉学   "Scinology"

huà'xué   化学   "chemistry"

zhé'xué   哲学   "philosophy"

Recursively, we even have kē'xuéjiā（科学家）, Hà'nxuéjiā（汉学家）, and huà'xuéjiā（化学家）with decreasing stress on the three syllables!

And with double recursion: in wù'lǐxuéjia（物理学家）, "physicist" tiā''nwé'nxuéjia（天文学家）, one might pedantically insist that lǐ is unstressed with regard to wù, and xué is unstressed with regard to wù'lǐ, and finally jiā is unstressed with regard to wù'lǐxué.

The important point to keep in mind is this: the stress patterns in all the above words are grammatically predictable and not lexically idiosyncratic. These patters should clearly be learnt by beginning students of Chinese.

In more complex words or word-like expressions, the system operates consistently at different levels of analysis. The stress in shè''huìzhǔyì'（社会主义）has to be on shè'huì（社会）, and this example shows how a detailed treatment of stress patterns must take account of the constituent structure of complex words and recognise different levels of stress assignment according to different levels of immediate constituent analysis. (Note the prosodic complexities in shè''huìzhǔyìzhě'（社会主义者）"socialist" which instantiates the very general tendency for long words or idiomatic expressions to be bounded by stressed syllables.)

Exceptions to this rule do have to be learnt separately as idiomatic stress, as in words like lǎ'oshǔ（老鼠）"rat; mouse", lǎ'obǎn（老板）"chief" where in fact the recurrent prefix receives clear stress for all speakers of Mandarin Chinese. I have no explanation for these cases. But such exceptions do not affect the general overriding rule that any free formations like lǎosā'n（老三）, lǎoLǐ'（老李）, and even lǎotó'uzi（老头子）have predictable stress on the non-grammaticalized second constituent.

3. Verb-object constructions (be they morphological or not, functioning verbally or nominally) have stress on all non-pronominal objects.

It is grammatically predictable that we must read yǒ'urén (有人) "some people", but definitely yǒuré'n (有人) "there is someone" (and entirely predictably we find the unidiomatically standard yǒu mǎ' (有马) "there is a horse"). The word rén (人) must be stressed as the object of the verb yǒu (有) for exactly the same reason that mǎ (马) has to be stressed in the same position. The following all have predictable stress:

(74) yǒuqiá'n   有钱   huíjiā'   回家

      yǒumi'ng   有名   bānjiā'   搬家

      yǒuwè'ir   有味儿   xíngli'   行李

      yǒuyì'sī/yǒuyì'si 有意思   suànmì'ng   算命

      pàré'n   怕人   kāihuì'   开会

      xiàoré'n   笑人   tóupià'o   投票

      zǒulù'   走路   shàngdà'ng   上当

      shuōhuà'   说话   hējiǔ'   喝酒

      dǎzhà'ng   打仗   zhíqiá'n   值钱

Even verbal objects of the wrongly so-called "auxiliary verbs" tend to receive regular predictable stress:

(75) yào zǒ'u   要走 "want to leave"

      yào qù'   要去 "want to go, want to attend"

      yào hē'   要喝 "want to drink"

      gāisǐ'   该死 "deserve to die"   cf. gāisǐ'de 该死的 "damned"

Note, however, that also in this general category there are idiomatic exceptions. The common stress pattern of jù'shuō (据说) "according to what people say" is not predictable by any rule governing word stress that I know of. It looks as if this pattern has to be learnt as an exception. And the general rule remains that we have yīncǐ' (因此) "therefore", rúcǐ' (如此) "like this", and yóucǐ' (由此) "from this" even in literary or bookish expressions. The stress patterns of modern Chinese are naturally transferred to literary Chinese.

4. Place nouns and time nouns after classical "empty words" receive stress.

(76) zhīqiá'n   之前

      zhīwà'i   之外

yǐqiá'n　以前

yǐhò'u　以后

yǐshà'ng　以上

5. Resultative verbs have stress on the final resultative complement.

(77) chībǎ'o　吃饱

xuéhuì'　学会

dǎpò'　打破

cāizhò'ng　猜中

dàomǎ'n　倒满

6. Adverbially modified verbs (as well as the nouns derived from these) tend to have final stress.

(78) miàntá'n　面谈　　shēnlǜ'　深绿

qiāngbì'　枪毙　　bìlá'n　碧蓝

kǒushì'　口试　　léngxià'o　冷笑

héchà'ng　合唱　　hānxià'o　憨笑

nènlǜ'　嫩绿　　chīxià'o　嗤笑

tōnghó'ng　通红　　wēixià'o　微笑

xuèhó'ng　血红　　shǎoyǒ'u　少有

wūhē'i　乌黑　　chángjià'n　常见

7. Verbs or stative verbs with postposed multisyllabic adverbs receive stress.

(79) kuà'iyīdiǎnr　快一点儿

mà'nyīdiǎnr　慢一点儿

guì'yīxiē　贵一些

But compare the emphatic exception jíle 极了 "to a high degree":

(80) hǎojí'le 好极了

8. Verbal as well as nominal synonym compounds tend to have stress on the second synonym, although this pattern has too many exceptions to be of much use:

(81) měilì'　美丽 "beautiful"　　fǔlà'n　腐烂 "rotten"

wěidà'　伟大 "great"　　xǐhuā'n 喜欢 "like"

zhěngqí'　整齐 "orderly"

Counterexamples come easily to mind. I mention just one of many:

(82) zhò'ngdà 重大 "significant, important"

The conditions under which synonym compounds receive stress on the first syllable deserve close attention.

9. Semi-grammaticalized prefixed passivising main verbs like kě (可), gòu (够), zú (足) are unstressed in the binomes or idiomatic phrases they form.

(83) kěkà'o	可靠	hǎotī'ng	好听	
kěà'i	可爱	hǎoyò'ng	好用	
kěpà'	可怕	nánchī	难吃	
kěliá'n	可怜	nánkà'n	难看	
kěxī'	可惜	nánshuō'	难说	
kěxià'o	可笑	nántī'ng	难听	
hǎochī'	好吃	gòuyò'ng	够用	"enough"
hǎowá'n	好玩	zúyò'ng	足用	"enough for use" (written
hǎokà'n	好看			Chinese, fairly rare)
hǎoxià'o	好笑			

Finally: Place names that end in generic nouns, surprisingly, seem to have regular final stress. Běijī'ng (北京) "Peking", Nánjī'ng (南京), "Nanking" seem to follow the same pattern as Xiānggǎ'ng (香港) "Hong Kong". But note Shǎ'nxī (陕西), Shā'ndōng (山东), Liá'oníng (辽宁), Guǎ'ngdōng (广东), etc.

One would like to know the reasons behind these prosodic patterns. Also, here as everywhere, one would also like to see the detailed empirical research to see exactly who, when and where maintains these stress patterns in a clear way. For example, it will be interesting to know whether speakers of Fujian Mandarin can or cannot distinguish between (84) and (85).

(84) Zhè shì bà'ochóu. "This is the salary."

(85) Zhè shì bàochó'u. "This is revenge."

More generally, it will be important to investigate whether they systematically hear their current word for "remuneration" as completely homophonous "revenge" and vice versa in contexts where both readings are plausible. And it will be important to investigate whether the thousands of minimal pairs which Peking Mandarin Chinese clearly distinguishes by contrasting stress patterns are all strict homophones in Amoy Mandarin Chinese.

4. Methodological Notes

Stress among tonal syllables is commonly optional in the sense that the underlying stress pattern of a word may not be realized in all the occurrences of that word. Thus when I ascribe stress [as in Hàʼnyǔ（汉语）"Chinese"], my criterion for this ascription of stress is not that the syllable marked for stress is in all or necessarily most contexts more prominent or longer than the other syllables. I define stress in modern Chinese by the following two criteria:

1. that the syllable marked for stress can be pronounced as very markedly longer and clearly more prominent than the unmarked syllable by the speaker(s) in question without this pronunciation becoming unacceptable.

2. that the syllable marked for stress can never be pronounced clearly shorter and far less prominently than the unmarked syllable by the speaker(s) in question.

One can test assignment of stress on a syllable by first grossly exaggerating its prominence to see whether the word remains recognizable, and by then unstressing the word in an exaggerated manner to see whether the word then becomes unrecognizable. Only when both these test yield clear results can one assign stress with any certainty. But disagreement between native speakers on these two "exaggeration tests" has turned out to be surprisingly limited when applied in such a way that respondents did not know what the issue that they were tested on was. Thus, even southern speakers, who will often deny that they have any stress in their Southern second-language Mandarin, turn out in practice to recognize a surprisingly large part of the stress distinctions discussed in this chapter when they are tested without knowing what they are tested on. (The way to insure that they cannot know this is simply to hide the question one is interested in among many that are unrelated to stress.)

One might add a third criterion, which, however, is hard to test and on which disagreement between native speakers is considerable:

3. that the syllable marked for stress is normally pronounced as more prominent or longer than the unmarked syllable(s) in rapid speech context. One will have to face the following situations:

a. that stress in Chinese is absent in many words (not all polysyllabic words of Chinese necessarily consist of stressed and unstressed syllables);

b. that stress in Chinese is not always a constant and regular feature of words but variable according to context;

c. that stress in Chinese typically is a matter of degree, and not simply a matter of "either-or".

In spite of the presence of these complicating features of stress in Chinese, the above criteria tend to provide a reasonably clear criterion to decide whether a given speaker does or does not have underlying stress on a given word.

Surely the case of Chinese is very different indeed from that of Polish with its rigid stress on the penultimate syllable, or of French with its relative stress on the last syllable.

If a reasonable number of the contrastive pairs listed up above turn out to be a real part of Peking Standard Chinese speech, then the following three features will turn out to have distinctive phonemic status in Modern Standard Chinese: (1) The distinction between tonal syllables and atonal syllables. The existence of the distinction is uncontroversial though there are many borderline cases. Optional neutralization of the last syllable is marked by a dot under the syllable which is marked as atonal (e.g. kànfa‧ 看法). (2) The relative stress among tonal syllables in binomes. This is undoubtedly wide-spread, but there are many variants among speakers of Peking Standard Chinese, and the scope of the distinction is less in other varieties of the Standard language. (3) The slight glottal closure or articulatory pause between the syllables as used when pronouncing literary Chinese words to indicate that they are to be taken in their old sense, marked by a hyphen or dash "-". This is common to all varieties of Chinese but often hard to identify in practice, although the characteristic pause between each syllable undoubtedly is a clear conventional signal in modern Chinese that the linguistic form one is using is literary and not part of the current daily language.

Chinese word stress is always a matter of degrees and varies significantly not only from dialect to dialect, but even from idiolect to idiolect (from one speaker to another) within one dialect group. In what follows I shall only indicate word stress where in Peking Modern Standard Chinese there seems to be no doubt on where a natural stress may fall.

A survey of Daniel Jones (Jones, 1967) in *Everyman's English Pronouncing Dictionary* (13th) shows variant pronunciations for a large majority of English words. There is also significant variation on stress in English (indo'cile/i'ndocile) in many words. This sort of phenomenon does not prevent us from teaching one of the standard forms to students of English.

The case is significantly different in Chinese. Speakers of southern varieties of Modern Standard Chinese have the even stress pattern in ré'nmí'n (人民) "the people" for a considerable number of words in which northern speakers of the language clearly stress one syllable or the other. Moreover, in all varieties of Chinese, including Peking Standard Chinese, the question of stress is one of degree rather than a question of the clear presence or absence of an absolutely distinct suprasegmental stress morpheme.

In addition, there are serious and pervasive problems of contextual variation: Zhīda·o (知道) may change according to context so that we may have bù zhidà'o (不知道) "does not know". Word stress can get into conflict with sentence intonation. For example, Běihǎi (北海) is definitely the standard stress pattern for the famous Peking park. But a question about where the Beihai Park is would sound like this: Bě'ihǎi zài nǎ'r (北海在哪儿).

Compare tā shō'udào le · yī'fēng xìn (他收到了一封信) versus yī'fēng xìn méi shō'udà'o (一封信没收到). This stress on unstressed syllables when these are phrase-final is regular and should not prevent us from taking it to be an important feature of zhīda·o (知道) that it has the stress on the first syllable. Along with the lexical ā'nquán (安全) we might hear bù ānquá'n (不安全). If any part of ré'nmi'n (人民) can be more prominent than the other, it tends to be rén (人) as in the possible Zhō'ngguó ré'nmín (中国人民). But then there is a prominent general tendency for four-syllable words to have stress on the first and third syllable. We can see that the problems of word stress are much more context-sensitive than in the common European languages. We do not, after all, significantly change the stress pattern of the word *population* according to the context in which the word occurs. On the other hand we have the standard stress *fiftee'n* versus the "iambic reversal" *fi'fteen me'n* even in English where stress is fairly stable across contexts.

In spite of all these complications it seems to me well worth recalling Karlgren (1918: 36):

"For a phonetic transcription of Chinese, which abounds in bewildering homonyms, we must be careful to render adequately the distribution of stress over the different syllables, for this is of the utmost importance if the transcription is to be perfectly understood. In my opinion, it is by no means sufficient to mark only the strong-stressed syllables and group all the rest under the heading of unstressed syllables...

"Instrumental research would of course enable us to distinguish a lot of degrees, but for all practical purposes three degrees will often be quite sufficient:

0) Unstressed syllables;

1) Weak-stressed syllables;

2) Strong-stressed syllables."

But consider the pronunciation of zǐ (子) in the following:

1. 鱼子 yúzǐ "roe"; lengthened elaborate stress (on the head of the construction).

2. 妻·子 qīzǐ "wife and children"; full tonal pronunciation

3. 老子 Lǎozǐ "proper name: Lǎozǐ"; weak tonal pronunciation

4. 孩子 háizi reduced atonal pronunciation close to "ze" with a very short "e"

5. 妻子 qīzi "modern suffixed noun: wife"; regular atonal pronunciation, close to "z" with very little of a vowel following it.

I concur in Bernhard Karlgren's judgment. And I am tempted to add that an interesting test whether a tonal syllable is weak-stressed is to try to pronounce. I believe that any account of Chinese language structure which disregards word stress or sentence stress is seriously deficient. Karlgren's perceptions were more acute than those of his successors.

Hoa (1983), concentrating on Peking Mandarin, has taken the crucial step of discussing matters of stress in connection with the different levels of immediate constituent analysis.

The first type, i.e., "secondary stress + primary stress", is most common, and it naturally invites further subclassification according to the stability of the reduction of the stress on the first syllable. This analysis has been carried out in a project of O. Švarný entitled *Dictionary of the most frequent monosyllabic sememes of Chinese* (see also the important work of Švarný's disciples Paul Kratochvil and Hana Třísková).

All stress types may occasionally take the standard form of the first type with the main stress on the second syllable. Conversely, one might insist that the lexical first stress type never has the second and third types as alternative forms. Thus the test of whether a word belongs to the second or third types is whether, outside conditions of contrastive stress, the word can be given these intonations in citation form.

We need to investigate stress contrasts as between lǎ'oshǔ (老鼠) "mouse" and lǎoyī'ng (老鹰) "eagle". One might point out that young speakers do seem to prefer lǎoshǔ' (老鼠) "mouse", but even these speakers agree that a common traditional form in Peking speech is lǎ'oshǔ (老鼠). On the other hand, no one is in any doubt that lǎoyī'ng (老鹰) has a clear stress on the second syllable. Lǎ'oyīng would not be understood as "eagle".

Similarly for lǎ'oshī (老师) "teacher" versus lǎomǔ' (老母) "mother": lǎoshī', though probably not the dominant form, is certainly comprehensible, while lǎ'omǔ, as noted above, is not recognised as a form having the meaning "mother".

The preface of Pǔ'tōnghuà Qī'ngshēng Cí' Huì'biā'n [《普通话轻声词汇编》 (1963)] claims that about 70% of the Standard Modern Chinese vocabulary conforms to pattern 1, about 23% conforms to pattern 2, and 7% conform to pattern 3.

Pattern 4, in a way represents the claim that clear stress in Chinese – as opposed to English – is not an invariable feature of words, and that in many words stress is not only variable but actually absent. Stress, I claim, is in fact not a pervasive feature of Chinese words. None the less, it is a significant feature of Chinese words.

There is no way in which the very important results reported in these publications can be incorporated into the present primer. The stress markings in this *Little Primer* have been reviewed by Yu Xiaoxing (于晓星) who grew up in Peking and left Peking four years after graduating from Peking University, and whose speech is as close to Peking Standard Chinese as I have been able to find here in Oslo. On the other hand, owing to the generosity of Dr O. Švarný of Prague, I have been able to make extensive use of his acoustic dictionary of all the words in Hànyǔ Pīnyīn Cíhuì (《汉语拼音词汇》) (1963)[①] which consists of more than 1700 hours of tapes recorded in 1967. If the indications of stress patterns in this primer serve to bring about free discussion about the relative acceptability of alternative stress patterns, they will have fulfilled their function.

5. Methodology Appendix

Mèng Zōng (孟宗) reports that in Public Radio Chinese, it is often hard to identify clear stress patterns. Even in *Bühnenchinesisch* "stage Chinese" stress patterns will only emerge to the extent that normal rapid speech is being deliberately imitated. It is in ordinary informal rapid speech that stress becomes pervasively prominent and regular in Peking Standard Chinese. Thus stress even in Peking Standard Chinese is not as pervasive and not as regular as in Standard English. Nonetheless stress is a crucial feature of colloquial Chinese.

The importance of stress is striking in pairs like the English *permi't/pe'rmit* (I introduce a dot under the stressed syllable in order to indicate stress). In English, such stress contrasts tend to be distinct and clear. Wrong stress produces radically unacceptable words. In French, by contrast, a reading *ci'vilisation* instead of the standard *civilisatio'n*, while non-standard, is not outrageous (*Ci'vilisation françai'se* is current), perhaps only motivated by some special prosodic context. The regime on stress is less strict in French than in English. In Chinese, word stress – which manifests itself most prominently not only in the loudness but even more in the length of a syllable – is certainly not a neat or clear matter. As in French, non-standard stress is unusual, but not really outrageous. It may be motivated by many kinds of prosodic and other

---

① 　中国文字改革委员会词汇小组编《汉语拼音词汇》(增订稿)，文字改革出版社，1963.

circumstances.

There is a fair amount of individual variation of Peking speakers when it comes to word stress (as there is among English speakers regarding such pairs as *resea'rch/ re'search*). Even within a single sentence the variation can be striking: yào fèizhǐ · jiù fè'izhǐ' (要废止就废止) "When they want to discontinue it they discontinue it." [Tang Junling sub verbo fè'izhǐ (废止)] Such common phenomena must be taken account of by any successful theory of stress.

Another point that needs to be taken into account is the rapid rate of change in the practice of using or not using stress. The older generation of Peking speakers of Mandarin, like the linguist and painter Wang Fangyu who has gone carefully through an early version of the present chapter, will recognise all the stress distinctions that are introduced in this section very clearly, but the younger generation of Peking speakers, while still making the distinctions, may tend to make these stress distinction less prominent in formal speech, whereas they bring out these distinctions very clearly indeed in rapid informal speech. For example, in 1966/7 Tang Yunling has produced more than 1200 hours of tapes on Hànyǔ Pīnyīn Cíhuì (《汉语拼音词汇》) (1963) and this material, which is extremely rich in rapid but clear colloquial Peking speech, provides ample evidence of the prominence of stress phenomena in the informal speech of young speakers of Peking Standard Chinese at that time.

Even when what presumably is the underlying lexical stress of a word is clear to a speaker, there is a significant tendency towards neutralisation stress features in certain contexts in Tang Yunling's speech. Moreover, there are many words like dà'xiǎ'o (大小) "size", chá'ngduǎ'n (长短) "length" where there is an **even** stress pattern with two equal peaks. (The use of two stress markers to indicate even stress is problematic because the dot does not in this context indicate primary stress. The notation is practically necessary only to differentiate in the manuscript between cases where I have not been able to make up my mind on stress patterns, and where I have decided that there is an even stress pattern.)

In English, you do have to choose between *resea'rch* and *re'search* and both these intonations are incompatible with the meaning of *re'-sea'rch* "search (e.g. a database) again". You cannot have an even stress on both syllables in any bisyllabic word in

English. Here we have an important contrast with stress in Chinese. On the other hand, even those speakers of English who always say *resea'rch* are well aware that those who use *re'search* will use this form only for the noun, not for the verb. In this way there are important similarities between stress distinctions in Chinese and in English. Compare the case of dādà'ng (搭档) "1. to cooperate; 2. partners" versus dā'dàng (搭档) "partner [as in lǎo dā'dàng (老搭档) 'old workmate']". The parallel with *resea'rch/re'search* is close.

On the other hand, there are cases in modern Standard Chinese where different stress patterns seem to be indifferent. Thus we have dǎ'bàn (打扮) "dress up" which can be read dǎban as well as dǎbà'n without apparently making any semantic difference; whatsoever, both words meaning the same thing: "dress up". It would be nice to chart the extent of this kind of phenomenon of free stress in Peking Mandarin Chinese, and then in Mandarin Chinese more generally. I have not found a great many cases in the material I have surveyed. But these cases need to be noted carefully. And it will be necessary to look out specifically for such cases of freely variable stress in Chinese words.

References

Arendt C. 1894. *Handbuch der nordchinesischen Umgangssprache. Mit Einschluss der Anfangsgründe des neuchinesischen officiellen und Briefstils. Erster Theil. Allgemeine Einleitung in das chinesische Sprachstudium. Mit einer Karte (=Lehrbücher des Seminars für Orientaische Sprachen zu Berlin*, Herausgegeben von dem Direktor des Seminars, Band VII, 1). Stuttgart & Berlin: W. Spemann, 1891; vol. 2, Stuttgart & Berlin: W. Spemann, 1894; vol. 3, Stuttgart & Berlin: W. Spemann.

Chao Y R. 1948/1961. *Mandarin Primer*. Cambridge: Harvard University Press.

Chao Y R. 1968. *A Grammar of Spoken Chinese*. Berkeley & Los Angeles: University of California Press.

Chen M. 2000. *Tone Sandhi: Patterns across Chinese Dialects*. Cambridge: Cambridge University Press.

Duanmu S. 2000. Stress in Chinese. In: Xu D B. *Chinese Phonology in Generative Grammar*. London: Academic Press, 117-138.

Duanmu S. 2000/2007. *The Phonology of Standard Chinese*. Oxford: Oxford University Press.

Duanmu S. 2014. Syllable structure and stress. In: Huang C.-T. J, Li Y.-H. A, Simpson A. *The Handbook of Chinese Linguistics*. Oxford: Wiley-Blackwell, 422-440.

Feng S L (冯胜利). 2016. Beijing dialect is a stress language (北京话是一个重音语言). *Language Science* (语言科学), (5): 449-473.

Harbsmeier C. 1992. *Modern Chinese Analytic Syntax* (vol. 1). Oslo: East Asian Institute.

Hoa M. 1983. *L'Accentuation en Pekinois*. Paris: Editions Langages Croises.

Hockett C F. 1947. Peiping Phonology. *Journal of the American Oriental Society*, (4): 253-267.

Hockett C F, Fang C Y. 1944. *Spoken Chinese*. New York: Henry Holt and Company.

Hyman L. 1977. Studies in Stress and Accent. *Southern California Occasional Papers in Linguistics 4*. Los Angeles: Department of Linguistics, University of Southern California.

Hyman L M. 1985. *A Theory of Phonological Weight*. Leiden: De Gruyter Mouton.

Isaenko В. Б.1957. Опыт китайско-русского фонетического словаря. Москва: Государственное издательство иностранных и национальных словарей.

Jones D. 1967. *Everyman's English Pronouncing Dictionary*. London: J. M. Dent & Sons.

Karlgren B. 1918. *A Mandarin Phonetic Reader in the Pekinese Dialect*. Stockholm: P.A. Norstedt & Söner.

Kratochvil P. 1974. Stress shift mechanism and its role in Peking dialect. *Modern Asian Studies*, (8.4): 433-458.

Kuraishi T (仓石武四郎). 1963. *Iwunumi Chugokugo jiten* (岩波中国语词典 Yánbō zhōngguó yǔ cídiǎn). Tokyo: Iwanami.

Lin Y-H (林燕慧). 2007. *The Sounds of Chinese*. Cambridge: Cambridge University Press.

Lyu S X (吕叔湘). 1980. *Xiandai Hanyu Babai Ci* (现代汉语八百词). Beijing: The Commercial Press.

Oshanin V M. 1952. Китайско-русский словарь. Около 65,000 слов и выражений / АН СССР. Институт востоковедения. Москва: Государственное издательство иностранных и национальных словарей.

Oshanin V M. 1955. Китайско-русский словарь. Более 70,000 слов и выражений. Москва: Государственное издательство иностранных и национальных словарей.

Oshanin V M. 1983-1984. Большой китайско-русский словарь по русской графической системе в 4 томах. Около 250,000 слов и выражений / АН СССР. Институт востоковедения. Москва: ГРВЛ.

Seidel A. 1901. *Chinesische Konversationsgrammatik*. Heidelberg: Julius Groos.

Shi Y X (石毓智). 2021. *A Comprehensive Grammar of Chinese Language* (汉语语法长编). Nanchang: Jiangxi Education Publishing House.

Švarný O. 1998-2000. *Učební Slovník Jazyka Čínského* (A Learner's Dictionary of Modern Chinese) (I-IV). Olomouc: Palacký University.

Třísková H. 2020. Is the glass half-full, or half-empty? The alternative concept of stress in Mandarin Chinese (玻璃杯半满抑或半空? 汉语重音的另类观). 韵律语法研究 (*Studies in Prosodic Grammar*) (第四辑), 2019 (2): 64-105. Beijing: Beijing Language and Culture University Press.

Wang F Y. 1944. *Spoken Chinese*. Edition prepared for the United States Armed Forces Institute. New York: Henry Holt and Company.

Yale University. 1966. *Dictionary of Spoken Chinese*. New Haven: Yale University Press.

Zhang B (张斌). 2010. *A Descriptive Grammar of Modern Chinese* (现代汉语描写语法). Beijing: The Commercial Press.

词重音和汉语词法的音乐性

何莫邪

哥本哈根学院跨文化及地域研究系

摘　要　本文详细介绍了晚清以来先贤学者对汉语重音的研究。研究重音的文献浩如烟海，本文对最有影响的著作进行了梳理，讨论了重音的定义，分析了制约普通话重音的普遍规律。汉语重音不仅因方言不同而异，也会因同一方言区的讲话者本人的不同而异。本文介绍的 MAID 在线系统可以对汉语方言的重音系统进行客观量化。但因为 MAID 搜集的语料都是由独白组成的，所以对话内容对重音有何影响这一问题尚待研究。

关键词　重音　词重音　形态学　汉学史　汉语语言学

Christoph Harbsmeier

Institute of Cross-Cultural and Regional Studies, University of Copenhagen

christoph.harbsmeier@ikos.uio.no

普通话"重—轻—重"组合同文异焦模式探微 *

——以 T1N(s)Tx 短句为例

曹 文 魏 伟

摘 要 本文以 T1N(s)Tx 短句为例，探讨普通话"重—轻—重"组合同文异焦模式。实验中一共有 5 位发音人，负载句为"他说（……）"；目标小句包含 4 种"重……重"声调组合、3 种轻声情况、2 种焦点位置，语音样本共 120 个。研究发现，音高在普通话"重—轻—重"组合同文异焦句的凸显焦点方面起着主导性作用，而表征"焦点后高音点骤降"的 $\triangle D$ 值具有稳定的统计显著性。结合"重重"组合类型，该值可以作为区分前焦和后焦模式的具有语言学意义的主要观察指标。

关键词 重音节 轻声 同文异焦 $\triangle D$ 语调 焦点 句重音 普通话

1. 引言

本文报告的是与词汇轻声相关的句重音研究成果。标题里的"重"指的是

---

* 本成果得到北京语言大学院级科研项目基金（中央高校基本科研业务费专项资金，23YJ170001）的资助。感谢匿名审稿专家的宝贵意见，文中如有不足，概由作者负责。

"非词汇轻声"的单位 / 音节。

吴宗济（1981/2004：143）把普通话句调中的单字调和二字调比作句调的"建筑材料"，并称之为"句调的基本单元"。"这些基本单元的调型在语句中虽然受语法、语气的影响而有所变动，但基本上不改变它们原有的模式——调型。"不无遗憾的是，吴先生虽关注到了单元内部的一致性，但并未考虑单元间组合时的问题。

沈炯（1982，1985：73～130）通过对声调音域序列的考察，研究重音和语调，最终提出了汉语语调的双线自主调节理论——高音线跟凸显语义的句重音有关，低音线跟标示节奏单位的完整性有关。他还特别指出句子重音后会发生高音线骤降。然而，到底要达到什么样的标准才叫"骤降"呢？

Gårding et al.（1983）、Gårding（1987）在借鉴瑞典语语调研究方法建立汉语语调栅格（grid）模型以及 Kratochvil（1998）在试图建立北京话语调的通道（channel）模型时，也都指出汉语句调的重音后成分会出现调域压缩；Xu et al.（2012）在做语调的类型学研究时，还把这种现象命名为焦点后压缩（post-focus compression，PFC）。但前述学者似乎皆未考虑过对这些"骤降"和"压缩"进行分类以及更加细致的研究。访日学者杨立明（1993）曾提出过一个"100 Hz"的骤降量级，可惜这一提法并未在学界引起足够的注意；另外，他以音高的绝对物理量（Hz）来解释组合中的相对关系确也不太有说服力。

Cao（2004）开始采用半音（semitone，st）标度对一组"同文异焦句"[①]进行考察，初步发现在 T3T4T3T4N 声调组合（如"马力买柚子"）中，焦点移位呈现较稳定的、区别性的重音后高音点骤降量级。此后，他借鉴吴宗济（1982/2004）的思路，设计了由四声调型两两组合而成的 SVO 短句，研究不同声调组合在承载句重音时单元内和单元间的情况，结果发现普通话语调中存在较为稳定的、具有某种程度递归性的"调核单元"(曹文，2006，2010)。无论是"前重型"调核单元还是"后重型"调核单元，都可以通过调核音节（即句重音）跟后接音节（包括无后接音节的情况）的高音差或时长比来实现及推导；而 10 多种声调组合前、后两型的高音差可以归纳为 4 个等级，分别是小落差（2 st 左右）、中落差（6 st 左右）、大落差（10 st 左右）和"逆差"(负值)。王瑞、曹文（2009）对双音节

---

① "同文异焦句"是指一组音段序列相同而焦点 / 重音位置不同的句子（参见吴宗济，1982/2004）。

句的研究结果也支持这些发现。王韫佳等（2016）以若干 7 音节句为实验样本，结果也发现焦点词之后的音高落差保持"恒定"。

然而，上述诸研究中皆未涉及或考虑句中轻声的情况。事实上，口语中轻声的使用率本就不低。据厉为民（1981），现代汉语每（说）5～7 个音节就会有一个轻声；吴宗济（1990/2004：292）还指出，"轻声（或轻读）在语调中也是一项构成成分，它具有突出语句核心的重点，作成与重读的强烈对比"；而 Chen & Xu（2006）和 Li et al.（2018）认为，轻声跟各个声调一样，有一定的目标值，但前者认为是中度值 M，后者认为是低度值 L；Třísková（2020）更是提出汉语口语里轻声的作用比重音更关键。由此可见，在对句重音模式或调核单元的研究中，有必要补充对含轻声组合的考察，进而将结果与无轻声组合的结果做对比，找出异同。如此方能"拼好版图"，一来丰富对轻声及其影响的研究，二来验证调核单元在汉语中的普适性和递归性。

2. 实验说明

实验目的：以 $T1N_{(s)}Tx$ 短句为例，探寻普通话"重—轻—重"组合短句的同文异焦模式。

2.1 基本情况

实验有 5 位女发音人，普通话标准（一级乙等），年龄 23～25 岁，文中编号为 F1～F5。

供发音人录音使用的文本都是专门设计的短句：用"他说（……）"作为相同负载成分，其后的目标句[①]由 3～5 个音节组成。目标句中的非轻声音节分居首尾，中间有 1～3 个轻声音节，分别以符号 N_1、N_2、N_3 表示，如表 1 所示。

表 1   实验目标句

句子	重—轻—重组合
哥哥高。	（$T1N_1T1$）

---

① 该语料按句法（文本）说是宾语从句，按语调说是语调主体——亦即赵元任先生所称"调体（body）"。

（续表）

句子	重—轻—重组合
哥哥们高。	（T1N$_2$T1）
哥哥们的高。	（T1N$_3$T1）
师傅沉。	（T1N$_1$T2）
师傅的沉。	（T1N$_2$T2）
师傅们的沉。	（T1N$_3$T2）
妖精美。	（T1N$_1$T3）
妖精们美。	（T1N$_2$T3）
妖精们的美。	（T1N$_3$T3）
疯子怪。	（T1N$_1$T4）
疯子们怪。	（T1N$_2$T4）
疯子们的怪。	（T1N$_3$T4）

　　表1中的每个短句都会产生两个同文异焦句，由不同的问句引出。比如："他说哥哥高"的两个同文异焦句中有一个是"他说谁高？"的答句，即前焦句；另一个是"他说哥哥怎么样？"的答句，即后焦句。理论上，焦点所在即句重音所在。

　　录音在某高校的专业录音室内进行。所有录音样本以波形文件格式（wav）直接存储到电脑里；采样频率为 16 kHz，采样精度为 16 bit。

　　配对的问答文本按照随机顺序排列，通过电脑显示器呈现发音人，每对问答的时间间隔约为 2 秒，实验仪器由录音人（本文作者之一）操控。

　　实验共有 5 位发音人，目标（答）句包含 4 种"重……重"声调组合、3 种轻声情况、2 种焦点位置，语音样本共 120（=5×4×3×2）个。

2.2　数据的测量与处理

　　本实验使用网络开放软件 Praat（http://www.fon.hum.uva.nl/praat/）进行测量与分析。测量的项目主要是音高和时长。

　　音高测量分两种情况："重"音节测量与"轻"音节测量。"重"音节记录韵母稳定段的起、中、末点音高；"轻"音节做整体测量[①]，记录轻声部分的起、中、末点音高[②]。Praat 语图显示界面的音高设置（pitch setting）直接选择以 100 Hz 为参考频率的半音（st_{100}），自动呈现音高曲线（见图 1）。另外，由于几位发音人的常态发音鲜有低于 100 Hz 的，上声中间如出现吱嘎声，一律折算为 0 st_{100}。

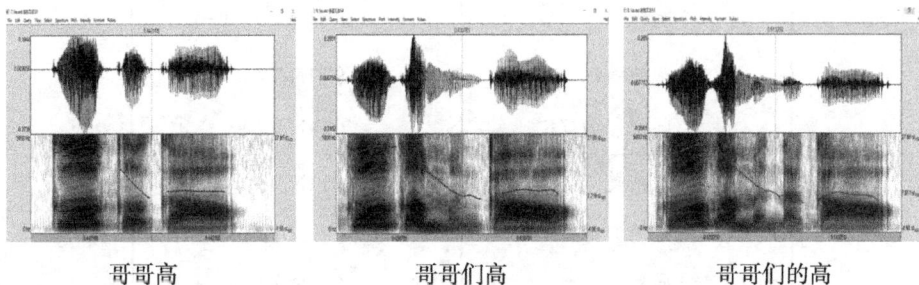

| 哥哥高 | 哥哥们高 | 哥哥们的高 |

图 1　一组前焦句的语图

注：以上三句的句重音均在第一个"哥"上。每幅小图的上半部显示的是目标句的波形，下半部显示的是对应的三维语图。浮在语图之上的横向延展细线是音高/调形曲线。

确定音节边界以记录原始时长时，根据语图、波形和听感综合判断。和音高测量时一样，本文将目标句中轻声音节的时长也看作一个整体进行测量。如 $T1N_2T1$ 句（"哥哥们高"），共测量三个时长值，分别是 T1（"哥"）、N_2（"哥们"）和 T1（"高"）的时长值。

测得原始时长后，继续计算相对时长。各音节的时长除以该音节所在句子的时长，得到该音节在全句时长所占的比例，该比例即为此音节的相对时长。

3. 结果与分析

首先对下文将出现的术语和代号做一交代。

[①]　本文并非要研究轻声本身，故而无须对每个轻声音节进行细致计算即可满足研究需要。另外，在音高方面，两个或三个轻声音节在语图上表现为连续平滑的基频曲线，与一个非轻声音节的基频曲线非常相似，因此，轻声的音高曲线在客观上也提供了将其看作一个整体计算的可能性。在时长方面，由于轻声音节很短，而且有元音弱化、清辅音浊化、连音等复杂的语音变化，有时不能清晰地划分出各个轻声音节。如果勉强将轻声音节分开计算，必更加烦琐。

[②]　轻声韵母段的起、末点为特征点，中点为过渡。

（1）句子编号

每个目标句包含三方面的信息：声调组合、轻声、焦点位置。焦点在前用 q 表示，焦点在后用 h 表示。例如，"哥哥们高"焦点为"高"时，句子编号是 $T1N_2T1h$。

（2）高音点和低音点

高音点是声调音系的区别性特征为 [+H] 的点。阳平的末点、全上声的末点和去声的起点都是高音点。阴平全调为 [+H]，考虑到其语音表现以中部最为稳定，故将其中点算作特征点。

低音点是声调音系的区别性特征为 [+L] 的点。比如，全上声的中点、半上声的末点和去声的末点。

（3）△D 值

△D 值（Cao，2004；曹文，2010：19）指两个音节的高音点之间的音高差值（前点减后点）。△D 值采用"平均值（±标准差）"来呈现。

下文将着重分析我们的实验结果。

3.1　$T1N_{(s)}T1$

实验中本组的目标句是：哥哥高、哥哥们高、哥哥们的高。$T1N_{(s)}T1$ 的前焦与后焦音高曲线如图 2、图 3 所示。

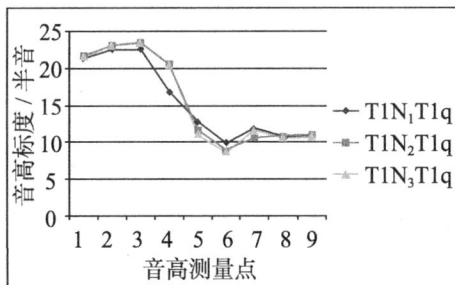

图 2　$T1N_{(s)}T1q$ 音高曲线图　　　　图 3　$T1N_{(s)}T1h$ 音高曲线图

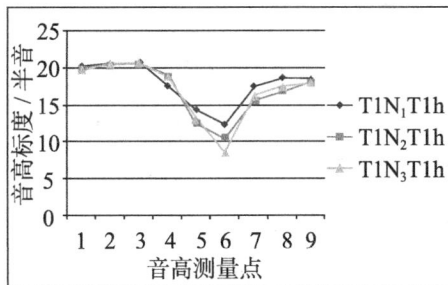

注：每个音节的韵母段都有起点、中点和末点 3 个点，例如，横轴点 1、点 2、点 3 分别是首音节 T1 的起点、中点和末点。其他 6 个点以此类推。图中显示的调形曲线是根据 5 位发音人的平均数据所制。以下图片如无特别说明，与此相同。

从图 2 和图 3 可以看出，当焦点位置相同时，轻声音节的数量仅对句中轻声本身的局部音高产生影响，而整体轮廓具有较明显的规律性。

前焦时（见图 2），三个目标句的首、末音节调形基本重叠。轻声部分起、中、末点的音高值在三句间皆表现出一定的差异，并具有统计显著性〔$F_{点4}(2, 12)=20.76$，$P=0.001$；$F_{点5}(2, 12)=7.25$，$P<0.05$；$F_{点6}(2, 12)=8.19$，$P<0.05$〕。其中，点 4 在 $T1N_1T1q$ 的音高显著低于其他两个同位的轻声起点〔$t_{n1-n2}(4)=4.94**$，$t_{n1-n3}(4)=5.33**$，$t_{n2-n3}(4)=0.37$〕，点 6 在 $T1N_1T1q$ 的音高显著高于其他两个同位的轻声起点〔$t_{n1-n2}(4)=3.94**$，$t_{n1-n3}(4)=2.71*$，$t_{n2-n3}(4)=1.96$〕，但点 5 的趋势并不明确〔$t_{n1-n2}(4)=1.22$，$t_{n1-n3}(4)=3.99**$，$t_{n2-n3}(4)=1.70$〕。首、末非轻声音节测量点在各自的纵向数据上都没有显著性差异（各点 P>0.05；具体 F 值文繁不附，下同）。首音节呈微升调势，前、后段音高[①]差异显著〔$t(14)=4.96***$〕，平均升幅 1.6 st；末音节大体为平，前、后段音高无显著差异〔$t(14)=1.23$〕。首、尾两个 T1 的高音点差异极其显著〔$t(14)=15.00***$〕，前高后低，△D 值为 12（±3）st。

后焦时（见图 3），三个目标句的首音节调形基本重叠，且调形趋平，前、后段音高无显著差异〔$t(14)=0.91$〕。首末音节测量点在各自纵向数据上都没有显著性差异（各点 P>0.05）。轻声部分中点有一定的差异〔$t_{n1-n2}(4)=1.22$，$t_{n1-n3}(4)=3.99*$，$t_{n2-n3}(4)=1.70$〕，末点的情况与中点类似〔$t_{n1-n2}(4)=1.44$，$t_{n1-n3}(4)=2.38*$，$t_{n2-n3}(4)=0.82$〕。此外，末音节调势微升，前后段音高差异显著〔$t(14)=4.04**$〕，平均升幅 1.68 st。首、尾两个 T1 的高音点差异显著〔$t(14)=4.11*$〕，前略高，△D 值为 3（±2）st。

对比图 2 和图 3 来看，前焦句首音节高音点较之后焦句的约高 2 st，统计检验表明这一差异非常显著〔$t(14)=6.71***$〕；后焦句末音节高音点（值）较之前焦句的差异极其显著〔$t(14)=11.89***$〕，后较前高约 7 st。而两个△D 值的差异也极其显著〔$t(14)=14.76***$〕。此外，轻声部分的起点值 $T1N_1T1q$ 与 $T1N_1T1h$ 无显著差异〔$t(4)=0.88$〕，但 $T1N_2T1q$ 与 $T1N_2T1h$ 差异显著〔$t(4)=2.80*$〕，$T1N_3T1q$ 与 $T1N_3T1h$ 差异显著〔$t(4)=3.13*$〕；而轻声部分的中点值仅 $T1N_3T1q$ 与 $T1N_3T1h$ 间有显著差异〔$t(4)=3.95*$〕，末点值则均无显著差异〔$t_{n1}(4)=1.61$，$t_{n2}(4)=0.39$，$t_{n3}(4)=0.23$〕。

---

① 根据统计检验需要而做此分段。所谓前段是取起点与中点的平均值，所谓后段是取中点与末点的平均值。后同。

时长情况见图4。

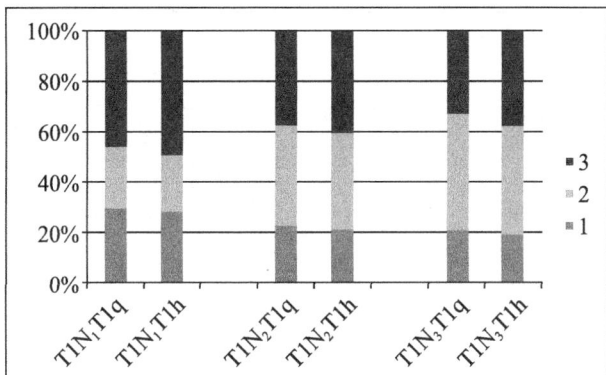

图4 T1N$_{(s)}$T1 相对时长柱状图

注：图中每根柱形从下往上的三段分别是首音节、轻声音节和末音节。

从图4可直观地看到，在同一种焦点情况下，轻声音节数量越多，轻声音节的相对时长值越大；当轻声音节数量相同时，前焦句和后焦句的整个句长无显著差异（P>0.05）——这些皆与常理相符。但是，各句内部皆呈现出末音节长于首音节现象，并具有很强的统计显著性（P<0.01），也就是说，在句子内部实际无法靠时长来区分焦点音节；而对相同音节在两种焦点句中的相对时长值进行比较后，我们发现它们也不存在显著差异（P>0.05）。上述结果表明，时长在T1N$_{(s)}$T1声调组合中无凸显重音的作用。

综合上述分析，我们可对T1N$_{(s)}$T1的同文异焦模式做如下小结：

（1）前焦的音高模式：前T1微升凸显，末T1维持平调而音高骤降，△D值为12（±3）st；轻声居间过渡，轻声音节数量=1时，轻声（起点）下降较快，末点较高。

（2）后焦的音高模式：前T1维持平调，后T1微升，△D值为3（±2）st；轻声居间过渡，无明确趋势。

（3）从聚合角度来看，焦点音节及其高音点的音高高于其在非焦点位置时的音高。

（4）时长在该组合中未表现出凸显焦点的作用。

3.2 T1N$_{(s)}$T2

本组实验句是：师傅沉、师傅的沉、师傅们的沉。T1N$_{(s)}$T2的前焦与后焦音高曲线如图 5、图 6 所示。

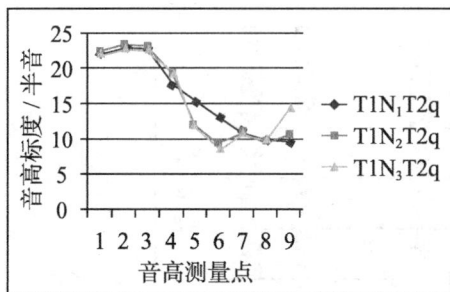

图 5　T1N$_{(s)}$T2q 音高曲线图

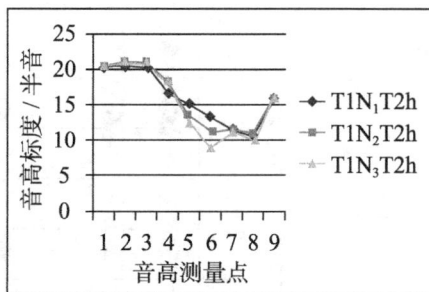

图 6　T1N$_{(s)}$T2h 音高曲线图

从图 5 来看，T1N$_{(s)}$T2 前焦时，首音节调形基本重叠，调形微升——前、后段音高差异极其显著〔t(14)=6.43***〕——虽幅度不大，在 1 st 左右。其他音节随轻声音节数量的不同而有所变化。其中，轻声部分的末点（点 6）统计上有显著差异〔t$_{n1-n2}$(4)=2.80*，t$_{n1-n3}$(4)=4.06*，t$_{n2-n3}$(4)=2.88*〕；结合音高均值来看，随着轻声音节数量的增加，轻声部分的末点依次下降。尾音节的末点（点 9）也体现出一定的差异〔t$_{n1-n2}$(4)=0.42，t$_{n1-n3}$(4)=3.08*，t$_{n2-n3}$(4)=2.46*〕，T1N$_3$T2 的末点显著高于其他两个前焦句的末点；相应地，尾音节的升幅（＝点 9－点 8）也有显著差异〔t$_{n1-n2}$(4)=0.74，t$_{n1-n3}$(4)=2.71*，t$_{n2-n3}$(4)=2.61*〕，结合音高均值来看，T1N$_3$T2 末音节的升幅比另两个句末 T2 的升幅大了约 3 个半音——这一结果应是由轻声音节数增加造成的，属于非音系性自然的"触底"反弹。这也使得整个 T1N$_{(s)}$T2q 组首、末两音节的高音点差异极其显著〔t(14)=16.35***〕，前高后低，△D$_{n1n2}$ 为 13（±4）st，△D$_{n3}$ 为 9（±2）st。但是无论 13 st 还是 9 st 皆为大级别落差，音系上不会构成差异。

从图 6 来看，T1N$_{(s)}$T2 后焦时，三个目标句调形的一致性好于前焦句，唯轻声部分的末点两两有别〔t$_{n1-n2}$(4)=2.21*，t$_{n1-n3}$(4)=3.99**，t$_{n2-n3}$(4)=3.69**〕；结合音高均值来看，随着轻声音节数量的增加，轻声部分的末点与前焦句中一样，依次下降。其余各点位的纵向数据间皆无显著差异（P>0.05）。首音节调形为平——前、后段音高无显著差异〔t(14)=0.77〕；末音节调形为升，前、后段音高差异极其显著〔t(14)=7.56***〕，后段平均升幅在 5 st 左右。音高落差方面，首、末音节的高音点有非常明显的差异〔t(14)=6.19***〕，前高后低，△D 值为 5（±2）st。

对比图 5 和图 6 来看，前焦句首音节高音点（值）与后焦句差异显著

〔t(14)=3.84*〕，前较后约高 2 st；后焦句末音节高音点（值）较之前焦句的差异
也很显著〔t(14)=4.52***〕，后较前约高 4 st。两个△D 值（见上文）差异也非常
显著〔t(14)=5.03***〕。此外，前焦句与后焦句在末音节（T2）的升幅上也有显著
差异〔t(14)=3.37*〕，具体数据可参见上文。而在轻声部分，仅 $T1N_2T2$ 轻声末点
音高在前焦句和后焦句间有显著差异〔t_{n2}(4)=2.47*〕。

时长情况（见图 7）分析如下。

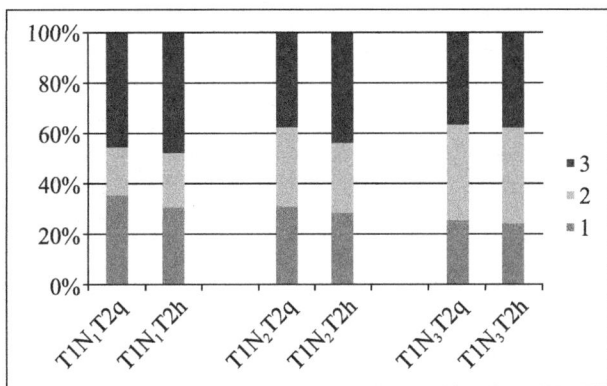

图 7　$T1N_{(s)}T2$ 相对时长柱状图

与 3.1 中发现的时长情况极其相似，在同一种焦点情况下，轻声音节越多，
轻声音节的相对时长越长；轻声音节数量相同时，前焦句和后焦句的整个句长也
无显著差异（P>0.05）。甚至 $T1N_{(s)}T2$ 各句内部也都呈现末音节长于首音节的现
象，并具有统计显著性（P<0.05），在其句子内部亦无法靠时长来区分焦点音节。
而对相同音节在两种焦点句中的相对时长进行配对样本 T 检验的结果表明：在同一
种轻声情况下，相同音节在前焦句和后焦句中的相对时长没有显著差异（P>0.05）。

综合上述分析，我们可对 $T1N_{(s)}T2$ 同文异焦模式做如下小结：

（1）前焦的音高模式：T1 调形微升，T2 后段升幅可有可无；随着轻声音节
数量的增加（到 3），似有末音节高音点抬升现象，但首—末音节的△D 值依然很
大，平均在 9 st 以上；轻声居间过渡，随着轻声音节数量的增加，末点依次下降。

（2）后焦句的音高模式：T1 保持平调，T2 后段升幅较大，平均为 5 st，首—
末音节的△D 值为 5（±2）st；轻声居间过渡，随着轻声音节数量的增加，末点
依次下降。

（3）从聚合角度来看，焦点音节高音点的音高高于其在非焦点位置时的音高。

（4）时长在本组句子中没有凸显焦点的作用。

3.3　T1N(s)T3

本组实验句是：妖精美、妖精们美、妖精们的美。T1N(s)T3 的前焦与后焦音高曲线如图 8、图 9 所示。

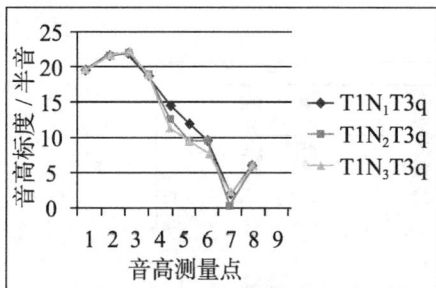

图 8　T1N(s)T3q 音高曲线图　　　图 9　T1N(s)T3h 音高曲线图

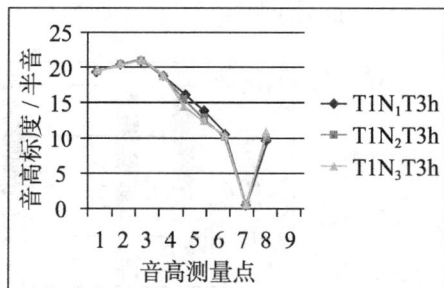

在 T1N(s)T3 三种前焦句（见图 8）的 9 个测量点中，轻声的中点（点 5）与末点（点 6）在纵向数据上的不同具有一定的统计显著性（P<0.05）——点 5 在三个前焦句中两两有别〔$t_{n1-n2}(4)=2.41*$，$t_{n1-n3}(4)=5.34**$，$t_{n2-n3}(4)=5.70**$〕，点 6 在 T1N₁T3 句中显著高于 T1N₂T3 和 T1N₃T3 中〔$t_{n1-n2}(4)=3.71**$，$t_{n1-n3}(4)=4.54**$，$t_{n2-n3}(4)=0.05$〕；其余各点位（的纵向数据）皆无显著差异（P>0.05）。首音节呈微升调势，前、后段音高差异显著〔$t(14)=7.03***$〕，平均升幅 2.3 st；末音节多呈降升调形，但也有下降调形，大多数发音样本中有吱嘎声，后段音高平均升幅为 4.6 st。首、末两音节的高音点差异极其显著〔$t(14)=15.24***$〕，前高后低，△D 值为 16（±4）st。

在 T1N(s)T3 三种后焦句（见图 9）的 9 个测量点中，除了轻声部分的末点（点 6）在纵向数据上具有某种程度的统计显著性〔$t_{n1-n2}(4)=2.54*$，$t_{n1-n3}(4)=6.75**$，$t_{n2-n3}(4)=0.55$〕——它在 T1N₁T3 里的音高明显高于在另两个后焦句里；其他各点位（的纵向数据）皆无显著差异（P>0.05）。首音节呈微升调势，前、后段音高差异显著〔$t(14)=5.77***$〕，但平均升幅仅在 1 个半音左右；末音节呈降升调形，所有发音样本中都出现了吱嘎声，后段平均升幅为 9.1 st。首、末两音节的高音点差异非常显著〔$t(14)=7.54***$〕，仍是前高后低，△D 值为 10（±5）st。

将前焦句和后焦句互相比较，前焦句首音节 T1 的高音点值比后焦句的高约

2 st，这一差别具有统计学意义〔t(14)=4.55***〕；句末音节 T3 的末点差异显著〔t(14)=4.13**〕，后高前低，差值约为 4 st；T3 的升幅也是前后焦有别（见上），差异显著〔t(14)=4.32***〕。上文提到的前、后焦△D 值的差异也是极其显著的〔t(14)=4.78***〕。在轻声部分，除起点（点 4）无差异〔t(14)=0.002〕外，中点（点 5）和末点（点 6）情况都较复杂：其中，T1N$_1$T3 前、后焦的点 5 无显著差异〔t(4)=1.22〕，但 T1N$_2$T3 前、后焦的点 5 差异显著〔t(4)=3.34*〕，T1N$_3$T3 前、后焦的点 5 也有显著差异〔t(4)=2.82*〕；而 T1N$_1$T3 前、后焦的点 6 无显著差异〔t(4)=1.63〕，但 T1N$_2$T3 前、后焦的点 6 差异显著〔t(4)=3.10*〕，T1N$_3$T3 前、后焦的点 6 也有显著差异〔t(4)=2.47*〕。

现在我们来分析一下时长的情况（见图 10）。

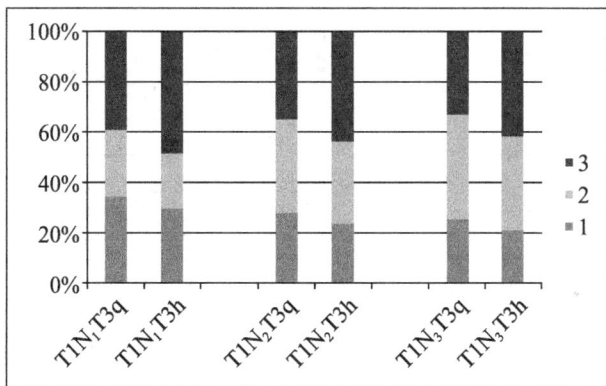

图 10　T1N$_{(s)}$T3 相对时长柱状图

首先，在同一种焦点情况下，除了 T1N$_1$T3q、T1N$_3$T3q 的首末音节时长无显著差异〔t$_{n1}$(4)=0.96，t$_{n3}$(4)=1.78〕以外，其他各句内部仍呈现出末音节长于首音节的现象，并具有很强的统计显著性（P<0.01），基本上，在句子内部依然无法靠时长来区分 T1N$_{(s)}$T3 的焦点音节。而在不同焦点情况下，前焦句首音节平均时长长于后焦句首音节的时长，且差异显著〔t(14)=2.69*〕；后焦句末音节的时长长于前焦句末音节的时长，并具有统计显著性〔t(14)=4.20***〕；但轻声的相对时长并无显著差异〔t(14)=1.70〕。综合看来，时长在 T1N$_{(s)}$T3 组有一定的凸显焦点的作用。

综合上述分析，我们对 T1N$_{(s)}$T3 的同文异焦模式做如下小结：

（1）前焦的音高模式：T1 微升凸显，T3 多实现为降升调，△D 值为 16（±4）st；轻声居间过渡，轻声音节数量为 1 时，轻声末点较高。

（2）后焦的音高模式：T1微升，T3全部为降升调，$\triangle$D值为10（±5）st；轻声居间过渡，轻声音节数量为1时，轻声末点较高。

（3）从聚合角度来看，焦点音节高音点的音高高于其在非焦点位置时的音高。

（4）时长在本组合中有一定的凸显焦点作用，焦点音节的时长显著长于该音节在非焦点位置时的时长。

3.4　T1N(s)T4

本组实验句是：疯子怪、疯子们怪、疯子们的怪。T1N(s)T4的前焦与后焦音高曲线如图11、图12所示。

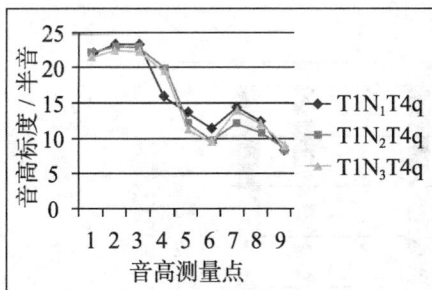

图11　T1N(s)T4q音高曲线图　　　图12　T1N(s)T4h音高曲线图

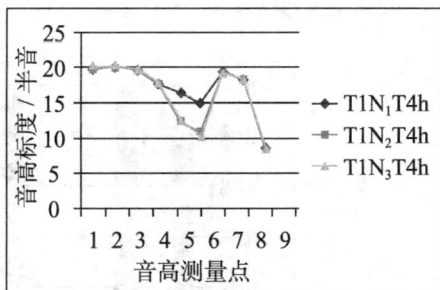

前焦时（见图11），非轻声音节的音高在各自点位的纵向数据均无显著差异（P>0.05）。与之形成对照的是，轻声部分的起、中、末点皆有显著差异（P_4=0.001，P_5<0.05，P_6<0.05）。结合图中数据可知，T1N1T4q点4的音高值明显低于其他两个同位的轻声起点〔$t_{n1-n2}(4)$=3.81*，$t_{n1-n3}(4)$=5.72**，$t_{n2-n3}(4)$=0.70〕。但是，中点的情况则相反〔$t_{n1-n2}(4)$=2.70*，$t_{n1-n3}(4)$=2.77*，$t_{n2-n3}(4)$=1.57〕，T1N1T4q点5的音高值明显高于其他两个同位点的音高；点6的情况与点5相似〔$t_{n1-n2}(4)$=2.46*，$t_{n1-n3}(4)$=3.15*，$t_{n2-n3}(4)$=0.42〕。首音节呈微升调势，前、后段音高差异显著〔$t(14)$=3.73**〕，但升幅有限，在1个半音左右；末音节调势为降，前、后段音高差异极其显著〔$t(14)$=9.43***〕，整个音节的降幅在5个半音左右。首、尾两个高音点差异极其显著〔$t(14)$=10.78***〕，前高后低，$\triangle$D值为10（±3）st。

后焦时（见图12），三个目标句的首、末两音节调形基本重叠，其测量点各自纵向的音高数据无显著差异（P>0.05）。至于轻声部分，其起点无显著差异（P>0.05）；中点有一定程度的差异（P<0.5），T1N1T4h点5的音高值显著高于其

他两个同位点的音高〔$t_{n1-n2}(4)=2.40*$，$t_{n1-n3}(4)=2.70*$，$t_{n2-n3}(4)=0.64$〕；末点则两两有别〔$t_{n1-n2}(4)=2.24*$，$t_{n1-n3}(4)=2.68*$，$t_{n2-n3}(4)=3.52*$〕。结合音高均值来看，再次观察到"随着轻声音节数量的增加，轻声部分的末点依次下降"这一现象。首音节调势为平，前、后段音高无显著差异〔$t(14)=0.11$〕；末音节调形降势鲜明，前、后段音高差异极其显著〔$t(14)=10.36***$〕，整个音节的降幅在 10 个半音左右。首、尾两个高音点无显著差异〔$t(14)=0.20$〕，△D 值为 0（±3）st。

比较前、后焦的情况来看，前焦句首音节高音点较之后焦句的高约 3 st，这一差异具有统计显著性〔$t(14)=6.37***$〕；前焦句末音节高音点较之后焦句的低约 7 st，这一差异同样具有统计显著性〔$t(14)=9.47***$〕。而前、后焦△D 值的差异同样极其显著〔$t(14)=11.00***$〕。但是，轻声部分的比较则呈现出非常复杂的结果。其中，轻声部分的起点在 $T1N_{(s)}T4$ 前、后焦之间无显著差异〔$t_{n1}(4)=1.80$，$t_{n2}(4)=2.08$，$t_{n3}(4)=1.16$〕；中点在 $T1N_1T4$ 和 $T1N_3T4$ 前、后焦之间差异显著〔$t_{n1}(4)=2.70*$，$t_{n3}(4)=3.05*$〕，但 $T1N_2T4$ 前、后焦的点 5 无显著差异〔$t(4)=1.63$〕；末点在 $T1N_1T4$ 和 $T1N_2T4$ 前、后焦间差异显著〔$t_{n1}(4)=3.27*$，$t_{n2}(4)=2.97*$〕，但 $T1N_3T4$ 前、后焦的点 6 无显著差异〔$t(4)=1.83$〕。

下面分析时长情况（见图 13）。

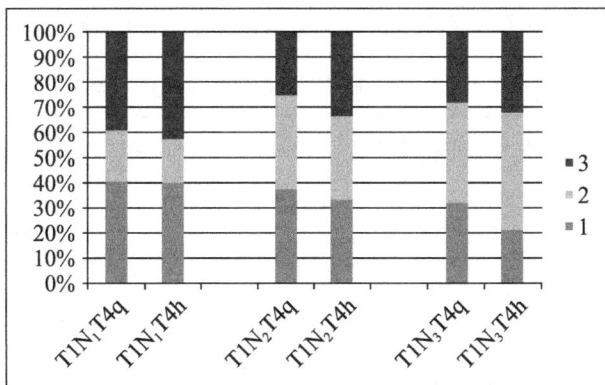

图 13 $T1N_{(s)}T4$ 相对时长柱状图

与 $T1N_{(s)}T1$、$T1N_{(s)}T2$、$T1N_{(s)}T3$ 不同的是，$T1N_{(s)}T4$ 各句内部首、末音节的时长皆无显著差异（P>0.05），因此自然也无法在句子内部靠时长来区分焦点音节。在同一种轻声情况下，比较相同音节在前焦句和后焦句的相对时长发现：$T1N_1T4$ 中，前焦句的末音节时长显著短于后焦句的末音节（P<0.05），其他音节

的相对时长无显著差异（P>0.05）；T1N$_2$T4 和 T1N$_3$T4 中，前焦句的首音节时长显著长于后焦句的首音节时长（P<0.05），末音节时长显著短于后焦句末音节的时长（P<0.05）。这表明，时长在 T1N$_{(s)}$T4 声调组中有一定的凸显焦点的作用，但不是在所有句子中都可发挥作用，也就是说，时长的作用并不稳定。

综合上述分析，我们对 T1N$_{(s)}$T4 的同文异焦模式可做如下小结：

（1）前焦的音高模式：T1 音高凸显，呈微升的趋势，T4 维持降调调势，但降幅中等（5 st），首一末音节△D 值很大，平均在 10 st 左右；轻声居间过渡，但轻声音节数量为 1 时，轻声起点较低，收点较高。

（2）后焦的音高模式：T1 保持平调，T4 高降，首一末音节△D 值在 0 st 左右。轻声居间过渡，随着轻声音节数量的增加，轻声部分的末点依次下降。

（3）从聚合角度来看，焦点音节高音点的音高高于其在非焦点位置时的音高。

（4）时长凸显焦点重音的作用不稳定。

4. 讨论

在开始讨论之前，我们先将本文的实验结果按"重……重"音节的声调组合顺序做一归纳，并与曹文（2006，2010）对不含轻声的多音节句和王瑞、曹文（2009）对不含轻声的双音节句的研究结果进行比对。请看表 2。

表 2　本文实验结果与已有研究相关结果对照表

声调组合		曹文（2006，2010）	王瑞、曹文（2009）	本文
T1T1	前焦	△D=9（±2）st，后 T1 变形降平	△D=9（±3）st，后 T1 变形降平	△D=12（±3）st，后 T1 降而不变调形
	后焦	△D=0（±1）st，后 T1 平	△D=0（±1）st，后 T1 平	△D=2（±2）st，后 T1 平
T1T2	前焦	△D=10（±1）st	△D=12（±2）st	△D=12（±3）st
	后焦	△D=3（±3）st，T2 升幅大	△D=3（±2）st，T2 升幅大	△D=5（±3）st，T2 升幅大
T1T3	前焦	未报告	△D=16（±4）st，T3 有时为半上	△D=16（±4）st，T3 有时为半上
	后焦	未报告	△D=10（±2）st，T3 全上，并有吱嘎声	△D=10（±5）st，T3 全上，并有吱嘎声

（续表）

声调组合		曹文（2006，2010）	王瑞、曹文（2009）	本文
T1T4	前焦	△D=2（±1）st	△D=2（±1）st	△D=9（±3）st
	后焦	△D=-2（±1）st	△D=-2（±0）st， T4 降幅大	△D=1（±2）st， T4 降幅大

注：表中数据皆取整数，不保留小数点，四舍五入。另，王瑞、曹文（2009）的研究涉及陈述和疑问两种语气，这两种语气的△D值绝大多数情况下没有显著差异；对有差异的数据，本文采录陈述语气的△D值。

不难发现，本文的研究结果与曹文等较早期的结果有同有异。该如何看待这些异同呢？下面进行一些有针对性的讨论。

4.1　△D 值及轻声影响

从表2可以看出，含轻声和不含轻声的同文异焦声调组合的绝大多数△D值是相近的。但是，我们同样可以观察到，轻声插入对 T1T1 和 T1T4 前焦的影响十分明显——尤其是对 T1T4 来说。"重重"组合的 T1T4 聚焦在前时，△D 值仅 2 st 左右，属小级别落差（SD）；而"重轻重"组合的 T1NT4 聚焦在前时，折算标准差，其△D 值则达 6 st ～ 12 st，变为中、大级别落差（MD-BD）。对 T1T1 的影响也是使"重重"组合原需的中、大级别落差（9±3st）变为绝对的大级别落差（12±3st）。应该指出的是，这一增大△D 值的需求不全是语音的作用，还包含了音系层面的影响。如果纯粹是语音作用的话，那么焦点后的 T1、T4 就当随着轻声的末点顺势而下——那样△D 值会更大。对这种变化最合理的解释是：随着轻声 [L] 特征插入两个 [H] 特征之间，后者产生了降阶（downstep）效应，加之原有的高音点落差要求，最终形成这样的结果。如果轻声 [L] 特征插入 [H] 和 [L] 特征之间，则不会触发△D 值降阶，从 T1（N）T2 和 T1（N）T3 可以清楚地看出这一点：前者是 [HH]([L])[LH]，后者是 [HH][L][LLH]，所以两种声调组合前焦的△D 值皆未发生显著的变化。

当然，这种 [L] 插入的降阶效应在后焦情形下也同样可以观察到。

至于表2首行对焦点后 T1 调形的不同变化所做的描述，反映了轻声介入（重音节之间）后，承担了焦点后骤降的压制力，使得句尾 T1 仍得以保持原调形。这主要是语音性表现。

在本小结的最后，我们认为有必要简单地谈一谈△D值与PFC在理论上的不同。

△D值用于表征"焦点后高音点骤降"，其理论来源是沈炯（1985）提出的语调双线模型。该模型认为，声调及声调序列音域的高音线和低音线有不同的功能，高音线用来实现跟语义相关的凸显，低音线用来实现跟节奏相关的凸显。△D值是属于高音线考察范畴的概念，所以"紧盯"高音点。而PFC并没有关注高音点/线和低音点/线是否有不同的功能。术语和概念上的细微差别代表了不同的理论认识：骤降≠压缩。后者如何进行量化的描写与归纳是一个不小的问题，而低音线的量化研究也还有待深入。

4.2 发声和时长作用

以往研究中，我们常常发现对于含有上声的声调组合，被试个体之间的发音差异较大，往往需要考察上声有无吱嘎声、调形是否曲折以及音节的时长等"参数"，并结合△D数据来综合判断焦点的位置。

本研究中，T1N$_{(s)}$T3的同文异焦结果同样符合以上"套路"。但真正有区别性的指标仍是△D值（参见表2），而吱嘎声、调形以及时长在前焦和后焦的表现皆有交叉、重叠。

马秋武（2017）提出汉语（包括方言）语调焦点重音的韵律实现有多种方式，我们表示认同。但他将普通话归为仅用音高手段来实现焦点的语言类型，以区别于其他使用时长手段来凸显焦点的方言。对于这一点，我们的看法有所不同。如同汉语的声调，虽属旋律型声调（林焘、王理嘉，1992/2013：123），但同时也具有高低型声调的高低特征或要求；普通话的语调固然以音高实现为主要手段，但时长、音质（发声）也都起到了重要的作用。

本实验中，时长与凸显焦点的关系有三种：（1）声调组合的音高聚焦信息不足，时长有重要的凸显焦点的作用，比如T1N$_{(s)}$T3；（2）声调组合的音高聚焦信息明晰，时长没有凸显焦点的作用，比如T1N$_{(s)}$T1和T1N$_{(s)}$T2；（3）音高聚焦信息明晰，时长起辅助性的凸显焦点的作用，比如T1N$_{(s)}$T4。

别的语言或方言我们暂不了解，但普通话肯定不只用音高来实现焦点。

4.3　轻声数量及其受重音节焦点移动影响而产生的效应

在上文 3.1～3.4 各小节分析实验结果时，我们注意到有关轻声的三种现象：

（1）轻声音节数量为 1 时，轻声（起点）下降较快，末点较高〔见于 T1N$_{(s)}$T1q 和 T1N$_{(s)}$T4q〕。

（2）轻声音节数量为 1 时，轻声（仅）末点较高〔见于 T1N$_{(s)}$T3q 和 T1N$_{(s)}$T3h〕。

（3）随着轻声音节数量的增加，末点依次下降〔见于 T1N$_{(s)}$T2q、T1N$_{(s)}$T2h 和 T1N$_{(s)}$T4h〕。

在本文的诸多同文异焦句中，唯有 T1N$_{(s)}$T1h 未出现明显的趋势。

然而，前两种现象皆与第三种交叉。如果暂不考虑统计显著性，只从平均值来看，上述三种现象可归纳为"随着轻声音节数量的增加，轻声部分的末点依次下降"。这样的话，T1N$_{(s)}$T1h 也不再例外。

未来的研究如果增加样本数的话，这一趋势也许会显得"鲁棒"（robust）起来。

本实验的研究结果不能确定是否存在 Chen & Xu（2006）和 Li et al.（2018）提到的某种稳定的轻声目标值。

4.4　"焦高于非"

本文的研究中还有一点发现与以往不同，即在不同焦点句的同位考察中，焦点音节高音点的音高皆高于其在非焦点位置时的音高〔参见 3.1～3.4 各小节的第三点小结〕——这里简称为"焦高于非"。

然而，"焦高于非"实际分两种情况。一种是焦点跟调尾比，即前焦句的末音节与后焦句的末音节比；另一种是焦点跟调头比，即前焦句的首音节与后焦句的首音节比。前一种因为跟△D 值相关，其理不难理解。要说的是后一种，如"师傅沉"与"师傅沉"中的两个"师"。前"师"比后"师"高 2 st 是得到统计检验支持的，但应该说，它仍只是语音现象而非音系现象或语言学现象。事实上也很难想象，我们不是在一句之内判断焦点所在，而是要在跟另一个未发出的句子进行比较后才能做出判断。

不同的实验设计造成了这一微量却稳定的结果。无论是曹文（2006，2010）还是王瑞、曹文（2009），他们的实验都未设计负载句；而本研究则将所有的目标句置于"他说（……）"之后。这个"他说（……）"在某种意义上起到了赵元任（Chao，1932/2002）所说的"调冠"（anacrusis）或英伦学派所谓的"前调头"（prehead）的作用。沈炯（1998）认为，调冠对焦点具有"烘托作用"。本文的实验结果恰好证明了这一观点。

5. 结论

通过本文的实验研究，我们发现，音高在普通话"重—轻—重"组合同文异焦句的焦点凸显方面起着主导性作用，而表征"焦点后高音点骤降"的△D值具有稳定的统计显著性。结合"重重"组合类型（或声调组合类型，因轻声不是声调），△D值可以作为区分前焦和后焦的具有语言学意义的主要观察指标。

参考文献

曹　文. 2006. 陈述句焦点—重音的韵律表现——普通话同文异焦句的实验研究. 北京大学博士学位论文.

曹　文. 2010. 汉语焦点重音的韵律实现. 北京：北京语言大学出版社.

厉为民. 1981. 试论轻声和重音. 中国语文，（1）：35-40.

林　焘，王理嘉. 1992/2013. 语音学教程. 王理嘉，王韫佳，增订. 北京：北京大学出版社.

马秋武. 2017. 汉语语调焦点重音的韵律实现方式与类型. 韵律语法研究（第二辑第1期）. 北京：北京语言大学出版社.

沈　炯. 1982. 普通话语调的音高构形分析. 北京大学硕士学位论文.

沈　炯. 1985. 北京话声调的音域和语调 // 林焘，王理嘉. 北京语音实验录. 北京：北京大学出版社.

沈　炯. 1998. 汉语语调分类和标记方法试说. 语言文字应用，（1）：102-104.

王　瑞，曹　文. 2009. 汉语普通话双音节句实验研究. 清华大学学报（自然科学版），49（S1）：1316-1321.

王韫佳，东孝拓，丁多永. 2016. 焦点和句末音高的恒定、变异及其相关问题. 语言学论丛（第五十四辑）. 北京：商务印书馆.

吴宗济. 1981/2004. 普通话语句中的声调变化 // 吴宗济语言学论文集. 北京：商务印书馆.

吴宗济. 1982/2004. 普通话语调规则 // 吴宗济语言学论文集. 北京：商务印书馆.

吴宗济. 1990/2004. 汉语普通话语调的基本调型 // 吴宗济语言学论文集. 北京：商务印书馆.

杨立明. 1993. 语句重音声学特征初探. 中国语学，（240）：1-10.

Cao W. 2004. A preliminary analysis of focus and ending in Chinese intonation. *Proceedings of Speech Prosody*. Nara, Japan.

Chao Y R（赵元任）. 1932/2002. A preliminary study of English intonation (with American variants) and its Chinese equivalents. 吴宗济，赵新那. 赵元任语言学论文集. 北京：商务印书馆.

Chen Y Y, Xu Y. 2006. Production of weak elements in speech-evidence from F0 Patterns of neutral tone in standard Chinese. *Phonetica*, 63.1: 47-75.

Gårding, E. 1987. Speech act and tonal pattern in standard Chinese: constancy and variation. *Phonetica*, 44: 13-29.

Gårding E, Zhang J, Svantesson J. 1983. A generative model for tone and intonation in Standard Chinese based on data from one speaker. *Working Papers*, 25: 53-65.

Kratochvil P (巴维尔). 1998. Intonation in Beijing Chinese. In: Hirst D, Cristo A. *Intonation Systems: A Survey of Twenty Languages*. Cambridge: Cambridge University Press.

Li A J, Li Z Q, Huang G, et al. 2018. Tonal target and peak delay in Mandarin neutral tone. *Proceedings of the Oriental COCOSDA*. Miyazaki, Japan.

Třísková H. 2020. Is the glass half-full, or half-empty? The alternative concept of stress in Mandarin Chinese (玻璃杯半满抑或半空？汉语重音的另类观). 韵律语法研究 (*Studies in Prosodic Grammar*) (第四辑), 2019 (2): 64-105. Beijing: Beijing Language and Culture University Press.

Xu Y, Chen S W, Wang B. 2012. Prosodic focus with and without post-focus compression: a typological divide within the same language family?. *The Linguistic Review*, 29: 131-147.

Preliminary Study on the Prosodic Pattern of Focus Distribution from the Evidence of the Chinese Sentences with S-W-S Tonal Combination: Taking $T1N_{(s)}Tx$ Short Sentences as Examples

Cao, Wen[1] & Wei, Wei[2]

1. Faculty of Linguistic Sciences at Beijing Language and Culture University

2. Chinese Department at the Second Middle School of Hohhot

Abstract: Cao (2004, 2006, 2010) and Wang & Cao (2009) found that there were consistent pitch dropping scales ($\triangle$ Ds) between tonal [H]s, which could prosodically predict the focus location in short Chinese sentences. However, all their observations were based on the word combination of normal tonal syllables (or to say "strong" syllables). What if there are in between "weak" syllables with neutral tones? This study aims to check if the focus model of short Chinese statement sentences with neutral tones are still bound to certain $\triangle$ Ds. An experiment has been designed to do the research.

Five speakers with high proficiency in *Putonghua* (Standard Chinese) participate in the experiment. Sentences designed are as follows:

Table 1　Focusing sentences in the experiment

sentences	s-w-s tonal combination
哥哥高。(Ge1ge0 gao1. Brother is tall.)	（$T1N_1T1$）
哥哥们高。(Ge1ge0men0 gao1. Brothers are tall.)	（$T1N_2T1$）
哥哥们的高。(Ge1ge0 men0de0 gao1. Brothers' are tall.)	（$T1N_3T1$）
师傅沉。(Shi1fu0 chen2. Master is heavy.)	（$T1N_1T2$）
师傅的沉。(Shi1fu0de0 chen2. Master's is heavy.)	（$T1N_2T2$）
师傅们的沉。(Shi1fu0men0de0 chen2. Masters' are heavy.)	（$T1N_3T2$）
妖精美。(Yao1jing0 mei3. Evil spirit is pretty.)	（$T1N_1T3$）
妖精们美。(Yao1jing0men0 mei3. Evil spirits are pretty.)	（$T1N_2T3$）
妖精们的美。(Yao1jing0men0de0 mei3. Evil spirits' are pretty.)	（$T1N_3T3$）
疯子怪。(Feng1zi0 guai4. Crazy man is weird.)	（$T1N_1T4$）
疯子们怪。(Feng1zi0men0 guai4. Crazy men are weird.)	（$T1N_2T4$）
疯子们的怪。(Feng1zi0men0de0 guai4. Crazy men's are weird.)	（$T1N_3T4$）

All these sentences are spoken out in answering certain questions with the beginning phrase "He says..." and focusing either on the subject, which is started with a Tone-1 syllable, or on the predicate, which is a one-syllable word with one of the four tones. There are accordingly one to three neutral tonal syllables between the first syllable of the subject and the ending predicate, which are labeled as N_1, N_2, and N_3. Main results are compared with former researches' as shown in the following table:

Table 2　Results comparing with Cao (2006, 2010) and Wang & Cao (2009)

tonal combination		Cao（2006, 2010）	Wang & Cao（2009）	Cao & Wei
T1T1	F-s	△D=9st	△D=9st	△D=12st
	F-p	△D=0st	△D=0st	△D=2st
T1T2	F-s	△D=10st	△D=12st	△D=12st
	F-p	△D=3st	△D=3st	△D=5st
T1T3	F-s	No report	△D=16st	△D=16st
	F-p	No report	△D=10st	△D=10st
T1T4	F-s	△D=2st	△D=2st	△D=9st
	F-p	△D=−2st	△D=−2st	△D=1st

The following conclusions can be drawn from the experiment: △D value, the difference between tonal [H]s, plays a crucial rule in identifying foci of the sentences; neutral tones in between don't make much difference from sentences without neutral tones except for T1NT4. The influence of duration and phonation is also discussed in the article.

Keywords: normal tone; neutral tone; focus; △D; pitch accent; intonation of Chinese; Putonghua

曹文

北京语言大学语言科学院

tsao@blcu.edu.cn

魏伟

呼和浩特市第二中学语文组

blcunicole@sina.com

粤语的同义多调字及其成因 *

江　荻　郭承禹

摘　要　同义多调字指一个汉字可读两个或多个不同声调而意思并无变化。关于同义多调字的成因，学界的解释多种多样，没有一个统一阐释的理论。本文列述了前贤有关粤语同义多调字产生的诸多原因——音变分化、古调继承、口语（词）造字、偏旁误读等，其中重要观点是音段音变（清浊声母、不同类型的韵尾等）导致音高变化并对应形成不同声调。系统地看，决定声调成为辨义单位的关键因素是母语社会群体的范畴化感知和社会约定。语音时刻在变，如果某字音高变化接近另一声调音高并在独立状态维持的时间够长，社会群体就可能对其重新约定，从而造成一个字拥有两种或多种声调的现象。这就是声调的本质，即声调是社会群体通过范畴化感知对音高形式的约定，而多调字是社会群体对音高变化感知进行多次约定的结果。

关键词　粤语　多调字　范畴化感知　群体约定

* 本文得到国家社科基金重大项目（21&ZD304）、国家自然科学基金面上项目（31271337）资助。暨南大学侯兴泉教授为本文的撰写提供了帮助，并提供了粤方言多音字表，特此致谢。

1. 引言

本文尝试回答现代粤语中有些字为何存在多种声调读音的问题。[①]汉字多声调读音属于常见现象，这种现象早在古代韵书中已经存在。例如《广韵》中"潦"字有两种反切注音，分别是"卢皓切"和"郎到切"，两者声韵一致，但调类存在上声与去声的区别。现代汉语普通话亦是如此，例如"荫"字究竟是读 yīn 还是 yìn 也存在争议。以上这些字属于"多音字"或"破读字"的一种，同时亦是汉语教学中的重点与难点。

关于汉字多声调读音的现象（以下简称"多调字"或"多调现象"），前贤研究大多关注不同调类所对应的词法或语义功能，而对于无意义区别的声调异读字则较少涉及。从历时的角度来说，周祖谟（1966）认为，一字多读的现象大概自东汉开始产生，后来随着六朝经师在注解古书时为其注音，才得以推广。王力（1980）也认为，这种"破读"字现象在当时的文学语言里的确存在。这里的"多读"或"读破"主要是指去声与非去声字的对立，两类不同声调读音往往具有语义或语法的区别。"去声别义"目前被认为是一种构词方式，与上古汉语的形态密切相关（梅祖麟，1980；孙玉文，2007）。不过也有学者认为汉语的声调不稳定，单字调在声调演变过程中的过渡状态造成了多调字的情况，与声调的构词功能无关（陈重瑜，2006）。

粤语中有相当一批无声韵、语法、语义、语用或文字等区别的声调异读字。例如"综"[zung1/zung3]和"刊"[hon1/hon2]，这些字的不同声调读音似乎找不到其固定词汇条件或语素意义差异，可以将之称为"同义多调字"或"声调异读字"[②]。随着粤语规范化活动的开展，一些学者开始研究无意义区别的异读字成因，多调字也是其中一种重要的现象。张群显（1991）搜集了 870 个粤语异读字，依据不同类型归纳其成因，这是最早系统地分析粤语异读字的成果。郑少玲（2012）研究了《粤语正读字汇》中的异读字，将多音现象的成因分为三类：依据《广韵》又读反切注音、受偏旁影响和受通假影响。而后也有学者详细讨论了粤语多音字的成因与具体规范原则（侯兴泉、吴南开，2017）。以上研究对粤语

---

① 本文讨论范围暂不包括因语义、语法造成的多调字。详见下文。
② 《现代汉语词典（第 7 版）》中，"异读"的释义为"指一个字表示同一个意义时习惯上具有的两个或几个不同的读法"。这里"声调异读字"实际上指仅在声调方面存在异读，并非声母与韵母的异读。

异读字的搜集和整理都有很大贡献。

近期有研究提出，字调不是单纯由音节的音高或音长等本体要素决定的，而是同一母语社会群体通过对音高形式的范畴化感知并在心理上达成共识和约定[①]而产生的（武波、江荻，2017；郭承禹、江荻，2020）。一个汉字读两个或多个不同声调也是由社会群体对音高变化的重新约定而产生的。本文以广州话为例，考察多类声调异读字的材料，亦尝试运用声调的社会约定性观点进一步探究多调字的根本成因，以及它在语言学上的普遍价值和意义。

2. 广州话声调异读字材料

广州话异读字的收集和整理工作主要是通过两次大规模的粤语规范化活动完成的。这两次粤语规范活动是由两个不同社会群体组织的。其一是香港教育署语文教育学院中文系组织成立的"常用字广州话读音研究委员会"，目的在于"减少小学语文教师因汉字广州话异读太多而产生的困扰"，并于 1992 出版了《常用字广州话读音表》（香港教育署语文教育学院中文系，1992）。其二是广东省中国语言学会和广东省广播电视学会于 1990 年联合成立的"广州话审音委员会"，而后在此基础上成立了"广州话正音字典编纂委员会"，并于 1995 年开始编写《广州话正音字典》（詹伯慧，1998），最终此书于 2002 年出版。除了大规模的社会群体组织，还有一些学者也对粤语的语音规范提出了意见与建议，例如饶秉才早在 1980 年就提出过若干条粤语"订音"的原则（饶秉才，1980）。异读字是语言规范化工作中重要的考察对象，这是因为某字有两种及以上的读音却又没有意义上的区别，显然会增加语言学习的难度或带来语言使用的困扰，而语言规范化的主要工作正是分辨出哪些读音是建议读音，哪些读音为异读或误读，以便逐步消除异读字。两次规范活动的原则都反映了这一点："无别义作用的异读，取最常用者为建议读音，颇常用者放入备注栏，不常用者不取。"（香港教育署语文教育学院中文系，1992）"审定粤语字音，宜贯彻同义异读尽量简化的原则。"（詹伯慧，1994）

本文利用以上两次规范化的异读字材料来考察粤语中的多调字现象，选用的多调字材料主要来自《常用字广州话读音表》的《异读分类整理（声调歧异）》

[①] 此处"约定"指的是元语言符号上的规约，例如共同的音系。凡是没有共同音系的群体都是不可能交际的，音系就是母语群体"约定"的编码和符号系统。声调也是符号感知层面的心理约定，而非人们日常交际的协议型主观约定。

字表。笔者筛选出其中备注为"又读"的词条，作为多调字的主要材料。此外，本文也选用了其他广州话的字汇和字典材料（详见表1），主要用以对照上文《异读分类整理（声调歧异）》所标注的读音①。以下材料按出版顺序排列。

表1　本文所用的其他广州话读音材料

材料（字汇/字典）	编者	出版时间	本文简称
《粤音韵汇》	黄锡凌	1941	《韵汇》
《广州音字典（普通话对照）》	饶秉才	1983	《字典》
《广州话标准音字汇》	周无忌、饶秉才	1988	《字汇》
《常用字广州话读音表》	香港教育署语文教育学院中文系	1992	《读音表》
《广州话正音字典：广州话普通话读音对照》	詹伯慧	2002	《正音字典》

需要说明的是，本文所引材料的声韵标音直接沿袭各种粤语材料的标音，并未转写为一致的标音方案。另外，本文的声调标音采用了香港语言学学会的《粤语拼音方案》（未刊）②，调类和调值如表2所示。

表2　广州话声调的调类和调值

调类			调值
阴调类	1	阴平	55，53
		上阴入	5
	2	阴上	35
	3	阴去	33
		下阴入	3
阳调类	4	阳平	11
	5	阳上	13
	6	阳去	22
		阳入	2

---

① 本文仅关注不同材料之间建议读音有差异的词条。若某异读字在几个材料中读音相同的话，不专门讨论。此外，本文并不区别其不同声调读音的"正误"，不同的异读正是多调字现象的表现。

② 转引自香港语言学学会网站（https://www.lshk.org/jyutping）。

3. 广州话多调字成因

3.1　中古调类的分化

广州话的多调字读音现象与中古调类的分化息息相关，主要是平上去入四声的阴调类与阳调类共存的声调异读，再次是阳调类之间的异读，阴调类之间的多调字现象比较零散。

首先是阴调类与阳调类的多调字现象（见表3），其中接近半数的字是中古次浊字，例如"髦、黏、竽、扰、绕、忍、阮、演、雳、跃"。"衅"虽为中古晓母字，其广州话读音和其他次浊字均为近音声母，也具有阴阳两调异读。这种喉部擦音演变为近音的现象在粤语中并不常见，属于特殊变化（黄玉雄，2016）。除次浊之外还有塞音声母字"雏、妥、贮、扮、栋、锻、滴、别（弊）"。只有"雏"属于中古浊声母字，其他字都属于中古清声母字。擦音声母字可以分为两类，即中古清塞音送气字"倩"和中古浊擦音字"汞、协"。

表3　广州话阴调类与阳调类的声调异读字

字形	读音	《广韵》	《韵汇》	《字典》	《字汇》	《正音字典》	分类
雏	[co1]			co1		tso1	阴平阳平异读
	[co4]	仕于切	ts₂ɔ4		tʃʰɔ4		
髦	[mou1]			mou1	mou1		
	[mou4]	莫袍切	mou4	mou4（又）	mou4（又）	mou4	
黏	[nim1]			nim1		nim1	
	[nim4]	女廉切	nim4		nim4	nim4（又）	
竽	[jyu1]			yu1（又）			
	[jyu4]	羽俱切	jy4	yu4	y4	jy4	
妥	[to2]	他果切	to2				阴上阳上异读
	[to5]			to5	tʰɔ5	to5	
贮	[cyu2]	丁吕切	ts₂y2				
	[cyu5]			qu5	tʃʰy5	tsy5	

（续表）

字形	读音	《广韵》	《韵汇》	《字典》	《字汇》	《正音字典》	分类
扰	[jiu2]					jiu2	阴上阳上异读
	[jiu5]	而沼切	jiu5	yiu5	jiu5		
绕	[jiu2]					jiu2	
	[jiu5]	而沼切①	jiu5	yiu5	jiu5	jiu5（又）	
忍	[jan2]			yen2	jɐn2	jan2	
	[jan5]	而轸切	jɐn5				
阮	[jyun2]			yun2		jyn2	
	[jyun5]	虞远切	jyn5		yn5		
演	[jin2]			yin2		jin2	
	[jin5]	以浅切	jin5		jin5		
扮	[baan3]	脯幻切②	ban3				阴去阳去异读
	[baan6]			ban6	pan6	baan6	
栋	[dung3]	多贡切	duŋ3	dung3	tʊŋ3	dung3	
	[dung6]			dung6（又）		dung6（又）	
锻	[dyun3]	丁贯切	dyn3		tyn3	dyn3	
	[dyun6]			dün6			
倩	[sin3]	七政切③	sin3	xin3			
	[sin6]			xin6（又）	ʃin6	sin6	
衅	[jan3]	许觐切	jɐn3				
	[jan6]			yen6	jɐn6	jan6	
汞	[hung3]				hʊŋ3	hung3	
	[hung6]	胡孔切④	huŋ6	hung6			

---

① "绕"还存在"人要切"的反切读音。

② "扮"还有平声"府文切"，上声"花伙切""方吻切""房吻切"的反切读音。

③ "倩"还有"仓甸切"的反切读音。

④ "汞"是浊上字，这里对应阳去调。这说明"汞"的多调现象产生于"浊上归去"之后。

（续表）

字形	读音	《广韵》	《韵汇》	《字典》	《字汇》	《正音字典》	分类
滴	[dik1]	都历切	dik1	dig1	tɪk1（又）		
	[dik6]			dig6（又）	tɪk6	dik9	
雳	[lik1]			lig1		lik7	
	[lik6]	郎击切	lik6		lɪk6		
惬	[hip3]	苦协切				hip8	阴入阳入异读
	[hip6]		hip6	hib6	hip6		
别	[bit3]	必袂切	bit3		pit3		
	[bit6]		bit6（别）	bid6		bit9	
协	[hip3]				hip3	hip8	
	[hip6]	胡颊切	hip6	hib6			
跃	[joek3]			yêg3（又）		joek8（又）	
	[joek6]	以灼切	jæk6	yêg6	jæk6①	joek9	

　　其次为阳调类之间的声调异读字（见表4）。具体来说是阳平调和阳上调之间、阳上调和阳去调之间存在异读现象。阳平调和阳上调的异读主要来源于中古浊上字"蓓、揆、挠、庚"，"闽"则是次浊平声字。而在阳上调与阳去调的多调字中，"饪、肾"则是浊上字，"邂、絮"属于去声字，"嚷"字未找到相应的中古反切。广州话的阳上调和阳去调的异读现象引起了一些学者的讨论。黄锡凌（1941）举出粤语中有部分字"尚游移于上和去之间"，如"伴、淡、断、在、坐、重、夏、造、善"，而且两种声调读音并没有意义差别。李小凡（2014）认为，这种由浊上字造成的异读现象可以"断定为是因方言接触而引发的叠置式音变"。

① "跃"在《广州话标准音字汇》中还有 [tʰɪk1]（同"趯"）的读音。

表4　广州话阳调类之间的声调异读字

字形	读音	《广韵》	《韵汇》	《字典》	《字汇》	《正音字典》	分类
闽	[man4]	武巾切①	mɐn4				阳平与阳上异读
	[man5]		mɐn5	men5	mɐn5	man5	
蓓	[pui4]			pui4		pui4（又）	
	[pui5]	薄亥切	pui5	pui5（又）	pʰui5	pui5	
揆	[kwai4]		kwɐi4	kuei4	kʰwɐi4	kwai4	
	[kwai5]	求癸切	kwɐi5	kuei5（又）	kʰwɐi5（又）	kwai5（又）	
挠	[naau4]		nau4	nao4	nau4	naau4	
	[naau5]	奴巧切②	nau5		nau5（又）		
庾	[jyu4]				y4		
	[jyu5]	以主切	jy5	yu5	y5（旧）	jy5	
任	[jam5]	如甚切	jɐm5	yem5	jɐm5（又）	jam5（又）	阳上与阳去异读
	[jam6]		jɐm6	yem6（又）	jɐm6	jam6	
肾	[san5]	时忍切	s_2ɐn5	sen5	ʃɐn5		
	[san6]			sen6（又）	ʃɐn6（又）	san6	
邂	[haai5]					haai5	
	[haai6]	胡懈切	hai6	hai6	hai6		
絮	[seoi5]			sêu5		soey5	
	[seoi6]	息据切③	sæy6		ʃøy6	soey6（又）	
嚷	[joeng5]		jæŋ5				
	[joeng6]			jêng6	jæŋ6	joeng6	

最后，阴调类之间的声调异读字较为零散（见表5）。"刊、妖"为中古清平字，"窜"为清去字，这三字在广州话均存在阴上调的异读。"岑（嵾）"在《广韵》

———————

① "闽"还有"无分切"的反切读音，与"武巾切"为重纽三等韵的关系。

② "挠"还有"呼毛切"的反切读音。

③ "絮"还有"尼据切""抽据切"与"乃亚切"三种反切读音。

中有"锄衔切"和"士减切"两读，即浊平与浊上两种异读，广州话里则变为阴上调[zaam2]和阴去调[zaam3]异读。"拷、烤"在《广韵》中无记载。"拷"在《集韵》中为上声读音"苦浩切"，现代粤语字音材料一般从"考"[haau2]音。但在粤语韵书《分韵撮要》中，"拷"属于"第十八交绞教"平声"交"小韵下辖字，与阴平调[haau1]的异读对应。

表5　广州话阴调类之间的声调异读字

字形	读音	《广韵》	《韵汇》	《字典》	《字汇》	《正音字典》	分类
刊	[hon1]	苦寒切	hɔn1	hɔn1（又）	hɔn1（旧）	hɔn1	阴平阴上异读
	[hon2]			hɔn2	hɔn2	hɔn2（又）	
妖	[jiu1]	丁乔切	jiu1	yiu1	jiu1	jiu1	
	[jiu2]			yiu2（又）		jiu2（又）	
拷	[haau1]					haau1	
	[haau2]		hau2	hao2	hau2	haau2（又）	
烤	[haau1]		hao1（又）			haau1	
	[haau2]		hau2	hao2	hau2	haau2（又）	
舛	[cyun2]				tʃʰyn2	tsyn2	阴上阴去异读
	[cyun3]	七乱切	tsyn3	qun3	tʃʰyn3（旧）		
崭	[zaam2]		dz̥am2	zam2	tʃam2	dzaam2	
	[zaam3]			zam3（又）	tʃam3（又）	dzaam3（又）	

表3～表5的39个声调异读字中，次浊声母字有16个，擦音声母字有10个，这两类字在广州方言声调系统分化中演变较为活跃，单字调类并不稳定。这些字之所以能在阴调类与阳调类之间，甚至是在阴调类或阳调类的内部形成相应的声调异读，说明了音变的无目的性，更像是由调值的不稳定性导致的结果，显得零散和杂乱。只有浊上字较为例外，似乎是由官话影响而造成系统的以声母为条件的声调异读现象。由此可知，在广州方言声调形成的过程中，字音的调值是不断变化的，特别是字音处在 A 调往 B 调演变的过渡阶段时，母语者对于音高的感知

处于两可的状态，这也是异读字或多调字现象产生的重要原因。而且这种变化涵盖了多种声母类型，其中次浊声母字和擦音声母字的音高变化更为明显。

3.2 中古多音字的继承

广州话的部分声调异读字来自中古多音字（见表6）。

表6 中古多音字与现代广州话多调字的对应

字形	读音	《广韵》	《韵汇》	《字典》	《字汇》	《正音字典》
壅	[jung1]	于容切	juŋ1	yung1	jʊŋ1（堵塞）	jung1
	[jung2]	于陇切	juŋ2	yung2（又）	jʊŋ2（又）	
	[ngung1]			ngung1		ung1/ngung1
淤	[jyu1]	央居切	jy1	yu1	y1	jy1
	[jyu2]			yu2（又）	y2（又）	
	[jyu3]	依倨切	jy3			
梵	[faan4]	房戎切		fan4		
	[faan6]	扶泛切	fan6		fan6	faan6
眩	[jyun4]	胡涓切		yun4		
	[jyun6]	黄练切	jyn6		yn6	jyn6
桦	[waa4]	户花切		wa4	wa4	waa4
	[waa6]	胡化切	wa6		wa6（正）	waa6（又）
怏	[joeng2]	于两切	jæŋ2	jêng2	jæŋ2	joeng2
	[joeng3]	于亮切	jæŋ3		jæŋ3（又）	
敛	[lim5]	良冉切				lim5
	[lim6]	力验切	lim6	lim6	lim6	
跨	[kwaa1]	苦瓜切		kua1	kʰwa1	kwaa1
		苦瓦切				
	[kwaa3]	苦化切	kwa3			
锭	[ding3]	丁定切	ding3			
	[ding6]	徒径切		ding6	tŋ6	ding6

中古平声与上声的多调字"壅",其在《广韵》中的平声读音"于容切"所对应的释义为"塞",上声的释义为"壅堨,亦塞也,障也",两种读音的释文相似。此外,"壅"在广州话中还有 [ngung1] 读音,这里不多讨论。

中古平声与去声的多调字有"淤、梵、眩、桦",后三字在广州话中都存在平声与去声的异读,"淤"除此之外还存在阴上调 [jyu2] 的读音。"淤"的平声读音"央居切"对应的释义为"淤泥",去声"依倨切"的释文为"浊水中泥也"。"梵"在《广韵》中的平声读音为"房戎切",所对应的释文为"木得风貌",去声读音"扶泛切"的意义与平声相近"眩"的平声读音"胡涓切"在《广韵》中解释为"乱也",去声读音"黄练切"则为"瞑眩,书曰若药弗瞑眩,厥疾弗瘳",两者语义略有差别。"桦"在《广韵》中的平声读音"户花切"对应的释义为"木名",与去声读音"胡化切"对应的释义相同。

中古上声与去声的多调字有"怏、敛"。"怏"在广州话中存在阴上调和阴去调的异读,其《广韵》上声读音"于两切"表示"怏怅也",去声读音"于亮切"义为"情不足也"。"敛"在《广韵》的上声读音为"收也,又姓,姚秦录有辅国将军敛宪",去声读音为"聚也"。"敛"在广州话中则为阳上调和阳去调的异读。

语义不同的多调字也是存在的,本文不赘述。同义多调字现象从古至今一直存在,以上大部分字在《广韵》时期就已经发展出多调的读音,通过表6粤语多调案例可判断其来自中古。

3.3 粤方言字的异读

与以上成因不同,粤方言字异读现象比较特殊,下文将详细论述。这里的粤方言字是狭义概念,指专门用以记录粤方言语素的字,包括自造字、古汉语字、假借字和训读字(侯兴泉、吴南开,2017)。粤方言字很多都是广州话的固有语素或词汇,其字形实际上是后来依据方言读音制定的,而且其中部分字存在异体字形,有待进一步整理和规范。以下粤方言多调字材料(见表7)主要以侯兴泉与吴南开编写的《信息处理用粤方言字词规范研究》的附录2《常见粤方言多音字表》为主,此外也参考了张群显和包睿舜合写的《以汉字写粤语》(The Representation of Cantonese with Chinese Characters)的三个附录材料。[1]

---

[1] "哨" [saau4] 和"㨢" [no4] 在《以汉字写粤语》中均无异读,而在《信息处理用粤方言字词规范研究》中存在声调异读现象。

表 7　粤方言字的声调异读现象

字	声调异读	释义	示例
掹（猛）	[mang1/3]	拉；拔出	～断咗条绳
㑊	[wu1/3]	俯下；弯腰	～低就头晕
髧	[jam1/4]	女孩前额的刘海	留～
挼（挼）	[no1/4]	用手指捻；揉搓	～成一粒粒
睄	[saau3/4]	扫视；略瞧	～佢一眼
睰（睰）	[lai3/6]	生气地盯着	唔好～住佢
撻	[taat1/3]	果馅饼	蛋～
嚓	[kwaak1/3]	圆圈；框架	一个～
嘭（嘭）	[baang1/4/6]	拟声词	～一声闩埋度门
㖞	[gut2/4/6]	拟声词	～一声饮
嘬	[cyut1/2/4/6]	拟声词	～一声

　　以上多数粤方言字的异读现象是广州话的四个平调[1]调型相近导致的。"掹（猛）"和"㑊"是高平调[55]和中平调[33]的异读字，"髧"和"挼（挼）"则属于高平调[55]和低平调[11]之间的异读字，"睄"是中平调[33]和低平调[11]的异读字，而"睰（睰）"是中平调[33]和中低平调[22]的异读字。此外，"撻"和"嚓"虽为入声字，但都属于上阴入[5]和下阴入[3]的异读字，调值也比较接近。实验语言学的证据表明，广州话平调之间的感知混淆很可能是从中平调[33]和中低平调[22]开始的（谢郴伟等，2017），例如表中的"睰（睰）"。

　　"嘭（嘭）、㖞、嘬"则属于拟声词。拟声词主要以其合适的声韵组合来模拟声响，而且多为非连续性的声响，因而音高在拟声的功能中并没有那么重要，拟声词也可以有多种声调读音。"嘬"甚至可以有四种不同的声调读音。

　　总之，粤方言字声调异读字属于比较特殊的一种多调现象。粤方言字的字音与字形仍未经严格的规范或审订，字音具有一定的随意性，不同粤方言使用者的读音可能存在差异；更重要的是，粤方言不同平调调类之间调型接近，如果音高稍有变化则容易感知为不同的调类，特别是中平调[33]和中低平调[22]。这种调值和调型的相似性会影响母语者对于声调的感知，比较容易形成多调字。

---

[1]　这四个平调分别为：阴平调[55/53]、阴去调[33]、阳平调[11]和阳去调[22]。

3.4 字符与偏旁的影响

由字符或偏旁引发的声调异读现象往往被视为"误读",这与语言使用群体息息相关。从根本上来说,汉字字音不断变化,如果字的读音与其声旁读音出现了不同调类的差异,那么语言使用群体在认字或读字时会受到较为简单易辨的声旁的影响,形成声调的异读。此类声调异读字以字符为单位,与成系统的调类之间的异读不同。例如表 8 中的"钏",声符"川"读作 [cyun1],其本字读为 [cyun3],部分人以声符"川"读"钏",多调字也因此产生。

表 8　由于字符或偏旁的"误读"产生的多调字

字形	读音	《广韵》	《韵汇》	《字典》	《字汇》	《正音字典》	多调来源
钏	[cyun1]			qun1（又）			川 cyun1
	[cyun3]	尺绢切	tsˀyn3	qun3	tʃʰyn3	tsyn3（又）	
综	[zung1]			zung1	tʃʊŋ1	二 dzung1	宗 zung1
	[zung3]	子宋切	dzuŋ3			一 dzung3	
绘	[kui2]		kui2	kui2（又）	kʰui2（又）	kui2	会 kui2
	[kui3]	黄外切		kui3	kʰui3		
侩	[kui2]		kui2	kui2（又）	kʰui2（又）	kui2	会 kui2
	[kui3]	古外切		kui3	kʰui3		
脍	[kui2]		kui2	kui2（又）	kʰui2（又）	kui2	会 kui2
	[kui3]	古外切		kui3			
茗	[ming4]		ming4	ming4	miŋ4（又）		名 ming4
	[ming5]	莫迥切	ming5		miŋ5	ming5	
酩	[ming4]		ming4	ming4（又）	miŋ4（又）		名 ming4
	[ming5]	莫迥切	ming5	ming5 ding2	miŋ5	ming5	
铭	[ming4]	莫经切	ming4		miŋ4	ming4	名 ming4
	[ming5]			ming5	miŋ5（又）	ming5（又）	
蕾	[leoi4]			lêu4		loey4（又）	雷 leoi4
	[leoi5]	落猥切	læy5	lêu5（又）	løy5	loey5	

（续表）

字形	读音	《广韵》	《韵汇》	《字典》	《字汇》	《正音字典》	多调来源
馒	[maan4]	母官切	man4		man4（旧）		
	[maan6]			man6	man6	maan6	曼 faan6
谊	[ji4]		ji4	yi4	ji4	ji4	宜 ji4
	[ji6]	宜寄切	ji6	yi6（又）	ji6（又）		
悍	[hon5]			hon5（又）		hon5	旱 hon5
	[hon6]	侯旰切	hɔn6	hon6	hɔn6		

声旁或字符的读音会影响一批与此声旁相关的字，这类字都会产生声调异读。例如声旁"会"导致了去声字"绘、侩、脍"读阴上 [kui2] 的异读；声旁"名"也导致了上声字"茗、酩"读阳平 [ming4] 的异读。值得一提的是，"铭"本来就是阳平调字，与"名"同音，但为什么产生阳上调 [ming5] 的读音却令人不解。

字符与字的声调读音区别在很多方言中都存在，普通话中也存在这一现象。例如普通话去声字"谊"在口语中经常读成阳平调 yí（刘祥柏、刘丹青，2017）。需要指出的是，由字符引起的声调异读的调类也与自身方言的声调分化相关。例如普通话中的浊上字已经归为去声调，因此浊上字"旱"与浊去字"悍"都是读去声调 hàn，并不存在声调异读。但"悍"字在广州话中仍存在阳上调 [hon5] 与阳去调 [hon6] 的异读。表 8 中的声旁影响字"川、宗、雷、曼"也都为广州话的读音。

4. 结语：声调的本质

迄今有关声调的产生和变化的讨论聚焦于音段与音高的关系（欧德利古尔，1954/1986；Hombert，1978；Ohala，1978；徐通锵，1998；江荻，1998；朱晓农，2009），如清浊声母、送气与否或不同韵尾引起的声调高低和升降；而上文多调字现象则大多反映声调变化与社会语用的关系。声调是汉语单音节词的别义特征和音系要素，不是单纯的音节物理音高特征。这意味着声调研究不能单纯依据自然语音特征来研究。

本文认为，在字段音高与声调单位之间还有一个未深入关联和探索的层次。这个层次可简述为范畴感知和母语社会群体约定，显然这是将感知者关联进来，从语言感知者对音高物理形式的心理反应来探究音高现象。再进一步，音高的个体感知必然存在差异，需要群体间相互协调将感知物（音高）类化为共同的认知体，这个过程称为社会约定，即将群体感知到的有一定物理差异的音高约定为同一共识单位。实验上把这样的感知称为范畴感知（Liberman et al.，1957；Wang，1976；Hallé et al.，2004；王韫佳、李美京，2010；石锋等，2016），所获得的语音单位即声调。因为音高是任一语言音段必含的属性，但并非一定成为语音辨义单位（Maddieson，1978），唯单音节声调语言将音高抽象为音高模式，并与意义结合为辨义单位。这个辨义单位并非由自然语言本体属性（基频或音高）所决定，而是基于说话人群体依音高模式约定的音高类别，并将其转化为心理上可识别的声调单位。

近期，跨方言的声调感知实验证实了声调的约定性（郭承禹、江荻，2020），提出声调的本质是社会群体通过范畴化感知对音高形式的约定。具体来说，相同方言人说话时采用范畴化声调感知机制，音高简约为有限数量的音系化声调，无听辨困难。当说话人感知异方言声调的时候，超出了自身音系心理约定范围，只能采用物理音高线索判断，造成听辨障碍。前者正是同区域语言或方言人（母语或母语方言人）通过范畴化感知达成声调约定，后者说话人互为异地关系，缺乏对音高的共识约定，所听物理音高不能转化为共有的声调类别。

由于声调以附载于单个音节字上的音高及其变化现象为基础，当一个字的声调音高值发生变化并靠近另一声调音高值，必然引起范畴感知的扰动。假设部分说话人，或逐渐过渡到所有说话人都接受某字新的音高值，就意味着在他们的范畴感知中该字可作为另一个声调类别来感知。换句话说，语音本体的变化促使说话人对该字的调类重新约定，结果该字获得了两种声调读音，即产生所谓多调字。声调约定性允许重新约定意味着同一个字可以读不同声调，这是多调字产生的理论依据。这个理论推定有大量事实的支持，下文以此理论对相关案例做进一步阐释。

第一，声调的音高值是不断变化的，中古以来就是如此，《广韵》时期的多调字就反映了这种情况。现代方言中也仍然如此，广州话中的一些异读现象可以视为音高值不稳定导致的。特别是阴去调 [33] 和阳去调 [22]，调型和调值十分相似，发音时音高值较高则被感知为阴调类，读低一些则被感知为阳调类，这是同义多调字现象形成的一个重要原因，同样也是调型和调值相近容易导致声调合并的原因（潘悟云，1982；曹志耘，1998）。当然，多调字并非只受自身方言声调格局的影响，例如广州话浊上字的异读是受官话影响而产生的（麦耘，2013）。

第二，声调约定现象离不开语言使用群体，不同的社会群体形成不同声调的心理约定结果。例如上文指出的由字符影响而形成的异读，这种异读实际上是因人而异的，文化水平较高的群体较少出现这种"误读"情况。此外，广州话的高升变调（张洪年，2000）也与语言使用者的文化背景相关。因为变调属于口语现象，具有更高文化水平的群体发音偏向于书面化，所以变调使用的频率就较低（姚玉敏，2010）。这种因不同人群而约定的不同读音必然会通过人群的交往扩散、相互接受造成多调字。

第三，针对语言使用群体之间的"不同读音"，或者是"误读"（"俗读"）的现象，语言权威机构开展了语言规范化工作。本文所述两次粤语规范化都遵循了"约定俗成"的原则，这一原则也是审音原则中最基础、最重要的原则。例如："字有正读俗读，而俗读为多数人所接受者，取俗读为建议读音。"（香港教育署语文教育学院中文系，1992）"审订现代广州话的音读既然是以今音为基础，对于某些通行的读音，尽管不合古音反切，甚至可能是错读的，只要社会上确已普遍使用，即所谓已经'积非成是'的，我们也就不好硬加摒弃，不妨仍作为俗读处理。"（詹伯慧，1994）饶秉才（1980）和詹伯慧（1994）将"约定俗成"作为广州话定音工作的第一个重要原则。单周尧（2012）认为："一些语音如果已错了几百年，甚至即使只错了几十年，由于已经约定俗成，即使不合反切，也没法子改，就不必再拘泥于反切了。"

总的来说，这两次大规模的社会活动无疑为粤语的规范化做了很大的贡献，将语言使用者共同的、隐性的心理"约定"读音作为建议读音，确立了一个新的读音规范。这种尊重语言事实并以此审订读音的行为，我们不妨称为显性的或广义的"声调社会约定"，即在语言使用群体"约定"读音的基础上，由语言权威团体承认或肯定读音的合理性。

第四，声调的社会约定现象也是随着群体的变化而不断变化的。施仲谋（2005）曾经调查了粤语读音倾向，笔者将之与广州话材料类比，如表9所示。

表 9　"声调约定现象"的变化

字形	读音	《韵汇》	《字典》	《字汇》	《正音字典》	1986 调查	2003 调查
倩	[sin3]	sin3	xin3			7%	1.1%
	[sin6]		xin6（又）	ʃin6	sin6	93%	98.3%
	其他					0%	0.6%
尷	[gaam1]	gam1	gam1 gai3	kam1	gaam1	21%	9.8%
	[gaam3]					79%	90.2%
拷	[haau1]				haau1	96%	87.1%
	[haau2]	hau2	hao2	hau2	haau2（又）	2%	12.2%
	其他					2%	0.7%

　　表 9 说明无论是显性还是隐性的社会群体约定都在不断地变化。从语言权威团体的角度来说，新的约定声调如"倩"[sin6] 和"拷"[haau1] 的声调，读音越来越符合语言发展规律，而"尷"读音 [gaam1] 也说明了显性与隐性约定的不同。另一方面，从隐性的声调约定趋势来看，"尷"的读音 [gaam3] 越来越受到大众的认可（增长 10% 以上），"拷"字的读音从原约定声调 [haau1] 慢慢地转向新的约定声调 [haau2]。

　　综上，广义的"声调的社会约定"包括语言使用群体的心理范畴化感知和权威学者语音规范化活动。无论如何，声调约定都无关音段的自然音高，而是群体的感知与使用的合作行为。也就是说声调具有一种特别的性质，是由母语社会群体共同对单字词产生的特定音高的约定现象，它既是人们对音高的选择又不等同于单音节字（词）的自然音高，唯有经过群体约定的单字音高才称为声调。

参考文献

曹志耘 . 1998. 汉语方言声调演变的两种类型 . 语言研究，（1）：89-99.

陈重瑜 . 2006. 多音多义字：不同的词位还是历史的层次 . 语言研究，（1）：40-53.

郭承禹，江荻 . 2020. 声调的社会群体约定性——来自跨方言单字调辨认实验的启示 . 语言科学，（6）：623-639.

侯兴泉，吴南开 . 2017. 信息处理用粤方言字词规范研究 . 广州：广东人民出版社 .

黄锡凌 . 1941. 粤音韵汇 . 上海：中华书局 .

黄玉雄 . 2016. 从"朽"的声母类型看粤语晓母字的历史层次 . 语言研究，（3）：55-62.

江　获 . 1998. 论声调的起源和声调的发生机制 . 民族语文，（5）：11-23.

李书娴 . 2008. 关于广州话阴去调和阳去调的听辨实验 . 方言，（1）：34-39.

李小凡 . 2014. 闽粤方言古全浊声母的文白异读和历史层次 . 语言学论丛（第五十辑）. 北京：商务印书馆.

李新魁，黄家教，施其生，等 . 1995. 广州方言研究 . 广州：广东人民出版社 .

刘祥柏，刘丹青 . 2017. 略说普通话异读词的审音原则 . 语言战略研究，（5）：65-70.

麦　耘 . 2013. 也谈粤方言梗摄三四等韵文白异读的来由 . 暨南大学学报（哲学社会科学版），（4）：35-39.

梅祖麟 . 1980. 四声别义中的时间层次 . 中国语文，（6）：427-433.

欧德利古尔 . 1954/1986. 越南语声调的起源 . 冯蒸，译 . 袁家骅，校 . 民族语文研究情报资料集（7）. 北京：中国社会科学院民族研究所语言室 .

潘悟云 . 1982. 关于汉语声调发展的几个问题——读王士元先生的 *A Note on Tone Development*. *Journal of Chinese Linguistics*, 10. 2: 359-385.

饶秉才 . 1980. 粤方言字音的订音问题 . 语文杂志，（5）：42-45.

饶秉才 . 1983. 广州音字典（普通话对照）. 广州：广东人民出版社 .

单周尧 . 2012. 正字与正音 . 能仁学报，（11）：1-16.

施其生 . 2004. 一百年前广州话的阴平调 . 方言，（1）：34-46.

施仲谋 . 2005. 语言教学与研究 . 北京：北京大学出版社 .

石　锋，王　萍，荣　蓉，等 . 2016. 汉语普通话阴平调的听感范畴 . 当代语言学，（1）：86-96.

孙玉文 . 2007. 汉语变调构词研究（增订本）. 北京：商务印书馆 .

王　力 . 1980. 汉语史稿 . 北京：中华书局 .

王韫佳，李美京 . 2010. 调型和调阶对阳平和上声知觉的作用 . 心理学报，（9）：899-908.

武　波，江　获 . 2017. 二声调语言呈现的轻重韵律模式 . 南开语言学刊，（2）：24-31.

香港教育署语文教育学院中文系 . 1992. 常用字广州话读音表 . 香港：香港教育署 .

谢郴伟，石　锋，温宝莹 . 2017. 广州话平调的感知 . 清华大学学报（自然科学版），（3）：299-305.

徐通锵 . 1998. 声母语音特征的变化和声调的起源 . 民族语文，（1）：1-15.

姚玉敏 . 2010. 也谈早期粤语中的变调现象 . 方言，（1）：18-29.

詹伯慧 . 1994. 广州话审音工作的进展 . 中国语文通讯，（32）：49-51.

詹伯慧 . 1998. 关于《广州话正音字典》. 学术研究，（6）：82-84.

詹伯慧 . 2002. 广州话正音字典：广州话普通话读音对照 . 广州：广东人民出版社 .

张洪年 . 2000. 早期粤语中的变调现象 . 方言，（4）：299-312.

张群显 . 1991. 粤语常用字字音异读研究 . 第三届国际粤方言研讨会论文集 . 澳门：中国语文学会 .

郑少玲 . 2012.《粤音正读字汇》所载日常错读字异读研究 . 能仁学报，（11）：489-583.

周无忌，饶秉才 . 1988. 广州话标准音字汇 . 香港：商务印书馆 .

周祖谟 . 1966. 问学集（上册）. 北京：中华书局 .

朱晓农 . 2009. 声调起因于发声：兼论汉语四声的发明 . 语言研究集刊：1-29.

Hallé P A, Chang Y C, Best C T. 2004. Identification and discrimination of Mandarin Chinese tones by Mandarin Chinese vs. French listeners. *Journal of Phonetics*, 32.3: 395-421.

Hombert J M. 1978. Consonant types, vowel quality, and tone. In: Fromkin V A. *Tone: A Linguistic Survey*. New York: Academic Press.

Kwan-hin C, Bauer R S. 2002. The Representation of Cantonese with Chinese Characters. *Journal of Chinese Linguistics* (*Monograph Series*), 18: 1-487.

Liberman A M, Harris K S, Hoffman H S, et al. 1957. The discrimination of speech sounds within and across phoneme boundaries. *Journal of Experimental Psychology*, 54.5: 358-368.

Maddieson I. 1978. Universals of tone. In: Greenberg J H. *Universals of Human Language (vol. 2)*. Stanford: Stanford University Press.

Ohala J J. 1978. Production of Tone. In: Victoria A. *Tone: A Linguistic Survey*. New York: Academic Press.

Wang W S-Y. 1976. Language change. *Annals of the New York Academy of Sciences*, 280.1: 61-72.

On the Multi-tonality of Cantonese Monosyllabic Words and Its Causes

Jiang, Di[1,2] & Guo, Chengyu[3]

1. School of Linguistic Sciences and Arts, Jiangsu Normal University

2. Chinese Academy of Social Sciences

3. Faculty of Arts and Sciences, Beijing Normal University

Abstract: A polytonal Chinese character is one that can be pronounced in two or more different tones without changing its meaning. The causes of polytonal Chinese characters have been variously interpreted by scholars; however, there is no single theory of interpretation. This article presents a list of the many reasons why polytonal characters exist in Cantonese, including phonetic differentiation, ancient tonal inheritance, oral (word) character creation, and misinterpretation of Chinese character components, among which the important point is that phonetic segmental changes lead to changes in pitch and emergence of different tones (by voiceless and voiced consonants, different types of word endings, etc.). Systematically, the key determinants of tone as a unit of differentiated meaning are the contextualized perceptions and social conventions of the native social group. Phonology is constantly changing, and if a word's pitch changes are close to that of another tone and remain independent for long enough, the social group may adopt it, resulting in a word having two or more tones. This is the nature of tone, i.e., tone is the agreement of the social group on the form of the pitch through category-based perception, and polytonal words are the result of multiple agreements on the perception of pitch changes by the social group.

In Cantonese, there are quite a series of polytonal Chinese characters which are the same between segment forms, grammar usages, meaning, and pragmatics. They can be coined as "characters with tone variants" or "synonymous characters with multi-tones". With the development of the standardization of Cantonese, some scholars have begun to study the causes of these characters with multi-tones. Consequently, multi-tones of characters are also one of the important phenomena.

Recent studies show that a Chinese character tone is not simply determined by the internal factor such as the pitch or length of syllable, but is shared by the same social group through the categorization of the pitch form with the psychological consensus or agreement (Guo & Jiang, 2020; Wu & Jiang, 2017). The pronunciation of two or more different tones of a Chinese character is also the result of the social group's re-arrangement of pitch changes. From this perspective, this article attempts to answer the question of why some characters in modern Cantonese have multiple-tone pronunciation. There are four main aspects to account for this:

The tonal split from Middle Chinese. Especially there are Cantonese characters can be pronounced with both "Yin" and "Yang" tones which correspond to high register and low register respectively. And there are also characters of pronunciation of different tones within "Yang" tones.

(1) 绕：[jiu2]/[jiu5]　　别：[bit3]/[bit6]　　肾：[san5]/[san6]

The multi-tones inherited from middle Chinese. Some multi-tones of Cantonese are found its source from *Guangyun* 《广韵》 which represents the Middle Chinese.

(2) 眩：[jyun4]— "胡涓切" 《广韵》　跨：[kwaa1]："苦瓜切" 《广韵》

　　　[jyun6]— "黄练切" 《广韵》　　　　[kwaa3]："苦化切" 《广韵》

The multi-tones of colloquial Cantonese words. This is a special kind of multi-tones. The pronunciation and graphs of Cantonese words have not been strictly standardized or reviewed. Therefore, the pronunciation of the characters is somewhat random, and the pronunciation of different Cantonese dialect speakers may be different.

(3) 掹：[mang1]/[mang3]　　搂(揉)：[no1]/[no4]　　瞴(靉)：[lai3]/[lai6]

The misleading of radicals from Character itself. The Multi-tones due to characters or radicals is often regarded as "misreading", which is closely related to the social group of native speakers.

(4) Characters: 综[zung1][zung3]　　悍[hon5]/[hon6]

　　Radicals:　宗[zung1]　　　　　旱[hon5]

Based on the facts above, the multi-tones in Cantonese are not necessarily corresponding with segments such as different types of consonants and codas. The changes of pitch or category might be the key to this phenomenon. Specifically, when the pitch value of a character changes and approaches another tone, it would probably cause disturbances in category perception. Assuming that some speakers, or gradually transition to all speakers, accept the new pitch value of a character, it means that in their category perception, the word can be perceived as another tonal category. In other words, the change of pitch prompts the speaker to re-agree on the tonal category of the character. As a result, the character acquires the status of having two tones, which is known as a polytonic character.

Phonological segments might play an important role in tonal changes, but social agreement and categorical perception are the key factors which decide phonological status of tone. If two kinds of pitch of one tone overlap for an extend period of time, the social agreement of tone may be reshuffled so that Chinese characters possess two pitch forms.

It is essential that tone is derived from social agreement in categorical pitch perception, and multi-tone Chinese characters resulted from the changing process of social agreement.

Keywords: Cantonese; polytonal Chinese characters; category-based perception; social convention

江荻

江苏师范大学语言科学与艺术学院 / 中国社会科学院

jiangdi@cass.org.cn

郭承禹

北京师范大学文理学院

guochengyu@bnu.edu.cn

普通话连续话语中轻重音的层级性和韵律表征

李智强　李爱军

摘　要　本文讨论普通话连续话语中轻重音的韵律表征和以韵律结构为基础的重音的层级性，根据声调实现域的确定，提出区分带轻声的和不带轻声的两类韵律词，分别确定各自的词重音位置。在连续话语中，轻声和轻读出现的频率远远高于词典中标注的轻声，说明前重后轻的重音格式在口语中是非常活跃的韵律模式。不带轻声的韵律词的重音位置受到韵律和结构因素以及上下文语境的影响。通过分析朗读语料，我们发现，连续话语中实词获得重音的概率一般要高于虚词，发音人在大多数情况下倾向使用前重的格式。

关键词　轻重音　核心重音　韵律层级　韵律表征

1. 重音和声调

重音是自然语言的一种韵律特征，代表语音单元之间横向的相对关系。一般来说，重音表现为音节在特定语音单元内在听觉感知上的凸显或加重。在语音研究中，一个或多个韵律词构成一个韵律短语，一个或多个韵律短语构成一个语调短语（Selkirk，1984；Nespor & Vogel，2007）。这种韵律结构的不同层级对应于不同等级的重音。一般来说，一个韵律词有一个词重音；一个韵律短语有一个韵律短语重音；一个语调短语有一个语调短语重音，又称为核心重音（nuclear stress）。如果一个句子只有一个语调短语，那么语调短语重音就是我们常说的句重音。句子中特殊的强调或对比还可以引起比一般句重音更显著的凸显。我们讨论普通话的重音首要要区分不同等级的重音，这是重音的韵律表征所决定的。

世界上很多语言的词重音位置是固定的，比如法语的词重音总是落在最后一个音节上，波兰语的词重音固定在倒数第二个音节上，而捷克语的词重音总是落在第一个音节上。[①] 有些语言的词重音在不同的词中可以落在不同的音节上，比如英语。英语词典里单词的注音包含重音位置，说明词重音的位置是不可预测的语音信息。[②] 很多语言的词重音在语音上都缺乏单一的声学关联量，带重音的音节和不带重音的音节在音高、音长、音强、音色等方面都可能发生变化。语音研究表明，英语词重音的感知跟音节的音高变化和时长变化关系密切，跟音强的关系最弱（Fry，1958）。

汉语是有声调的语言，每个汉字，即单念的音节，都有一个声调，即使没有本调的轻声音节在单念时也要念阴平。阴阳上去四个单字调构成了普通话的声调系统，每个单字调不仅有特定的调型或音高模式，而且声调的实现需要足够的持续时间，尤其是升调和降调这种曲折调（Sundberg，1979；Xu，1997）。普通话不带轻声的双音节词之间的轻重常常不容易判断，这是因为两个音节都有声调。如果两个音节的持续时间都足够长，也都有对应于各自声调的音高模式，结果就是两个音节都符合上面提到的重音的声学条件，所以从理论上说，双音节词在这种情况下比较难判断出哪一个音节更重，这一点已有学者指出（端木三，1999）。带轻声的双音节词呈现出明显"前重后轻"的重音格式。轻声音节读得轻和短，发音倾向于弱化（lenition），表现为元音发音趋向于央元音，不送气的塞音声母发

---

① 审稿人指出："这里的'词重音位置是固定的'，法语落在最后一个音节上的重音是词重音还是短语重音？同理，其他的语言也是词重音吗？"我们认为，重音的一个特点是层级性，一个词可以是一个句子，此时词重音既是短语重音，也是核心重音。

② 准确地说，英语词干（stem）或词基（base）部分的重音位置是不可预测的，如"content、content、apple"。在词基加上词缀生成一个新词的过程中，有些词缀可以改变词基的重音位置，如 -ity 和 -ize，"public"的重音在第一个音节，"publicize"的重音转移到倒数第二个音节。这种构成过程中的重音转移是有规律的，是词汇音系学（Lexical Phonology）的一个研究专题，有兴趣的读者可以参看 Mohanan（1996）。感谢审稿人指出这一点。

生浊音化等（端木三，1999）。从声学的观点看，前边的音节有固有的音高模式，后边的轻声音节失去了固有的阴阳上去的调值，音高由前边音节的声调决定，而且时长大致是前边音节的60%左右（林茂灿、颜景助，1980；林茂灿，2012）。在这种情况下，音高和时长作为重音的两个声学条件都在起作用，重音格式就比较容易判断。

由于重音和声调在声学上存在相通之处，我们比较普通话和英语这两种韵律系统的时候要首先确定跟意义有关的音高变化的最小范围，即声调的实现域（tonal domain）。普通话的音节有阴阳上去四个声调，轻声音节在韵律上附属于前边的音节，音高由前边的声调决定。不管后边有几个轻声音节，只有第一个音节带四声。对普通话而言，这个最小范围构成一个声调实现域，可以是一个带四声的单音节，或者一个带四声的单音节加上后边的轻声音节，如（1）所示。

（1）$T_i\,T_0$

[σ σ] (i = 1, 2, 3, 4)

音高变化其实也是英语词重音的主要声学特征之一，表现为一种特定的音高模式（Goldsmith，1981）。在自主音段表达式里一个单词里获得主要重音的音节跟高调（H）连结，其他音节跟低调（L）连结，重音用下划线表示，如（2）所示：

（2）(L) H L　　　　(L) H　L　　　　(L) H L

Ala <u>bam</u> a　　　un <u>tou</u> cha ble　　　coat

在语调的自主音段节律理论（Autosegmental-Metrical Model，AM）中，音高重音（pitch accent）出现在词重音的位置（Pierrehumbert，1980；Ladd，2008）。上边的例子可以表述为H*L%，带星号的H*为音高重音，L%为边界调。[①]对英语来说，音高变化的最小范围同样构成一个声调实现域，可以是一个单音节词或者多音节词。

从以上的分析我们可以看出下面几点：第一，重音域和声调实现域在普通话和英语里是相等的。一个英语单词可以有一个或多个音节，但是主要词重音只有

---

① 审稿人指出："音高重音有两类，一类是单独调（如H*和L*），一类是组合调（如H*+L、H+L*），应该是音高重音中的标星调与词重音相联结。"我们认为，英语单词单念时一般采用降调，所以调型组合为（L）H*L%，带星号的H*跟词重音位置的音节相联结。H+L*并不出现在一般单词单念的情况下。

一个，承载重音的音节跟 H*L% 音高模式中的高调相连。普通话带四声的单音节因其固有的音高模式，都是重读的。一个带四声的单音节加上后边的轻声音节，带四声的音节承载重音，轻声音节失去固有的阴阳上去四声。两种语言的区别在于，普通话带轻声的双音节的重音分布只能是"前重"格式，而英语就相对自由得多，见（2）中的例子。这种分析跟 Duanmu（1995）对上海话和闽南话的分析是一致的。第二，每个重音域都有一个最重的音节，带一个声调或者音高重音。这一点也符合 Duanmu（2007：249）提出的"声调—重音原则"，即"每个重读音节都带一个声调或音高重音，非重读音节不带声调或音高重音"。第三，从韵律层级的角度看，英语单词的韵律表征跟普通话带四声的单音节和带轻声的双音节或多音节词类似。王洪君（2008：317～322）认为：在英语的韵律层级中，韵律词是一级枢纽性的单位；而在汉语的韵律层级中，韵律字是一级枢纽性的单位，韵律字就是指带四声的单音节。我们再加上带轻声的双音节或多音节词。简单来说，英语的韵律词一般指连续话语中的一个语法词加上前后的弱读成分。它和汉语的单音节都有显著的韵律标记，比如完整的音高模式。林焘曾经指出，在分割"我买了一个茶杯"这句话时，"/ 买了 /""/ 一个 /""/ 茶 /""/ 杯 /"四个语音单位处于同一个层次，"了"和"个"读轻声，"我们的书"应该先分成"/ 我们的 /"和"/ 书 /"（林焘，1990：23）。这两个例子在韵律上的共同之处是每个分割出来的语音单元都只包含一个带四声的单音节，相当于一个声调实现域。在连续话语中，"/ 买了 /"和"/ 一个 /"、"/ 我们的 /"和"/ 书 /"分别构成一个韵律词，"/ 茶杯 /"也构成一个韵律词。我们讨论普通话的词重音，首先要把这两类韵律词分开，带轻声的只有一个声调实现域，不带轻声的单音节就是一个声调实现域。第一类韵律词的重音位置容易判断，第二类韵律词的重音位置不容易判断。

需要指出的是，汉语的词和短语的界限常常是不清楚的，既有典型的词，又有典型的短语，还有接近词或者接近短语的结构。在连续话语中，韵律词是更具操作性的概念，而且本身就是韵律层级的一个单位。例如，"来了"和"我的"都是带轻声的韵律词，二者的形态句法结构完全不同。

从韵律类型学的角度，英语和汉语处于一个连续体的两端（Hyman，2009）：英语音系的一个典型特点是重音系统（Chomsky & Halle，1968），而声调是汉语音系的显著特征。我们在讨论普通话重音的时候，可以把英语作为一个参考。我们看到，英语有不少合成词的重音位置也不容易判断，跟普通话不带轻声的双音节词的情形类似（Duanmu，2007：130～132）。一般的英语多音节词在词典里都要标注重音位置，这是词汇信息的一部分，跟普通话带轻声词的情形类似。两种结构有相同的重音域和声调实现域，是产生这种类似关系的韵律条件。因此，至少在词重音层面英语和普通话是可以做有意义的比较的。

2. 轻音和轻声

重音是相对轻音而言的，反之亦然。林焘在 1957 年和 1962 年发表的两篇文章中使用了轻音的概念（林焘，1990）；路继伦、王嘉龄（2005）提出区分重音层面和声调层面，轻音表示重音层面上的非重读音节，轻声表示声调层面上的中和声调（neutral tone）。为了方便讨论，我们下面还是沿用"轻声"的说法，除了在必须区分轻音和轻声的时候。

轻声在构词中的作用是参与构成双音节词的最小语音对立体，即后音节是否读轻声是区别词义的唯一因素。我们这里讨论的是语音对立，所以像"蛇头"和"舌·头"（轻声音节在汉字前加小圆点，下同）、"报仇"和"报·酬"这种前后汉字不同的例子，也符合语音对立条件。下面的例子是文献中经常引用的。

（3）轻声构成最小语音对立

买卖—买·卖	东西—东·西
火烧—火·烧	老子—老·子
地道—地·道	大意—大·意
莲子—帘·子	行礼—行·李
报仇—报·酬	蛇头—舌·头
服气—福·气	本市—本·事
利器—力·气	粒子—粟·子

轻声的分布特点是只能出现在后音节，所以带轻声的双音节词符合"前重后轻"的重音格式，跟不带轻声的双音节词形成对立，如"地道"和"地·道"、"利器"和"力·气"，区别仅在于后音节是否读轻声。实际上，轻声出现的范围不限于词典中标记出来的轻声词。有些可读轻声的词，如"医生"的"生"词典中未标轻声，但也常常按照轻声来读，词义不发生任何变化。另外一些词在词典中同时标记本调和轻声，如"知·道""管·家"。（4）中所列表达一定句法功能的

词或短语一般要读轻声，这些例子大都不是典型的词，而是比词大的结构。这说明带轻声的词或结构远比词典里轻声词的数量多，而且像动补结构和其他几个虚词、助词的出现频率在连续话语中也是非常高的。林焘（1990：26～34）把这种跟语言结构层次关系密切的轻声称为"结构轻音"，以区别于只跟句子语气有关的"语调轻音"。

（4）轻声的例子〔部分例子出自董少文（1955）和林焘（1990）〕

    a. 方位词：屋·里　书·上　底·下　他·那儿

    b. 动词重复：看·看　看·一·看　谢·谢

    c. 动补结构：拿·来　进·来　拿·出·去　写·得好　写·不好

    d. 动态助词：来·了　等·着　去·过

    e. 其他虚词：这·么　什·么　多·少　我·们　记·得　坐·吧　是·吗

      她·呢　这·个

李爱军（2021：293）报告了中国社会科学院"汉语口语语篇库"中不同场景对话语料的基本语言学标注信息，一共55小时的录音材料，场景包括话剧、面对面自由交谈、网络聊天和服务行业的客服电话。声调分布的统计结果显示：去声是四个声调中出现比例最高的；其次是上声；轻声的比例为16%～18%，高于阳平和阴平。轻声如此高的出现频率反映了口语与书面语的差异，同时说明轻声在口语中是非常活跃的韵律范畴。

多个轻声音节连续出现的例子也很常见，如（5）。

（5）a. 她来·了。（一个轻声音节）

    b. 她来·了·吗？（两个轻声音节）

    c. 请站·起·来。（两个轻声音节）

    d. 请站·起·来·吧。（三个轻声音节）

    e. 他走·了·过·来。（三个轻声音节）

    f. 你把苹果放在篮·子·里·了·吧。（四个轻声音节）

轻声和非轻声的轻重交替在连续话语中可以作为消除句子歧义的主要韵律手段。（6）中的两个句子在字面上完全相同，区别仅在于其中的一个音节是否读轻声，整个句子的意思就变得不同了（冯胜利，2016）。

（6）a. 我考过了。（"过"读轻声，意思是参加过考试了）

    b. 我考过了。（"过"重读，意思是通过考试了）

　　"前重后轻"的重音格式不仅是词典里标注轻声的双音节词的韵律标记，也是后词汇（post-lexical）阶段连续话语常常使用的韵律手段，如（4）～（6）中列举的例子。一般来说，母语者对轻声音节的感知和判断清晰而且稳定。重音最重要的两个声学条件——音高和时长在普通话里都被用来表征阴阳上去四个声调了，了解轻声的实现方式对理解普通话的重音系统就显得更重要了。双音节中轻声音节的时长跟前边带阴阳上去四声的音节和同处后音节的非轻声音节相比，都有明显的缩短，大致是带声调的单音节时长的 60% 左右。在音高方面，轻声音节有不同于阴阳上去四个单字调的音高模式，所以说轻声的表层语音表现也是有声调的，只是不同于阴阳上去四声的音高模式。普通话带四声的音节可以构成音系对立，轻声跟非轻声音节也可以构成音系对立。这两类对立关系要体现在音系层面。

　　在音系表达式（7）里，非轻声音节占据两个时长单位，一般用莫拉（mora，单位记作 μ）表示，轻声音节占据一个时长单位。上声分"半上"和"全上"，"全上"只能出现在单念时或句末，是四声中最长的音节。上声表达式中的高调特征（H）是一个漂浮调（Milliken，1989），只在"全上"时出现，或者出现在后边的轻声音节上。

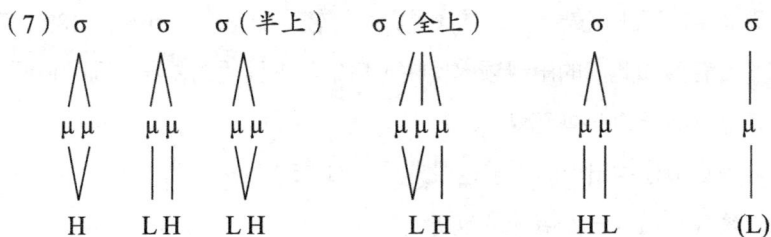

（7）σ　　　σ　　　σ（半上）　　σ（全上）　　　σ　　　　　σ

　　∧　　　∧　　　∧　　　　　／∣∣　　　∧　　　　∣

　μμ　　μμ　　μμ　　　　μμμ　　　μμ　　　μ

　　∨　　　∣∣　　∨　　　　∣∣∣　　∣∣　　∣

　　H　　　LH　　LH　　　　LH　　　HL　　　(L)

　　轻声音节在音系表达式里没有声调，原本带四声的音节变成轻声后跟其他轻声音节有相同的韵律表现，底层声调的删除和时长缩短可以通过一个"轻音规则"完成（路继伦、王嘉龄，2005）。轻声的表层音高模式一般被认为是在阴阳去声后是低调，在上声后是高调（Chao，1968：36）。在（8）给出的描写中，上声后轻声的 H 从高度上更接近阴平的 H，而去声的 H 实际的音高值要高很多。上声后如果有两个轻声音节，如"奶·奶·的"，那么表层音高模式变为 L-H-L，也就是说，最后一个轻声还是实现为低调。关于轻声音节低调赋值的来源，请参考（Li A. & Li Z.，2022）。

（8）轻声音高模式

　　a. 低调　　阴平＋轻声　　H-L　　　（哥·哥）

　　b. 低调　　阳平＋轻声　　LH-L　　　（爷·爷）

　　c. 高调　　上声＋轻声　　L-H　　　　（奶·奶）

　　d. 低调　　去声＋轻声　　HL-L　　　（弟·弟）

　　上声本质上也是一个低调，出现在非上声音节前，调值为21。"全上"形式出现在句末或单念的时候，调值为214。一般来说，上声单念的时候很难达到214的调值，通常的读法是212，而在句末时"半上"的低调形式也经常出现，除非有特殊强调（Duanmu，2007：239）。例如，做名词用的"赛马"里的"马"可以读"半上"，而动宾结构的"赛马"里的"马"既可以读"半上"，也可以读"全上"。根据这种分析，"多少"里的"少"有三种读法，分别对应不同的意义。

　　（9）a. 轻声：多·少，疑问代词。如：有多少人？

　　　　b. 半上：多少，副词。如：这句话多少有点儿道理。

　　　　c. 全上：多少，短语。如：能穿多少穿多少。（"少"重读，意思是尽量少穿点儿）

（9）c 里两个"多少"的"少"都是强调形式，读"全上"，而且第二个"穿"前边还要插入一个小停顿。这句话里的"少"如果读轻声，就变成了相反的意思，如（10）。

　　（10）能穿多·少穿多·少。（"少"读轻声，意思是尽量多穿点儿）

　　在四声里，上声的"全上"形式时间最长，调型也最复杂，听起来是最重的声调，所以是强调的形式。"半上"是低调，在四声里时间最短，所以是听感上最轻的声调。轻声音节是最轻的。如果按照音节的时长单位划分，"全上"占三个莫拉，"半上"占两个，轻声占一个。这种三分法，即"全上""半上""轻声"，可以解释（11）的词语中"子"的不同发音：

　　（11）a. 轻声：老·子　旗·子　栗·子　嫂·子

　　　　b. 通常念半上：妻子　老子　庄子　方舟子

　　　　c. 可以念全上：妻子　棋子　粒子　原子

　　（11）a 中，念轻声的"子"除了音节时长短以外，前音节如果是上声的话，轻声音节读高调或半高调，符合（8）c 的音高模式；在音段方面，元音有明显的央化。元音弱化是音节不承载重音的一个主要的语音特征，元音是否发生弱化是英语中判断重音位置和构词过程中重音能否发生转移的一个重要条件。英语中不承载重音的音节里的韵母会发生弱化，例如"Alabama/ˌæləˈbæmə/"，这里的主重音和次重音在国际音标里分别用上标和下标表示，单词的第二个和第四个音节里的韵母都发生了弱化，变成一个央元音（schwa）。英语还有一个"重音转移"（stress shift）规则，即一个次重音在前、主重音在后的单词出现在另一个带重音的音节前面的时候就会造成"重音冲突"（stress clash），解决的办法是"重音转移"，这时次重音就变为主重音，而原来的主重音变为次重音，例如"Chi'nese 'restaurant → 'Chinese 'restaurant（中餐馆）""rac'coon 'coat → 'rac͵coon 'coat（浣熊外套）"。后例把前面的词换成"ma'roon"以后，"ma'roon coat（深红色的外套）"就不会发生重音转移，这是因为 maroon 里的第一个音节韵母弱化，变成了央元音。重音转移是一种节奏交替现象，是消除重音冲突的一种方式，但是重音不能转移到韵母弱化的音节上。因此弱化的韵母是我们判断轻重音的一个指标。（11）a 中的"子"都有明显的弱化，它们的发音跟（11）b 中的"子"有明显的不同，而且这组"子"出现在上声音节后的时候使前音节发生了连上变调，我们比较"老·子（口语中的父亲或男性自称）"和"老子（道教创始人）"，两个"子"在时长上的差别不易判断，因为"半上"也很短，但是前者的调型是 L+H（半上＋高调），后者是 LH-L（上声变调＋半上）。①

　　徐世荣（1982）和冯胜利（2016）都认为轻声音节还可以再细分为轻声和次轻声，或轻音节和最轻音节。这里涉及（11）b 里"妻子"（男女两人结婚后，女子是男子的妻子）的"子"是读轻声还是"半上"。《现代汉语词典》（第 7 版）把"妻·子"标为轻声，同时列出另一个词条"妻子"（妻子和儿女）。（11）b 中的四个"子"中发音上有一个共同点，就是没有发生元音的央化，相反，舌尖元音 /ɹ̩/ 的音色很清楚。可以比较"妻子"和"嫂子"里"子"的发音，后者听起来更像 [tsə]。（11）c 中的"子"在停顿前可以念"半上"，也可以念"全上"，而（11）b 中的"子"念"全上"听起来不自然。

　　上声的"半上"形式是低调，而轻声音节的表层语音形式也是低调。在音节时长差别不显著的情况下，需要依靠音段和变调方面的信息来判断。Cheng

---

① 审稿人指出："上声位于双音节词中的第二个音节时与上声变成轻声时有无差别？从（9）、（11）和（12）感觉不出来有什么差别。比如，在'这句话多少有点儿道理'中的'少'字读成轻声或非轻声似乎都是可以的。正如文中所说的，口语里多采用轻声形式，非轻声的音节在口语体中变成轻声是常有的事。"我们在下面的讨论中提出，上声的"半上"形式是低调，而轻声音节的表层语音形式也是低调。在音节时长差别不显著的情况下，需要依靠音段和变调方面的信息来判断。但是在没有音段和变调的征兆的情况下，如审稿人例子中的"多少"，其中的"少"到底是"半上"还是"轻声"并不容易判断。

（1973：45～46）注意到"小姐"和"姐姐"不同的变调形式。他认为"小姐"中的"姐"本调是上声，通过连上变调规则使"小"变为阳平，然后再通过轻音规则变为轻声音节。路继伦、王嘉龄（2005）也支持这种分析。Duanmu（2007：242～243）认为，"小姐"中的"姐"其实是"半上"，而非轻声。我们可以用例子（12）来进一步说明"半上"的分析更合理，也更简单：（12）a是亲属称谓词，后音节读轻声，在上声后音高特征为高调；（12）b是两个上声，前上变为阳平，后上为"半上"；（12）c是动词重叠式，是后词汇过程的产物，先变调，然后后音节读轻声，这点我们同意路继伦、王嘉龄（2005）的分析。"想想、扫扫、听听、尝尝"都属于这种前重后轻的发音模式。[①] 不过，黄靖雯、李爱军（待刊）指出，来自不同结构的轻声在轻重方面构成一个连续统，这可以说明我们在轻声的判断方面需要考虑多种因素。

（12）a. 姐姐　嫂嫂（上声＋轻声）

　　　b. 小姐　表嫂（连上变调，后音节读半上）

　　　c. 想想　扫扫（连上变调，后音节读轻声）

3. 影响重音感知的韵律和结构因素

每个带阴阳上去四声的音节都是有重音的，轻声音节没有重音。双音节"前重后轻"的重音格式在构词过程中通过后音节是否有重音形成音系对立，表达不同的词义，见（3）中的例子。以这种韵律手段构词的前提条件就是母语者能够清楚地辨析哪个音节读轻声。普通话的事实告诉我们，"前重后轻"的重音格式在连续话语中也是非常活跃的。从韵律层级的角度来说，带四声的音节和带轻声的双音节或多音节词处于同一个语音层次，都包含一个声调实现域，见（1），韵律标记都是在一个声调实现域内出现显著的音高模式变化。这类韵律词的重音格式在构词阶段和连续话语中都是比较清楚的。

不带轻声的双音节词是普通话词重音讨论的焦点，学者们研究的重点是两字组在单念时、在承载句中和在连续语句中的重音分布规律（曹剑芬，2008）。王志洁、冯胜利（2006）利用声调对比法得出北京话的词汇可以有四种重音类型：重轻、重中、不分和中重。Hoa（1983）也给出了大量的重音判断，包括双音节和多音节。

---

① 感谢审稿人指出这点。

　　我们在前面指出，重音主要靠音高变化和足够的音节时长来表征，因此两个都带四声的音节不太容易判断出哪个听起来更重一点儿。从某种意义上讲，这是由人耳的听觉特性决定的。带四声的双音节组合可以是词典里的词，也可以是短语，或者介于二者之间的结构。在连续话语中，它们可以形成韵律词。这类结构的重音格式更多地表现出韵律短语重音的特点，受形态句法结构和所处韵律位置，甚至声调类型的影响，还可能受到上下文语境的影响。

　　Duanmu（2007）提出的"辅重原则"适用于短语。根据这个原则，动宾结构的宾语重，而偏正结构的修饰成分重。例如，Chao（1968：55）注意到"有井"经过连上变调后表层声调变为阳平＋上声，但是跟"油井"还是有所不同。Duanmu（2007：148）指出，这是因为"有井"是动宾结构，宾语更重，可以读"全上"，而"油井"是偏正结构，修饰语更重，"井"一般不读"全上"。

　　另一个影响重音分布的因素是韵律位置，一般来说，一个韵律结构的边界位置对发音有影响。单元起始位置的音节发音较充分，音高较高（Barnes，2002；Dilley et al.，1996），而结束位置的音节时长会延长一些（Klatt，1975，1976）。林茂灿等（1984）对单念的带四声的双音节词做的听辨实验显示大部分词都被判断为后重型。一般的解释是后音节的延长现象使人们觉得后音节听起来更重。对于带四声的音节来说，上声读"全上"一定需要更多的时间，所以只能出现在大的韵律边界位置。其他声调在韵律边界位置的时候是否要读得长一些以增强重音的感觉，还要取决于其他因素，如声调类型。换言之，并不是在韵律边界的声调就自动变为最重的。

　　Meredith（1990：134～135）注意到普通话的四个声调里去声和阴平最重，上声（半上）最轻，并据此提出了一个声调的"重度等级"（Stressability Hierarchy）。殷治纲（2011）研究了声调类型对轻重音感知的影响。他把四声按声调特征分为稳态调和动态调，阴平是高调，上声是低调，二者调域范围很窄，所以是稳态调；阳平和去声都是动态调，调域范围大，尤其是去声。通过对二字调的16种组合（实际为15种，上上跟阳上合流）进行重音听辨，他发现去声最重，阴平、阳平次重，上声最轻。值得注意的是"阴平＋上声"组合中阴平的轻重感知得分跟去声差不多，而"阴平＋阴平"中前一个阴平听起来就不如后一个重。作者的解释是，阴平是高调，上声是低调，这种音高上的"高—低"组合跟去声的音高模式一样，而且是跨两个音节，后边的低调突出了前边的高调。这是一种逆向的声调协同发音作用（Xu，1994），轻声音节前四声的整体调域比非轻声前四声的整体调域要大，也是同样的逆向作用（Li A. & Li Z., 2022）。陈娟文等（2003）分析上海话和普通话的词重音时也发现，韵律位置是影响声调重读的一个因素，重音落在前音节时，普通话的去声最容易重读，其次是阴平和阳平，上声最不容易重读。杨辰（2005）也指出，普通话中上声是最不容易获得重音的音节，去声和阴平比阳平更容易获得重音。

有些"辅重原则"不好解释的例子可以通过声调的重度等级得到解释。文献中常见的例子是"炒饭"，它本身是有歧义的，可以是动宾结构，也可以是偏正结构。如果是动宾结构，根据"辅重原则"，"饭"重于"炒"；如果是偏正结构，"炒"重于"饭"（冯胜利，2016）。实际上，普通话的母语者基本上都会认为两个结构的读音相同，都是"饭"更重。这种现象可能是声调的重度等级造成的：因为这里"炒"是上声，读低调的"半上"，而"饭"是去声，显然去声听起来更重。

我们再看（13）。

（13）a. 管家，T3+T1，动宾短语

　　　b. 管家，T3+T1/T0，偏正式合成词

（13）a 是动宾短语，动词是上声，宾语是阴平，"辅重原则"和声调重度等级都指向做宾语的"家"更重；（13）b 是偏正式合成词，"家"可以读阴平或轻声，两种读法不区分词义。"家"的轻声读法导致"管"更重，这样从重音格式上满足了"辅重原则"的要求。

后音节轻化或轻读是一种常见的调整重音的韵律手段。另一韵律手段是保留本调，通过降阶（downstep，降低声调音高的高音点）使前音节或者后音节听起来轻一些。"去声＋去声"组合常常使用降阶的办法。例如，单念"创造"时，一般是"造"更重一些，后音节的去声实现得更充分。但是当"创造"出现在"创造天才"这样的动宾短语里的时候，"造"的去声就要比"创"低一些，也就是说，"创"比"造"更重。对于双音节中出现的更普遍的降阶现象，可以参考杨辰（2005）的研究。"去声＋去声"组合另一种调整重音的手段是第二个去声轻化，如"技术""艺术""重要"；但是动宾短语或动宾式合成词往往通过前音节的降阶来满足宾语重的要求，如"计数""念旧"等。

4. 语调重音和重音判断

研究重音不能脱离韵律结构，韵律结构有层级，重音也有层级。一个语调短语

中等级最高的重音是语调短语重音，或称核心重音，它出现在语调短语里韵律显著性最高的音节上。从韵律词的词重音到韵律短语重音，再到核心重音，体现了重音的层级性。核心重音是一个句子里凸显程度最高的重音，在连续话语中，常常起到影响句子的结构意义和语用意义的作用。我们以"他们都走了"为例〔见（14）〕：

    （14）a. 他们<u>都</u>走了。

        b. 他们都<u>走</u>了。

        c. <u>他们</u>都走了。

这句话可以有三个不同的核心重音位置，用下划线表示。在一定的语境下，如朋友聚会，（14）a 强调的是每个人都离开了，"都"带重音是这种句式的一般重音模式；（14）b 强调的是已发生的动作；（14）c 强调的是一部分人离开了，如果聚会的主人看到所有的客人都离开了，然后说"<u>他们</u>都走了"，听起来就非常奇怪。通过（14）我们可以看到，在句法结构和每个音节的声调都没有改变的情况下，核心重音位置的改变对语用意义产生了明显的影响。同时，对重音位置的音节和重音位置以外的音节也产生了不同的影响，在声调调类不改变的情况下，表现为声调实现方式的变化。这句话里的"都"分别处于核心重音位置〔（14）a〕、核心重音前〔（14）b〕和核心重音后〔（14）c〕，虽然声调还是阴平，但是表层调型明显不同。图 1 给出了这句话三种重音模式的基频曲线图，发音人为男性，每个音节的韵母部分按照相同间隔在 10 个点提取基频，基频单位为赫兹（Hz）。

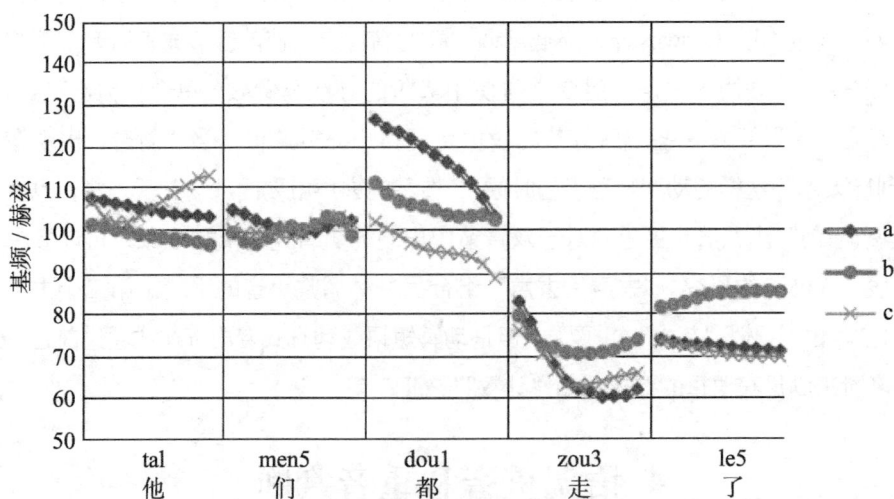

图 1 "他们都走了"三种重音模式的基频曲线

同理，"看起来不错"可以有两个重音位置，我们暂且称之为短语重音，因为这是一个对应于韵律短语的结构。（15）a是这种结构一般的重音模式，短语重音落在"不错"上，表达对语境中的主语某种程度的认可和肯定；而（15）b是一种对比重音模式，短语重音落在"看"上，跟另一个动词形成对比，如"这种小吃，看起来不错，吃起来一般"。如果比较一下（15）a和（15）b中"看"和"错"的读音，我们就会注意到这两个去声音节都保持了去声的调型，但是获得重音的去声实现得非常充分，不但调型听起来很完整，而且音节时长可能也长一些，跟短语里没有获得重音的去声相比，二者在轻重程度上的差别很明显。图2给出了这两种重音模式的基频曲线图，发音人和基频提取方式跟图1相同。

（15）a. <u>看起来不错</u>

　　　b. <u>看</u>起来不错

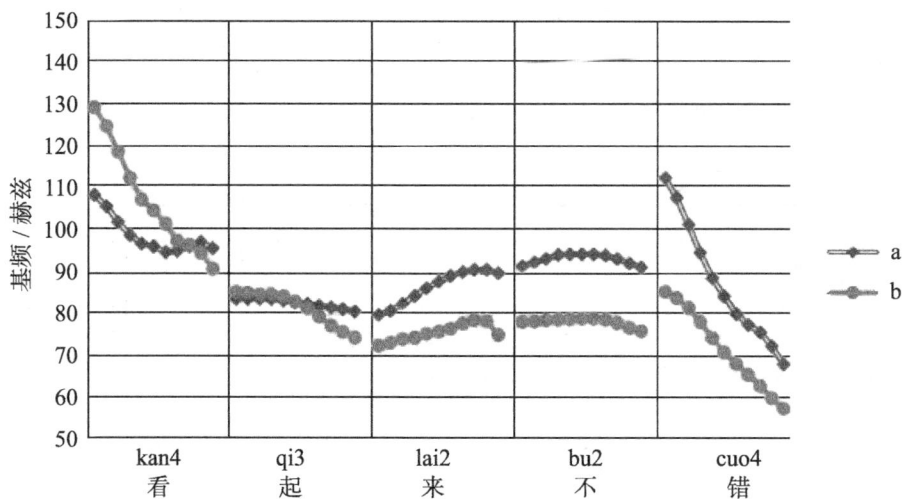

图2　"看起来不错"两种重音模式的基频曲线

（14）和（15）这两个例子至少可以说明在韵律短语和语调短语的层面，我们对于核心重音的语感是非常清晰的，否则就难于分辨因重音位置改变而引起的意义变化。从言语理解和交际的角度看，能够完成这种信息编码功能的一个前提条件是核心重音产生的语音变化有足够的韵律显著性，这样才能有助于说话人和听话人之间言语交流的顺利进行。

核心重音位置可以改变整个语调短语的音高模式。以往汉语语调研究发现，焦点位置的强重音导致重音位置的声调调域扩展，焦点位置后的声调调域变窄，而焦点位置前的声调调域基本保持不变（沈炯，1994；Xu，1999），也就是说要突出语调短语中重的部分，还需要后边的部分变轻。核心重音的这种实现方式恰恰说明重音是一个相对的韵律范畴。我们以（16）为例来进一步说明核心重音对声调实现的影响。

（16）a. 他家<u>就</u>在附近

　　　 b. 他家就在<u>附近</u>

（16）是一个语调短语，可以有两种读法。（16）a 核心重音落在去声的"就"上，"在"的本调是去声，在核心重音后读轻声，"附近"依然是两个去声，并未变成轻声，但是去声音高的高点远远低于"就"，而且调域变窄，两个去声几乎等重。（16）b 核心重音落在"附近"上，强调家的位置不远，"近"是整个语调短语最凸显的位置，而"就"的声调虽然没有轻化，但是去声音高的高点比"附近"都要低。图3给出了两种读法的基频曲线图，发音人和基频提取方式跟图1相同。从这个例子我们可以看出，"附近"在非核心重音位置的时候几乎等重，但是一旦出现在核心重音位置，重音格式就变得很清楚了。

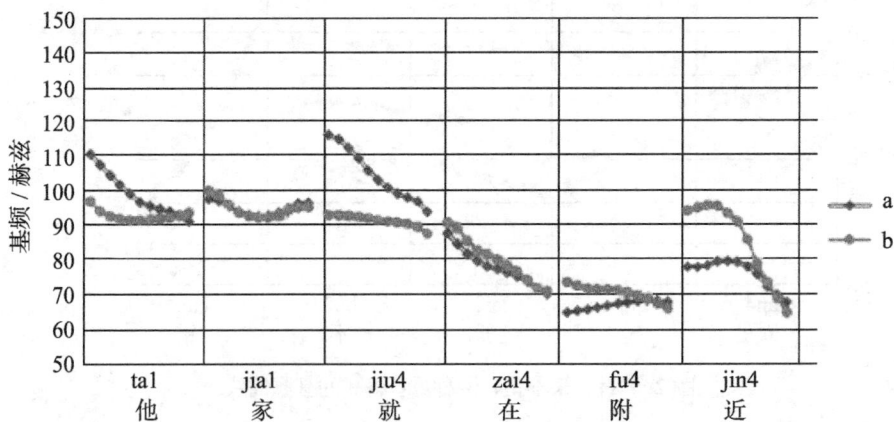

图3　"他家就在附近"两种重音模式的基频曲线

核心重音对于重音判断的意义在于韵律凸显导致声调调域扩大、音节时长加长，有利于母语者借助更突出的声学信号对不带轻声的韵律词的重音位置做出相对准确的判断。（16）中的"附近"就是一个例子。

5. 连续话语中的重音分布与词类的关系

近年来，对于普通话重音的研究开始关注连续话语中的重音分布现象，例如王韫佳等（2003）发现连续话语中双音节词的重音感知特点受到词所在的韵律边界的显著影响，又在随后的研究中通过实验的方法考察了自然语句中焦点重音和语义重音的分布（王韫佳等，2004），结果发现，焦点重音具有明显的后置倾向，在主谓句中倾向于落在谓语部分，在有宾语的句子中倾向于落在宾语部分，在宾语部分，焦点重音倾向于落在定语上。他们的结论基本上验证了"辅重原则"。陈娟文等（2003）统计了多人普通话朗读语料中双音节韵律词的重音分布，结果显示前重比率占61%。殷治纲（2011）发现，普通话韵律词有"左重"趋势，韵律短语有"中重"趋势，语调短语有"右重"趋势。

我们利用中国社会科学院语言研究所制作的朗读语篇语料库ASCCD考察在朗读语篇中重音在不同词类中的分布情况以及与词类的关系，另外考察在双音节词结构中构词结构对重音分布的影响，以及不同发音人对重音处理的异同问题。ASCCD的内容包括18篇文章，体裁覆盖记叙、议论、通讯、散文等常见文体。语料库的基本信息参见李爱军（2021：279～282），韵律标注采用C-ToBI，由专业标注人员通过观察语图并结合听感标注重音（韵律词重音、韵律短语重音和语调短语重音）和韵律边界（韵律词边界、韵律短语边界和语调短语边界）。

本文分析的数据取自数据库的8篇朗读语料，一共包括4254个音节，重音标注在C-ToBI的基础上，综合每个人语篇的重音情况，给出了4级绝对重音的标注（殷治纲，2011）：0（轻读）、1（正常）、2（略重）、3（很重）。我们同时标注词类，参照《现代汉语词典》和《现代汉语八百词》分为12类：形容词、连词、副词、数词、名词、介词、量词、代词、助词、动词、语气词、熟语①。我们分析其中一位女性发音人（F01）和一位男性发音人（M01）的数据。

表1给出了不同重音等级的音节个数及占总数的百分比。数据的一个显著特点是无重音的音节占60%，有重音的占40%，两位发音人的数据几乎完全一致。男性发音人在句子里特别凸显的音节（3级重音）要多于女性发音人，这反映出

---

① 指常用的固定短语。

两个人在韵律上不同的发音特点。

表1 不同重音级音节个数及占总数的百分比

重音级	F01		M01	
	个数	比例	个数	比例
0	2552	60.00%	2555	60.06%
1	897	21.09%	721	16.95%
2	326	7.66%	333	7.83%
3	479	11.26%	645	15.16%
总数	4254	100.00%	4254	100.00%

不同重音等级的音节在时长上也有区别，图4给出了音节和声韵母的时长，以毫秒为单位。基本上，不同重音等级的音节在整体时长上有明显不同，男性发音人更明显。两位发音人在2级和3级之间时长上并未表现出差别。但从音高上限跟重音的关系看（见图5），音节音高上限和重音级别成正相关——随着重音级别的提高，音高上限也升高。重音级别从1级升到3级，音高上限呈现加速上升趋势，说明高级别重音可能主要是通过音高上限的升高实现的。可见从自然音节（1）到轻读音节（0），可能是通过时长缩短等实现的，其音高上限不一定下降。在时长足够长的3级和2级重音情况下，音高是更重要的韵律表征。

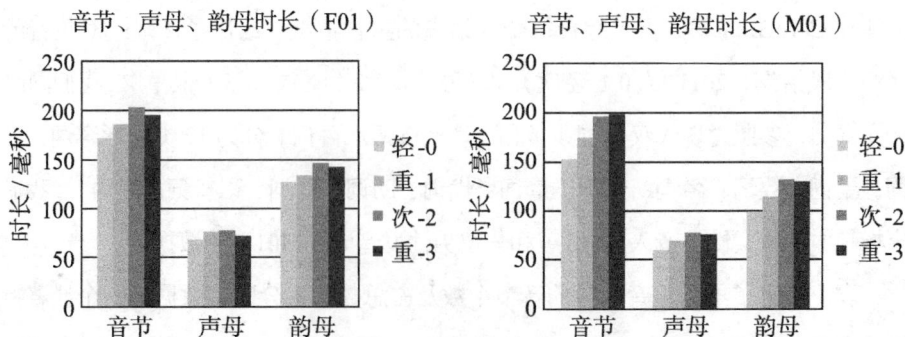

图4 两位发音人不同重音级音节和声韵母时长值

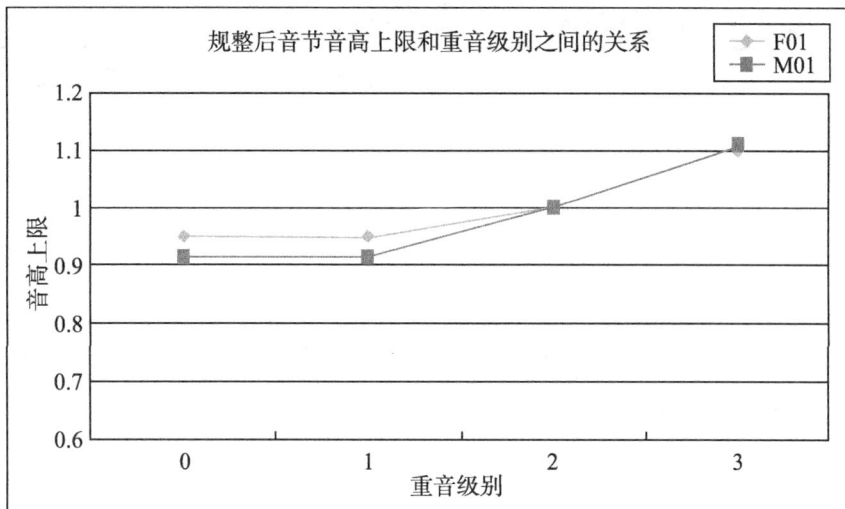

图5　两位发音人音高上限和4级重音的关系（殷治纲，2011）

我们统计了语料中词的音节数，单音节和双音节词占全部音节数量的91%，而三音节和三音节以上（多音节）的词仅占9%。重音在词中的分布及重音所占比例见表2。单音节词一共有1278个，两位发音人读重音的比例分别是40%和38%。双音节词一共1090个，大部分都带词重音。

表2　重音在词中分布及所占比例

词的类型	个数	F01		M01	
		个数	比例	个数	比例
单音节词	1278	509	40%	487	38%
双音节词	1090	910	83%	942	86%
多音节词	241	222	92%	227	94%

表3给出了不同词类在语料中的出现比例，并按照音节数分类。在音节总数里，实词的比例远远高于虚词，其中名词和动词的比例最高。语气词、助词、量词、介词大多数为单音节词，名词在双音节和多音节里比例最高，动词主要是双音节和单音节的。

表3　不同词类占总数的比例及不同音节个数的词在不同词类中所占比例

词类	全部出现比例	单音节词所占比例	双音节词所占比例	多音节词所占比例
形容词	4.5%	1.9%	8.8%	0.8%
连词	2.1%	1.4%	2.4%	0.4%
副词	8.8%	11.8%	7.6%	1.2%
数词	4.2%	6.9%	1.5%	2.9%
名词	31.3%	9.5%	46.5%	73.4%
介词	3.7%	6.9%	0.8%	0.4%
量词	4.8%	9.5%	0.2%	0.4%
代词	6.6%	8.1%	6.1%	0.0%
助词	11.0%	22.7%	0.0%	0.0%
动词	21.7%	21.0%	26.1%	6.6%
语气词	0.1%	0.1%	0.0%	0.0%
熟语	1.2%	0.0%	0.0%	13.7%

不同等级的重音在不同词类中表现出不同的分布规律，两位发音人在句重音的选择上也有不同的特点，见表4。

表4　单、双音节词中在不同词类中重音、次重音、最重音的分布比例

词类	1级重（单音节词）		1级重（双音节词）		2级次重		3级最重	
	F01	M01	F01	M01	F01	M01	F01	M01
	重	重	重	重	次重	次重	最重	最重
形容词	3%	3%	10%	10%	5%	4%	1%	4%
连词	4%	4%	2%	2%	4%	2%	5%	2%
副词	18%	20%	8%	8%	17%	24%	23%	31%
数词	7%	7%	2%	2%	10%	13%	9%	13%

（续表）

词类	1级重（单音节词）		1级重（双音节词）		2级次重		3级最重	
	F01	M01	F01	M01	F01	M01	F01	M01
	重	重	重	重	次重	次重	最重	最重
名词	11%	12%	44%	45%	13%	13%	12%	11%
介词	9%	9%	1%	1%	5%	2%	6%	3%
量词	6%	5%	0%	0%	6%	5%	6%	1%
代词	11%	12%	6%	5%	7%	11%	3%	10%
助词	1%	0%	0%	0%	1%	0%	1%	0%
动词	30%	28%	27%	27%	32%	26%	34%	25%
语气词	0%	0%	0%	0%	0%	0%	0%	0%

由表4可以看出，女性发音人的1级重音主要落在动词、副词、名词和代词上；短语以上的2级重音以动词、副词和名词居多；句重音为3级，以动词、副词和名词居多。男性发音人的1级重音以动词、副词、名词和代词居多；短语以上的2级重音以动词、副词、名词和数词居多；句重音为3级，以副词、动词和数词居多。代词出现重音时，男性发音人短语重音和句重音的比例明显高于女性发音人。形容词和连词里出现重音的情况比较少，介词也比较少。根据重音分布的"辅重原则"，在定中结构中，修饰语容易获得重音，而形容词做修饰语的概率较高，所以我们实际上期待形容词获得重音的比例更高。总的来看，名词、副词和动词获得各级重音的概率远远高于其他词类。

　　我们进一步分析了双音节词中的重音在不同结构中的分布情况，数据见表5。双音节词共有296个标记为定中结构，女性发音人的数据中前重的占69%，男性发音人的数据中定语获得重音的比例高达76%。述宾结构一共有57个，两位发音人的数据里前重的比例远比后重的高。联合式在双音节词里出现频率最高，其中70%以上都是前重式。重叠式的双音节词都是前重的，说明重叠式后音节都是轻声。根据我们前面对"想想"重叠式的分析，发生连读变调说明后音节是一个读"半上"的上声，而不是轻声。在不考虑结构的情况下，双音节词中词首位置出现重音的分别占 70% 和 77%，后重的分别占 14% 和 10%，后重的比例低于无法判断重音的情况。这说明结构对重音位置的影响并不像我们预测的那么明显，发音人在大多数情况下使用前重的格式。

表5　双音节词中重音位置在不同结构中的分布

结构	F01						M01					
	前重		后重		无重		前重		后重		无重	
	出现个数	占该结构比例	出现个数	占该结构比例	出现个数	占该结构比例	出现个数	占该结构比例	出现个数	占该结构比例	出现个数	占该结构比例
定中	203	69%	46	16%	47	16%	224	76%	36	12%	36	12%
状中	68	62%	28	26%	13	12%	80	73%	19	17%	10	9%
联合	276	71%	43	11%	69	18%	295	76%	33	9%	60	15%
述宾	32	56%	9	16%	16	28%	39	68%	7	12%	11	19%
述补	68	79%	10	12%	8	9%	73	85%	4	5%	9	10%
主谓	5	71%	0	0%	2	29%	7	100%	0	0%	0	0%
后缀	90	73%	12	10%	21	17%	98	80%	3	2%	22	18%
前缀	4	67%	2	33%	0	0%	4	67%	2	33%	0	0%
重叠	9	100%	0	0%	0	0%	9	100%	0	0%	0	0%
单纯	8	89%	0	0%	1	11%	9	100%	0	0%	0	0%

我们最后分析双音节词中重音分布和词类的关系，数据见表6。在双音节词中，名词、动词、形容词、副词获得重音的概率最高。单音节词中，也是动词、名词、副词获得重音的概率最高。形容词以双音节为主，单音节形容词数量较少。

表6　双音节词中重音位置在不同词类中的分布

词类	F01						M01					
	前重		后重		无重		前重		后重		无重	
	出现个数	占该词类比例	出现个数	占该词类比例	出现个数	占该词类比例	出现个数	占该词类比例	出现个数	占该词类比例	出现个数	占该词类比例
形容词	67	70%	21	22%	8	8%	82	85%	9	9%	5	5%
连词	20	77%	2	8%	4	15%	17	65%	5	19%	4	15%

（续表）

词类	F01						M01					
	前重		后重		无重		前重		后重		无重	
	出现个数	占该词类比例	出现个数	占该词类比例	出现个数	占该词类比例	出现个数	占该词类比例	出现个数	占该词类比例	出现个数	占该词类比例
副词	54	65%	17	20%	12	14%	58	70%	18	22%	7	8%
数词	7	44%	8	50%	1	6%	8	50%	7	44%	1	6%
名词	354	70%	56	11%	97	19%	392	77%	38	7%	77	15%
介词	7	78%	2	22%	0	0%	7	78%	1	11%	1	11%
量词	2	100%	0	0%	0	0%	2	100%	0	0%	0	0%
代词	46	70%	5	8%	15	23%	43	65%	1	2%	22	33%
助词	0	0%	0	0%	0	0%	0	0%	0	0%	0	0%
动词	207	73%	35	12%	43	15%	231	81%	23	8%	31	11%

　　根据以上的分析，我们看到在朗读语料中两位发音人的韵律表现基本一致，差异主要表现在单音节词中句重音在不同词类间的分布和每类词的百分比上。语料的标注分为三级重音，分别对应于韵律词重音、韵律短语重音和语调短语重音，语调短语重音即核心重音或句重音。双音节词的重音分布和词的结构方式之间的关系与重音理论的预测有不小的差距，这是需要进一步研究的问题。从词类的角度看，无论是单音节词还是双音节词，实词获得重音的比例最高（比如名词、动词、副词），双音节的形容词获得重音的比例也很高。

6. 结语

　　本文主要讨论了轻重音在连续话语中的韵律表征和重音的层级性，并根据声调实现域的确定，提出区分带轻声的和不带轻声的两类韵律词，分别确定各自的词重音位置。在连续话语中，轻声和轻读出现的频率远远高于词典中标注的轻声，说明前重后轻的重音格式在口语中是非常活跃的韵律模式。不带轻声的韵律词的重音位置受到韵律和结构因素以及上下文语境的影响。通过分析朗读语料，我们发现，连续话语中实词获得重音的概率一般要高于虚词，发音人在大多数情况下倾向于使用前重格式。

声调和轻重音一起构成了普通话丰富的韵律系统。轻重音在韵律词的层面构成音系对立，在韵律短语和语调短语的层面上通过重音分布调整语调短语内各个音节的音高实现方式，核心重音的位置对句子的结构语义和语用意义都会产生影响。我们研究汉语的重音不能脱离韵律结构，考察对象由孤立的词到连续话语的转变有助于我们深入理解韵律现象。

参考文献

曹剑芬. 2008. 汉语普通话词重音问题再探. *Report of Phonetic Research*. Phonetic Lab, Institute of Linguistics, Chinese Academy of Social Sciences: 20-29.

陈娟文，李爱军，王　霞. 2003. 上海普通话和普通话词重音的差异. *Report of Phonetic Research*. Phonetic Lab, Institute of Linguistics, Chinese Academy of Social Sciences: 268-273.

董少文. 1955. 语音常识（改订版）. 北京：文化教育出版社.

端木三. 1999. 重音理论和汉语的词长选择. 中国语文，（4）：246-254.

冯胜利. 2016. 北京话是一个重音语言. 语言科学，（5）：449-473.

黄靖雯，李爱军. 轻声与非轻声之间轻重的连续统关系. 世界汉语教学，待刊.

李爱军. 2021. 汉语口语语篇库：建构与标注. 北京：中国社会科学出版社.

林茂灿. 2012. 汉语语调实验研究. 北京：中国社会科学出版社.

林茂灿，颜景助. 1980. 北京话轻声的声学性质. 方言，（3）：166-178.

林茂灿，颜景助，孙国华. 1984. 北京话两字组正常重音的初步实验. 方言，（1）：57-73.

林　焘. 1990. 语音探索集稿. 北京：北京语言学院出版社.

路继伦，王嘉龄. 2005. 关于轻声的界定. 当代语言学，（2）：107-112.

沈　炯. 1994. 汉语语调构造和语调类型. 方言，（3）：221-228.

王洪君. 2008. 汉语非线性音系学——汉语的音系格局与单字音（增订版）. 北京：北京大学出版社.

王韫佳，初　敏，贺　琳. 2004. 普通话语句重音在双音节韵律词中的分布. 语言科学，（5）：38-48.

王韫佳，初　敏，贺　琳，等. 2003. 连续话语中双音节韵律词的重音感知. 声学学报，（6）：534-539.

王志洁，冯胜利. 2006. 声调对比法与北京话双音组的重音类型. 语言科学，（1）：3-22.

徐世荣. 1982. 双音节词的音量分析. 语言教学与研究，（2）：4-19.

杨　辰. 2005. 声调与元音对汉语非轻声两字组凸显感知的交互作用. 天津师范大学硕士学位论文.

殷治纲. 2011. 汉语普通话朗读语篇节奏研究. 中国社会科学院博士学位论文.

Barnes J. 2002. Domain-initial strengthening and the phonetics and phonology of positional neutralization. *Proceedings of the North East Linguistic Society*, 32.1: 1-20.

Chao Y R. 1968. *A Grammar of Spoken Chinese*. Berkeley: University of California Press.

Cheng C C. 1973. *A Synchronic Phonology of Mandarin Chinese*. Mouton: The Hague.

Chomsky N, Halle M. 1968. *The Sound Pattern of English*. New York: Harper & Row.

Dilley L, Shattuck-Hufnagel S, Ostendorf M. 1996. Glottalization of word-initial vowels as a function of prosodic structure. *Journal of Phonetics*, 24: 423-444.

Duanmu S. 1995. Metrical and tonal phonology of compounds in two Chinese dialects. *Language*, 71.2: 225-259.

Duanmu S. 2007. *The Phonology of Standard Chinese* (2nd ed.). Oxford: Oxford University Press.

Fry D B. 1958. Experiments in the perception of stress. *Language and Speech*, 1: 126-152.

Goldsmith J. 1981. English as a tone language. In: Goyvaerts D. *Phonology in the 1980's*. Ghent: E. Story-Scientia.

Hoa M. 1983. *L'Accentuation en Pekinois*. Paris: Editions Langages Croises.

Hyman L M. 2009. How (not) to do phonological typology: the case of pitch-accent. *Language Sciences*, 31.1-2: 213-238.

Klatt D H. 1975. Vowel lengthening is syntactically determined in a connected discourse. *Journal of Phonetics*, 3: 129-140.

Klatt D H. 1976. Linguistic uses of segmental duration in English: acoustic and perceptual evidence. *Journal of the Acoustical Society of America*, 59.5: 1208-1221.

Ladd D R. 2008. *Intonational Phonology* (2nd ed.). Cambridge: Cambridge University Press.

Li A J, Li Z Q. 2022. Prosodic realization of tonal target and F0 peak alignment in Mandarin neutral tone. *Language and Linguistics*, 23.1: 47-81.

Meredith S. 1990. *Issues in the Phonology of Prominence*. Ph.D. dissertation, MIT.

Milliken S. 1989. Why there is no third tone sandhi rule in Standard Mandarin, paper presented at the Tianjin International Conference on Phonetics and Phonology, Tianjin Normal University, June 7th-10th.

Mohanan K P. 1996. *The Theory of Lexical Phonology*. Dordrecht: D. Reidel Publishing Company.

Nespor M, Vogel I. 2007. Prosodic Phonology: with a New Foreword. Berlin: de Gruyter Mouton.

Pierrehumbert J. 1980. *The Phonology and Phonetics of English Intonation*. Ph.D. dissertation, MIT.

Selkirk E O. 1984. *Phonology and Syntax: The Relation between Sound and Structure*. Massachusetts: MIT Press.

Sundberg J. 1979. Maximum speed of pitch changes in singers and untrained subjects. *Journal of Phonetics*, 7: 71-79.

Xu Y. 1994. Production and perception of coarticulated tones. *Journal of the Acoustical Society of America*, 95: 2240-2253.

Xu Y. 1997. Contextual tonal variations in Mandarin. *Journal of Phonetics*, 25: 61-83.

Xu Y. 1999. Effects of tone and focus on the formation and alignment of f0 contours. *Journal of Phonetics*, 27: 55-105.

The Hierarchical Nature and Prosodic Features of Stress in Continuous Speech in Mandarin

Li, Zhiqiang[1] & Li, Aijun[2]

[1]University of San Francisco

[2]Institute of Linguistics, Chinese Academy of Social Sciences

Abstract: The paper is primarily concerned with the prosodic hierarchy of stress and prosodic features of strong and weak stress, as manifested in continuous speech in Mandarin. Since Mandarin used tones to distinguish lexical meanings, it is necessary to determine how tone and stress interact at some level of the prosodic hierarchy, especially given that they share similar acoustic cues such as pitch and duration variations on the syllable that carries a tone or stress. We establish that a tonal domain is also a stress domain in Mandarin, in line with Duanmu's (1995) analysis of Shanghai and Southern Fujian dialects. We distinguish, prosodically, two types of words in Mandarin. The stress pattern in the first type is S-W pattern, where the first syllable is in one of the four lexical tones (S) and the second in the neutral tone (W). The stress pattern in the second type is S-S, where both syllables are said in one of the four tones. Between the two strong syllables, which one has the greater stress has been the focus of debate.

The S-W pattern is first motivated by minimal pairs of disyllabic words distinguished by the second syllable in examples such as "mǎi mài" (buying and selling) and "mǎi mai" (business). Although such pairs are small in number, the S-W pattern is widely adopted at the phrasal level. For example, the directional complement after the verb is always in neutral tone. The pattern is even more extensively attested in continuous speech. According to Li (2021), the percentage of syllables in neutral tone is as high as 16%–18% in recorded scripted and unscripted conversations. The percentage is much higher than the percentage of neutral-tone syllables in entries recorded in dictionaries. What this fact entails is that the S-W pattern is a strong, productive prosodic pattern in continuous speech. The alternation of S and W can also be used as a prosodic means of disambiguation. In the example below, the two sentences carry different meanings as a result of the metrical status of the syllable "guo", in the S-W pattern in a. and in the S-S pattern in b.

(17) a. Wǒ kǎo guo le.

    I   test par par

    "I took the test."

b. Wǒ kǎo guò le.

    I   test pass par

    "I passed the test."

The S-S pattern distinguishes itself from the S-W pattern in that both syllables bear one of the four lexical tones. The controversy centers around whether word-level stress pattern can be unequivocally established as in the S-W pattern. If the answer is yes, then what it is. Three sub-patterns have been proposed in the literature, S-S (i.e., equal-level stress), M-S and S-M, where M refers to the stress level between W and S (Cao, 2008; Wang & Feng, 2006). It is worth pointing out that since both syllables in this pattern carry a lexical tone, stress does not play a contrastive role. For example, disyllabic words can be distinguished by varying tones in the first or second syllable, as in liù jí (level 6) and liú jí (fail to move up to the next grade), or sì jì (four seasons) and sì jí (level 4). In these examples, tones are the only distinctive element. To determine which syllable is said with more stress, the judgement has to be based on auditory signals that contain pitch and duration variations, which are more subtle to differentiate in syllables bearing one of the four tones.

We propose in the paper that the stress pattern of S-S combinations, which can be word entries in a dictionary or phrasal structures, is more readily defined in metrical terms in a prosodic hierarchy. At the level of prosodic word, prosodic position and tone type are found to impact the surface stress pattern. In a disyllabic word, the final syllable tends to be longer and the extra length is conducive to stronger stress perception. Meredith (1990) put forth the Stressability Hierarchy of Tones in Mandarin. Yin (2011) studied the effect of tone types on the judgement of stress in disyllabic words. They both identified Tone 4, the high falling tone in Mandarin, as the strongest tone, and the half Tone 3, the low tone with the final rise, as the weakest tone. Combining tone type and prosodic position, previous research (e.g., Chen, Li & Wang, 2003) found that Tone 4 in the first syllable is more likely to be stressed in Mandarin, as in "měi shù" (art). At the level of prosodic phrase, the Non-head Stress Principle (Duanmu, 2007) places the phrase-level stress on the non-head in a phrasal structure. For example, in a verb-object (VO) structure the object receives more stress while in a modifier-noun (MN) structure, the modifier is more prominent. Disyllabic phrases such as chǎo fàn are structurally ambiguous. When it means "to cook rice" it is a VO structure; when it means "cooked rice", it is a MN structure. However, more people would agree fàn is more stressed than chǎo in both readings. We suggest that tone type and prosodic position are involved in the determination of stress here. In the half Tone 3 and Tone 4 combinations, Tone 4 carries more stress than the half Tone 3.

Another important factor that contributes to the surface stress pattern of the S-S combinations is the placement of the nuclear stress. At the level of the intonational phrase, placement of the nuclear stress is also dependent upon contextual information such as focus structure of the sentence. The judgement of stress in a disyllabic S-S word can be enhanced greatly when the nuclear stress falls on the word.

In our analysis of a read speech corpus, we found that morphosyntactic structure, tone type and prosodic position are relevant in determination of the stress position in prosodic words. In addition, lexical words are more likely to receive stress than function words in continuous speech. There is also a strong tendency to use the S-W pattern in disyllabic prosodic words in the data.

Keywords: strong and weak stress; nuclear stress; prosodic hierarchy; prosodic features

李智强

美国旧金山大学文理学院

zqli@usfca.edu

李爱军

中国社会科学院语言研究所

liaj@cass.org.cn

闽南方言揭阳话核心重音规则的句法效应 *

林晓燕

摘　要　基于韵律语法理论研究闽南方言揭阳话的核心重音规则（NSR）以及与此有关的韵律句法的互动现象，本文研究发现:（1）核心重音的承担者是保持词汇调的成分;（2）揭阳话的核心重音规则是核心重音由句中主要动词指派给其直接管辖的补述语;（3）揭阳话核心重音范域内存在"前轻后重"的韵律结构要求（"对"字句中主要动词不能挂单；若句中的复杂动词或动词带补语结构后带宾语，则该宾语必须提到主要动词之前）。

关键词　闽南方言　揭阳话　核心重音规则　韵律　句法

1. 引言

核心重音（nuclear stress）指"一个句子在没有特殊语境的情况下所表现出来

* 本文为"北京语言大学研究生创新基金（中央高校基本科研业务费专项资金）"项目（21YCX120）成果。承蒙王丽娟老师启发，笔者注意到揭阳话中韵律和句法的互动现象，从而对其进行深入研究。本文部分内容在北京市语言学会第 14 届学术年会暨 2020 年学术前沿论坛中做过小组报告，获得了黄瑞玲等老师的修改建议。本文也得到了匿名评审专家以及马宝鹏老师的修改建议。在此，向各位老师一并致谢。如若本文仍有错漏，实为笔者一人之责。

的重音结构"（冯胜利，2000：49）[①]。目前学界发现的核心重音规则（Nuclear Stress Rule）有几种不同的类型，如：Liberman & Prince（1977）指出核心重音通过"相对凸显"（relative prominence）实现，Cinque（1993）提出深重原则（Depth Stress Principle），Zubizarreta（1998：19）指出德语的核心重音规则是一种基于"选择关系"的核心重音规则（Selectionally-based NSR），Feng（1995，2003）提出普通话的核心重音规则为"管约式核心重音规则"（Government-based NSR）。[②] 学界对闽南方言的核心重音规则鲜有研究。

揭阳话属于潮汕闽南话的分支方言之一，主要为广东省揭阳市（现辖榕城区、揭东区、惠来县、揭西县，代管普宁市）的人所使用。闽南方言的核心重音规则是否也如普通话那样是基于管辖关系的？笔者通过考察闽南方言揭阳话语料[③]，对比宽域焦点句及窄域焦点句的变调模式，认为揭阳话的焦点可以通过音高或音长手段[④]凸显，核心重音与句中保持词汇调的成分有关，进一步指出核心重音范域位于句末谓语部分、以主要动词为中心建立起来的结构中，最终推导出揭阳话的核心重音规则，并发现核心重音规则的两种句法效应。

本文第 2 节首先介绍与揭阳话重音和变调相关的语言现象，第 3 节回顾以往学者关于闽南方言中重音实现的研究概况，第 4 节论证了揭阳话实现核心重音的韵律手段、核心重音规则及核心重音规则的句法效应，第 5 节为结语部分。

2. 语言现象

李艳惠、冯胜利（2015）认为，北京话是一种轻重相对的韵律型语言，而台湾地区闽南方言则倾向于韵律上的平重，名词短语中的成分不存在轻读（destress）的现象，因此轻重对立在台湾地区闽南方言中不易被察觉。但本文指出，闽南方言名词短语中的"轻读"需要进一步考察与具体化（分析见下文）。闽南方言是一种单音节语言（monosyllabic language），其单音节语素一般有两种声调形式——底层调 T（underlying tones）与派生调 T'（derived tones），但有的语素还有另一种形式，即出现在底层调后、变调边界前的，为弱读调 T⁰（neutral

---

① 原文称"核心重音"为"普通重音"。
② 上述关于核心重音规则的几种类型的总结引自冯胜利（2013a）。
③ 笔者来自揭阳市代管的普宁市，文中例句为日常口语对话。
④ 由于本文主要讨论音高手段，音长手段暂且不谈。

tone）①，因而这类语素有三种声调变体。揭阳话的语素也存在三种声调变体。林晓燕（2020）指出，揭阳话的变调规则为：在一个变调组 α 中，派生调 T' 音节发生在底层调音节之前，底层调音节之后可有弱读调 T⁰ 音节，即弱读调音节出现在底层调音节之后、变调组的末尾。相关规则可以形式化为（1）。

（1）揭阳话的变调规则：

     a. $T \rightarrow T' / \underline{\quad\quad} T\ (T^0)\ ]\alpha$

     b. $T \rightarrow T^0 / T\ \underline{\quad\quad}]\alpha$　　　　　　　　　　　（林晓燕，2020）

另外，揭阳话每个底层调都有其固定的调值变化，参考 Xu（2007）对揭阳话连读变调具体调值变化的研究，本文将其重新整理并列例字，见表1。

表1　揭阳话变调的调值变化表

调类	例字	底层调	派生调	弱读调
阴平	分、书	33	33	11
阳平	陈、人	55	11	11
阴上	看、好	53	35（①类前）② 24（②类前）	213
阳上	近、上	35	21	21
阴去	对、爱	213	53（①类前） 42（②类前）	21
阳去	害、画	11	11	11
阴入	急、铁	2	5（①类前） 3（②类前）	2
阳入	学、读	5	2	2

从表1可知，弱读调的调型有低降的特点。林伦伦、陈小枫（1996：22）认为，这种变调不是由前字引起的，而是由社会约定俗成的，且变调的结果都是

---

① 施其生（2011）根据变调成分在变调组中线性序列上的位置将其分为本调、前变调、后变调，Xu（2007）将其分为 basic tone、anterior tone sandhi、posterior tone sandhi，但本文基于这三种声调的不同地位，采用 Chen（2001：50）的分类方法，认为底层调为原调，派生调与弱读调为进入词或短语组合后在表层的声调变体，故而采取此名称。

② ①类调类为阴上、阳平、阳入，②类调类为阴平、阴去、阴入、阳上、阳去。

低降性质，类似于普通话的轻声，所以把这种声调变化现象视作"轻声"。但需要明确的是，这里的"轻声"（即弱读调）对应的是普通话中的"轻音/轻读"与"轻声"。"轻声是声调层面的失调音节，属于词汇现象，没有明确、系统的音系规律性"（冯胜利、王丽娟，2018：50）。如"东西"的"西"、"先生"的"生"读轻声，属于词汇现象。而"轻音是重音层面的弱读现象，属于句法现象，具有相对清晰的规则，可以预测"（冯胜利、王丽娟，2018：50）。如"看看""起来"的第二个音节为轻音，因为"看看"是词的重叠形态，"起来"是述补短语，二者都不是词汇现象，而是句法结构的弱读现象。林伦伦、陈小枫（1996：22～27）提到，某些时间名词如"年""月"（"前年""十月"）、某些表方位的名词语素（或词缀）如"头""块"（"边头""许块"）、某些做补语的数量短语如"两碗"（"食两碗"）、趋向补语如"来""去"（"起来""出去"）、做宾语的人称代词如"我"（"送我"）、助词"着、了、过"（"惊着""好了""去过"）等读"轻声"。依据冯胜利、王丽娟（2018：50）对"轻音"与"轻声"的定义，我们将上述例子分为两类：一类为词汇现象的"轻声"，如某些时间名词、表方位的名词语素（或词缀）；一类为句法层面的"轻音"，如数量短语、趋向补语、人称代词及助词。由于"轻声"并无明确的音系规律，本文不讨论该类现象，本文讨论的主要对象是与句法结构相关的"轻音"。

李艳惠、冯胜利（2015）所说的闽南方言的名词短语中无"轻读现象"，更具体来说，应该是在宽域焦点句中，名词短语内没有"轻音成分"，而非轻声成分。在此背景下，我们进一步提出问题：闽南方言的焦点能否通过韵律手段来凸显？施其生（2011）指出，普通话可以通过轻重读以强调某些词语，而汕头话[1]可以通过改变连调模式表示强调。同样，揭阳话也可通过改变变调模式来表达信息的焦点，如（2）[2]所示：

（2）a. 阿$^{33\text{-}33}$妈^{55}# 叫$^{213\text{-}53}$阿$^{33\text{-}33}$弟^{35}# 去$^{213\text{-}53}$买$^{53\text{-}35}$水^{53}。（宽域焦点句）

　　　妈　妈　叫　弟　弟　去　买　水

　　　"妈妈叫弟弟去买水。"

---

① 汕头话、揭阳话同为潮汕闽南话的分支方言之一。
② 上标数字如"53-35"，表示53为该字底层调，35为其派生调或弱读调；下划直线表示保持词汇调，波浪线表示弱读调，读派生调的音节则不进行标记；字体加粗表示焦点成分；"#"表示变调边界，下文同。

b. 阿 ³³⁻³³ 妈 ⁵⁵# 叫 ²¹³⁻⁵³ <u>阿 ³³⁻³³ 弟 ³⁵</u> 去 ²¹³⁻²¹ 买 ⁵³⁻²¹³ 水 ⁵³⁻²¹³。（窄域焦点句）

　　妈　妈　叫　弟　弟　去　买　水

"妈妈叫弟弟去买水（，不是叫我）。"

宽域焦点句（2）a 的主语"阿妈"和宾语"阿弟""水"保持词汇调[1]，其他成分都发生了句法层面的变调；而在窄域焦点（2）b 中，焦点"阿弟"之前的成分变调模式与（2）a 相同，但其后的成分（波浪线部分）改变了变调模式，即"去买水"改成弱读调。弱读调低、降的特点正好凸显了前面保持词汇调的焦点。可见，揭阳话的焦点可以通过改变变调模式来凸显。本文认为，揭阳话虽没有如普通话一样存在明显的轻重对立，但可以通过保持词汇调与变调形成相对凸显，以标记焦点，实现重音。

既然焦点重音可以用韵律手段标记，那么当整句为焦点时，该句的核心重音如何实现？目前鲜有关于闽南方言核心重音的研究，因此下文主要介绍学界关于闽南方言重音实现的相关研究及其局限性，进而论证揭阳话核心重音与保持词汇调的成分是否有关。

3. 闽南方言重音实现的韵律研究概况

闽南方言如何实现重音？有学者从轻重音节与变调的关系角度探讨了闽南方言重音的韵律表现。Duanmu（1993，1995）将"重音节—保音 / 轻音节—变音"这一语言普遍趋向应用到作为声调语言的汉语普通话、上海话及厦门话中。钟奇（2007）则认为，厦门话的词语重音属于重音节—调高不限、轻音节—低调型。但上述文献只谈及变调组或词重音的音节表现，未谈及句重音的情况。

有学者通过声学、感知实验研究了音强、音高、音长的韵律手段在实现闽南方言重音方面的作用。Xu et al.（2012）对台湾地区的闽南方言进行了语音实验研究，主要关注焦点的不同是否会影响音高、音长、音强的变化走向。该文通过声学实验比较宽域焦点句、疑问窄域焦点句[2]中这些韵律要素在语流中的具

---

① "保持词汇调"在本文中指词在组合构成短语或句子时能保持单个词时的变调模式，例如："苹果"的词汇调是"31-53"，"食"的词汇调是"5"，在短语"食苹果"中，其变调情况为"2=31-53"，因此，"食"改变了词汇调，而"苹果"则保持词汇调。（"-"表示词内部成分组合；"="表示短语间成分组合）

② Xu et al.（2012）中疑问焦点答句：A1：图中你看到什么？　　B1：<u>妈妈在摸猫咪</u>。
　　　　　　　　　　　　　　　A2：谁在摸猫咪？　　　　B2：<u>妈妈</u>在摸猫咪。
　　　　　　　　　　　　　　　A3：妈妈在干什么？　　　B3：妈妈在<u>摸猫咪</u>。

体数值走向，结果显示台湾地区的闽南方言主通过音长凸显窄焦，即焦点处音节音长大于非焦点处音节音长，不存在北京话那样的"焦点后压缩"（post-focus compression）现象；通过感知实验发现，台湾人对闽南方言焦点的敏感性不如北京人对北京话焦点的敏感性强。但 Xu et al.（2012）并没有进一步研究台湾地区闽南方言的核心重音。

上述学者主要研究厦门话的词重音（如 Duanmu，1995；钟奇，2007）或台湾地区闽南方言的焦点重音（如 Xu et al.，2012），虽不涉及本文所要研究的核心重音，但给予我们极大的启发：闽南方言的重音可以通过音长与音高（变调、保调的相对凸显）实现。在上述研究的基础上，本文将探讨揭阳话的核心重音的韵律表现，并推导揭阳话的核心重音规则。

4. 揭阳话的核心重音规则及句法效应

4.1　揭阳话核心重音规则的凸显方式

前人研究发现，闽南方言变调组内重音/词重音可通过"变调、保调"[①]凸显。而揭阳话的窄域焦点句，如上文（2），也可以通过"变调、保调"形成相对凸显实现焦点重音，但此处的"保调"是保持词汇调[②]，如以"阿弟"为单位保持词汇调，"变调"为焦点后成分改弱读调。又如：在（3）"连"字句中，焦点"阿明"保持词汇调，而其后为弱读调；在（4）"是"字强调句中，焦点"阿姐"保持词汇调，其后都为弱读调。

（3）连 $^{55-11}$ 阿 $^{33-33}$ 明 ^{55} □[to]$^{33-11}$ 训 $^{2-2}$ 坐 $^{35-21}$ 过 $^{213-21}$ 飞 $^{33-11}$ 机 $^{33-11}$。

连　阿　明　都　曾　坐　过　飞　机

"连阿明都曾坐过飞机。"

（4）是 $^{35-21}$ 阿 $^{33-33}$ 姐 ^{53} 在 $^{33-11}$ 煮 $^{53-213}$ 饭 $^{33-11}$。

是　姐　姐　在　做　饭

"是姐姐在做饭（，不是别人在做饭）。"

---

① 揭阳话的焦点凸显可以通过音长、音高实现，且两种韵律手段可以同时使用，但当焦点无法通过音高凸显时，则只能通过焦点成分的停延加以凸显，如（2）的动词"买"为焦点时，该句变调模式与宽域焦点句的变调模式相同，只有延长"买"的音长加以凸显〔详细分析见林晓燕（2020）〕。

② 前人由于只研究某变调组/某词的重音，所以只是关注到某个音节是否保调或变调；而本文讨论的是句重音，即核心重音、焦点重音，关注的是句子层面中词的保调与变调的情况。

（5）（语境：怎么回事？厨房怎么那么吵？）①

阿 $^{33\text{-}33}$ 姐 ^{53} # 在 $^{33\text{-}33}$ 煮 $^{53\text{-}24}$ 饭 ^{33}。

姐姐　　　在　　做　饭

"姐姐在做饭。"

那核心重音的凸显手段是什么？（5）为宽域焦点句，主语和谓语切分为两个变调组：主语"阿姐"保持词汇调；谓语部分"在""煮"读派生调，"饭"保持词汇调。（4）中的焦点"阿姐"保持词汇调，并弱化其后非焦点成分"煮饭"以凸显焦点。因此，焦点不同，韵律（变调）不同。（5）整句为焦点，正常变调（即按照揭阳话宽域焦点句变调组的构建规则变调）②，因此谓语部分"饭"前成分为派生调，"饭"保持词汇调。由此看来，当词进入句子后，不仅需要根据句法位置进行变调，其焦点位置也可能会影响其变调模式。

上述例子说明焦点可能与保持词汇调的成分有关③，以此作为旁证，我们认为保持词汇调是宽域焦点成分所在的前提条件。另外，本文赞同 Duanmu（1993，1995）关于词内"重音节保调"原则，而推及短语或句子层面，即"核心重音为保持词汇调的成分"④。下一小节将逐步推导揭阳话的核心重音规则。

4.2　揭阳话的核心重音规则

首先，揭阳话核心重音与保持词汇调的成分相关，但并非所有保持词汇调的成分都承担核心重音。揭阳话宽焦句中，主谓之间都有变调边界〔如（5）〕，主语及谓语部分都有保持词汇调的成分，但主语并不承担核心重音。冯胜利（2013b：54）提到，关于核心重音，大多数学者认为其特点是"后重"，如 Behaghel（1909）的"强信息居后法则"（Das Gesetz der wachsenden Glieder）、Quirk et al.（1972）的"尾重原则"（Principle of End-weight）、赵元任（1980/2002：20）提到的汉语"最后的音节最重"。因此，根据核心重音"后重"的普遍原则，我们可排除揭阳话主语承担核心重音的可能。但揭阳话的句子是不论句子结构，

---

① 为了明确例句的焦点位置，笔者会在下文中的所有例句前增设其所处的语境。

② 揭阳话宽域焦点句变调组的构建规则（第二版）：除了当 XP 为 C- 统制其词汇核心词的修饰语以外，在每一个 XP 的右边界标"#"。（林晓燕，2020）

③ 上文提到有些焦点〔如（2）中的"买"〕不能通过音高手段凸显，需要通过音长的停延加以凸显，但这并不影响我们推断宽焦的凸显手段，核心重音是在没有特殊语境下所表现出来的重音，句中不存在音节的停延时间无故加长的情况，因此音高手段的对比凸显尤为重要。

④ 此处"核心重音为保持词汇调成分"，然而保持词汇调成分未必是核心重音所在，论证具体见下文。

一律"后重"吗？Feng（1995，2003）提出的关于汉语普通话的"管约式核心重音"规则指由句子最后一个动词指派重音给其直接管辖的成分。那么，揭阳话的核心重音规则如何？

根据冯胜利（2009：91），核心重音只约束句子未加修饰语以前的基础结构①。因此我们在研究揭阳话宽域焦点句中承载核心重音的成分时，排除了所有的修饰语，只研究基础结构中的成分（即主语、谓语、宾语、补语）。通过分析光杆动词做谓语、形容词做谓语，以及动宾结构、动补结构、双宾结构充当谓语的句子，我们归纳出七种结构的宽焦句，如表2所示。

表 2 揭阳话宽焦句的七种基础结构类型表

序号	结构类型	举例及变调情况	保持词汇调成分
1	$[_{TP}DP[_{T'}T\ VP]]$ 句的变调	阿 $^{33-33}$ 明 ^{55} #走 ^{53} 了 $^{213-21}$。 "阿明离开了。"	V
2	$[_{TP}DP[_{T'}T\ AP]]$ 句的变调	杯 $^{33-33}$ 茶 ^{55} #酷 $^{2-3}$ 烧 ^{33}。 "这/那杯茶很热。"	Adj
3	$[_{TP}DP_1[_{T'}T[_{vP}V\ DP_2]]]$ 句的变调	阿 $^{33-33}$ 明 ^{55} #惊 $^{33-33}$ 蛇 ^{55}。 "阿明怕蛇。"	DP_2
4	$[_{TP}DP[_{T'}T[_{vP1}V_1\ VP_2/AP]]]$ 句的变调	阮 ^{53} #打 $^{2-5}$ 赢 ^{55} 了 $^{213-21}$。 "我们打赢了。" 阿 $^{33-33}$ 明 ^{55} #起 $^{53-24}$ 晚 ^{213} 了 $^{213-21}$ "阿明起（床）晚了。"	VP_2/AP
5	$[_{TP}DP_1[_{T'}T[_{vP}V_复^②\ DP_2]]]$ 句的变调	阮 ^{53} #打 $^{2-5}$ 赢 $^{55-11}$ 球 ^{55} 了 $^{213-21}$。 "我们打赢球了。"	DP_2
6	$[_{TP}DP[_{T'}T[_{vP}V\ [_{PP}P\ LP^③]]]]$ 句的变调	阿 $^{33-33}$ 弟 ^{35} #企 $^{53-42}$ 在 $^{33-33}$ 床 $^{55-11}$ 顶 ^{53}。 "弟弟站在床上。"	DP_2
7	$[_{TP}DP_1[_{T'}T[_{vP}V_i[_{vP}DP_2[_{v'}t_i\ DP_3]]]]]$ 句的变调	阿 $^{33-33}$ 明 ^{55} #送 $^{213-53}$ 同 $^{55-11}$ 学 $^{5-2}$ #本 $^{53-42}$ 书 ^{33}。 "阿明送同学一本书。"	DP_2、DP_3

---

① 基础结构实则为提纯的结构，即谓语部分只含有一个主要谓语动词的结构，暂不讨论宽焦兼语或宽焦连调等结构。

② "$V_复$"指的是由动词和动词（如"打""赢"）或动词和形容词（如"起""晚"）组合而成的复杂动词 V〔参考何元建（2011：280～282）关于动结式的讨论〕。

③ LP 为方位词（localizer）短语。

　　根据表 2，谓语部分如果有宾语，则宾语保持词汇调，如表中第 3、5、6、7 种结构类型；谓语部分如果没有宾语，则动词后的补语（不含趋向补语）保持词汇调，如第 4 种结构类型；当光杆动词或形容词充当谓语时，该动词或形容词保持词汇调，如第 1、2 种结构类型。因此除了第 7 种双宾句结构（两个宾语都保持词汇调，我们另再讨论）外，似乎保持词汇调的成分都在句末谓语部分内嵌最深的位置。根据 Liberman & Prince（1977）的相对凸显规则，句末重音范域应为一对轻重组合，即核心重音的指派者与承担者。表 2 中句子的谓语部分都是动词性结构[1]，动词是否为核心重音的指派者？英语中，无论 PP 为修饰语还是补述语，只要 PP 为深嵌结构，则 P 的补述语为核心重音所在[2]。但是在揭阳话的核心重音句中，修饰语 PP 不能出现在谓语动词之后〔如（6）a〕，只有在修饰语 PP 作为焦点时才被允准出现在句末〔如（7）所示〕。

　　（6）（语境：A 问"你笑什么？怎么回事儿？"，B 回答如下。）

　　　　a. * 阿 $^{33\text{-}33}$ 明 ^{55} # 画 $^{11\text{-}11}$ 了 $^{53\text{-}35}$ 个 $^{55\text{-}11}$ 人 ^{55} # 在 $^{33\text{-}33}$ 你 $^{53\text{-}24}$ 面 ^{11} 块 $^{213\text{-}21}$ 。

　　　　　　阿明　　　画　了　个　人　　在　　你　脸　L

　　　　　　"* 阿明画了一个人在你脸上。"

　　　　b. 阿 $^{33\text{-}33}$ 明 ^{55} # 在 $^{33\text{-}33}$ 你 $^{53\text{-}24}$ 面 ^{11} 块 $^{213\text{-}21}$ # 画 $^{11\text{-}11}$ 了 $^{53\text{-}35}$ 个 $^{55\text{-}11}$ 人 ^{55} 。

　　　　　　阿明　　　在　　你　脸　L　　画　了　个　人

　　　　　　"阿明在你的脸上画了一个人。"

　　（7）（语境：A 没听清楚，问"你说什么？在哪儿画了？"，B 回答如下。）

　　　　阿 $^{33\text{-}33}$ 明 ^{55} # 画 $^{11\text{-}11}$ 了 $^{53\text{-}35}$ 个 $^{55\text{-}11}$ 人 ^{55} # 在 $^{33\text{-}33}$ 你 $^{53\text{-}24}$ 面 ^{11} 块 $^{213\text{-}21}$ 。

　　　　　阿明　　　画　了　个　人　　在　　你　脸　L

　　　　　"阿明画了一个人在你脸上（，不是在别处）。"

　　（6）a 谓语部分为 [V ClP[3] PP] 结构，如果按照揭阳话宽域焦点句变调组的构建规则（以下简称"变调规则"）变调，即 PP 内 P 读派生调，P 所管辖的 LP 中的"面"保持词汇调，这种变调模式在回答（6）中的宽焦问题时不合法，该变

---

① 何元建（2011：293）指出，形式句法学认为形容词兼有动词性质，形容词做谓语与动词做谓语的性质一样。因此我们将表 2 中第 2 种形容词谓语句也归入动词性结构中。

② 例子如：

　　a. PP 为补述语：John worked on the paper.

　　b. PP 为修饰语：John worked on the table.

③ "Cl"为"classifier"（量词）的缩写，ClP 表示量词短语。

调模式只适合回答（7）中的问题，即凸显窄焦"在你面块（在你脸上）"时才是合法的，同时伴随"面"音节的音长延长。既然宽域焦点句中这种句末 PP 结构的变调模式不能出现在动宾结构之后，即 P 的补述语 LP 不能保持词汇调，那么 P 不能作为句末结构核心重音的指派者。

如若要表达宽焦语义，该结构则需调整为 [PP V ClP]，将 PP 提前，此时句末为动宾结构，按变调规则，V 读派生调，而 ClP 中的 NP 保持词汇调，如（6）b。如果该结构的 NP 为核心重音的承担者，那么它前面的 V 则为核心重音的指派者，核心重音指派域为 [V ClP]。然而当 PP 作为谓语动词的补述语时，如表 2 中的第 6 种结构，介词也必须紧贴动词，动词与介词之间不能有变调边界，动介必须合并为一个复合词。综上，介词 P 不能单独作为核心重音的指派者。

另外，我们发现揭阳话宽域焦点句句末主要动词[①]后不能出现两个保持词汇调的成分。

（8）（语境：A 问"怎么回事儿，这个月电话费怎么那么高？"，B 回答如下。）

a. *阿<u>$^{33\text{-}33}$</u>明<u>^{55}</u>#一<u>$^{5\text{-}2}$</u>日<u>^{5}</u>#打<u>$^{2\text{-}3}$</u>电<u>$^{35\text{-}21}$</u>话<u>^{11}</u>#五<u>$^{35\text{-}21}$</u>次<u>^{213}</u>。

阿明　　　一　天　打　电　话　　　五　次

"*阿明一天打电话五次。"

b. 阿<u>$^{33\text{-}33}$</u>明<u>^{55}</u>#一<u>$^{5\text{-}2}$</u>日<u>^{5}</u>#打<u>$^{2\text{-}3}$</u>五<u>$^{35\text{-}21}$</u>次<u>$^{213\text{-}42}$</u>电<u>$^{35\text{-}21}$</u>话<u>^{11}</u>。

阿明　　　一　天　打　五　次　　电　话

"阿明一天打五次电话。"

（9）（语境：A 问"今天发生什么奇怪事儿了？"，B 回答如下。）

a. *阿<u>$^{33\text{-}33}$</u>明<u>^{55}</u>#今<u>$^{33\text{-}33}$</u>日<u>^{5}</u>#遇<u>$^{35\text{-}21}$</u>着<u>$^{5\text{-}3}$</u>三<u>$^{33\text{-}33}$</u>个<u>$^{55\text{-}11}$</u>同<u>$^{55\text{-}11}$</u>学<u>^{5}</u>#四<u>$^{213\text{-}42}$</u>

阿明　　　今　天　遇　到　三　个　　同　学　　四

次<u>^{213}</u>。

次

"*阿明今天遇到三个同学四次。"

b. 阿<u>$^{33\text{-}33}$</u>明<u>^{55}</u>#今<u>$^{33\text{-}33}$</u>日<u>^{5}</u>#遇<u>$^{35\text{-}21}$</u>着<u>$^{5\text{-}3}$</u>我<u>$^{53\text{-}24}$</u>四<u>$^{213\text{-}42}$</u>次<u>^{213}</u>。

阿明　　　今　天　遇　到　我　四　次

"阿明今天遇到我四次。"

（8）a 动词后带了两个保持词汇调的成分——宾语和数量补语，生成的句子不合法，假若动词后的宾语"电话"承担核心重音，保持词汇调，那么其后的数量

---

① 这里的动词暂不包含三元动词，即双宾句另再讨论。

补语则不能出现〔结构如（10）〕。该结构改为（8）b 则合法，即把频率补语"五次"变成"电话"的修饰语，此时，NP "电话"保持词汇调，NP 前成分读派生调〔结构如（11）〕。

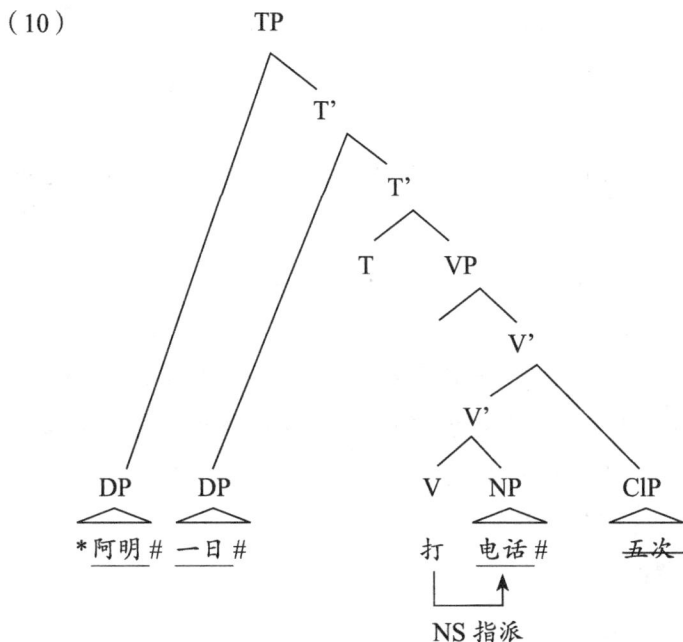

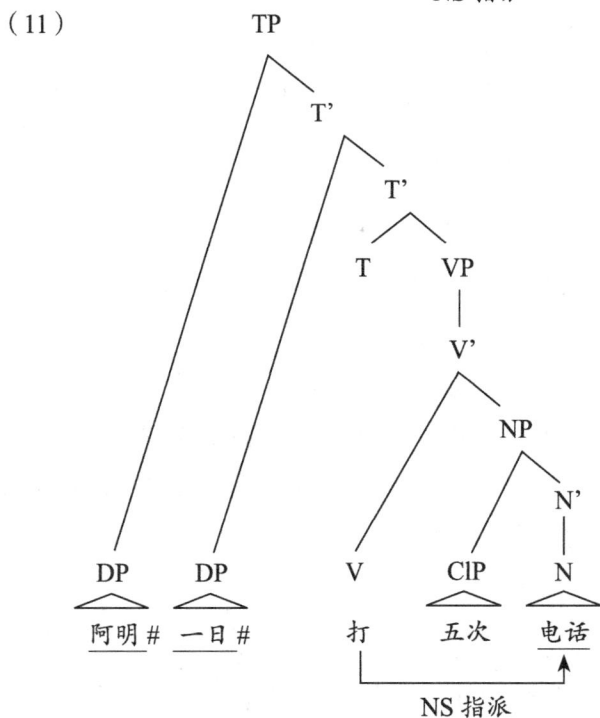

（10）

```
                        TP
                       /  \
                          T'
                         /  \
                        T'
                       /  \
                      T    VP
                          /  \
                             V'
                            /  \
                          V'    \
                         / \     \
          DP    DP      V   NP    CIP
          /\    /\      |   /\    /\
        *阿明# 一日#    打  电话#  五次
                           └──┐ ↑
                              └─┘
                          NS 指派
```

（11）

```
                        TP
                       /  \
                          T'
                         /  \
                        T'
                       /  \
                      T    VP
                            |
                            V'
                           /  \
                              NP
                             /  \
                                 N'
                                 |
          DP    DP      V   CIP   N
          /\    /\      |   /\   /\
        阿明# 一日#    打  五次  电话
                          └────┐ ↑
                               └─┘
                          NS 指派
```

又如（9）a，动词后有定数名词宾语和动量补语时，依据变调规则变调，同样生成不合法的句子，而当定数名词宾语"三个同学"改为（9）b的代词"我"时，由于代词为非重读成分（读派生调），其后的动量补语保持词汇调，该句子合法。由此证明，当动词将核心重音指派给其后直接管辖的补述语时，完成核心重音指派，至此句末位置已定，其后就不能再有第二个保持词汇调（不可轻读）的成分了，否则句子不合法。

根据上述研究，我们可以得出以下结论：（1）核心重音需在结构中通过句法成分的相对凸显关系实现。（2）揭阳话的核心重音范域在谓语部分。（3）揭阳话中并非任一结构都可出现在宽域焦点句句末，只有动词性结构才能成为核心重音的指派域。由前三点推论出核心重音在句末动词性结构中，该结构内的主要动词V与其补述语有相对凸显关系（即变调与保调的关系），并且由动词指派核心重音到其补述语上。（4）宽域焦点句中主要动词之后不能有两个不可轻读成分，因此推论出动词只能给其直接管辖的成分指派重音，一旦完成重音指派，句子的句末位置就确定了。综上，我们可以得到揭阳话的核心重音规则。

（12）揭阳话核心重音规则：

　　　　句末主要动词直接管辖的补述语获得重音，亦即保持词汇调。

核心重音规则在揭阳话中如何发挥作用？接下来我们将从揭阳话的两种句法结构——"对"字句以及复杂动词带宾或动补结构带宾句——入手进行探究。

4.3　揭阳话核心重音规则的句法效应

4.3.1　效应一："对"字句中动词不能挂单现象

揭阳话的"对"字句相当于普通话的"把"字句。在这类句子中，主要动词不能挂单。陈传佳（1996）通过分析介词"对、将"的提宾现象指出，这些介词和普通话中的"把"一样，要求动词前后要带其他成分，不能只是一个单音节动词，如"你对只件事呾（你把这件事说）"[①]不合法，而应改为"你对只件事呾一下（你把这件事说一下）"[②]，如（13）和（14）所示。但是陈文中只是描述了这种现象，却没有解释为什么动词不能挂单。

---

① 陈传佳（1996）原文例句为"你将只件事呾"，但笔者与黄瑞玲老师讨论后，认为目前揭阳话口语中不用"将"，因此将此处改用"对"，感谢黄老师的提示。

② 陈传佳（1996）指出韵文不受此限制，如"将伊拍（将他打）""将你骂"。

（13）a.* 你对只件事呾。（* 你把这件事说。）

　　　b. 你对只件事呾呾 / 呾一下。（你把这件事说说 / 说一下。）

（14）a.* 老板对块招牌收。（* 老板把那块招牌收。）

　　　b. 老板对块招牌收收起。（老板把那块招牌收了起来。）

（15）

```
              vP
           /      \
         DP        v'
                 /    \
                v      VP
                     /    \
                   DP      V'
                   /\      |
                  /  \     V
             *对只件事#   呾
                重       轻
```

（16）

```
              vP
           /      \
         DP        v'
                 /    \
                v      VP
                     /    \
                   DP      V'
                   |      /   \
              对只件事#  V     CIP
                        呾    /\
                        NS   一下
```

结构（15）中，"对只件事"位于核心重音范围内，但由于"对只件事"在韵律上为双分支结构，而核心词 V 为单支，形成了"前双后单"的韵律结构。核心重音本应由动词指派给其右边的姊妹节点，但在这个结构中，由于其右边并无其他成分，因此核心重音落在动词上。此时不分支的"呾"无法与同在核心重音范围内的双支结构"对只件事"抗衡，造成了"前重后轻"的韵律结构，违背了核心重音规则"前轻后重"的要求,因此该句非法。然而当动词后有其他成分时,如(16),双分支结构增加了 V 的韵律重量。冯胜利(2013b:52)指出,功能性成分以及定指成分在韵律规则的操作系统中都是隐形成分。(16)中的"只件事"(这件事)是定指成分,在核心重音范围内是韵律上的隐形成分,另外 CIP"一下"也是非重读成分,所以核心重音落在动词上。这样就不会造成韵律上的双重单轻、前重后轻的结果。虽(15)和(16)句法结构相同,但(15)非法而(16)合法,原因在于(15)违背了"前轻后重"的韵律要求,可见韵律直接决定着句子的合法性,换句话说,这就是韵律规则的句法效应。

4.3.2 效应二:动补结构带宾的提宾现象

在揭阳话中,宾语一般在谓语动词之后〔如(17)〕,但也存在宾语前置的现象。陈传佳(1996)在研究潮汕方言宾语前置时提到这种前置现象,例如:(18)a 的宾语"担物(这/那担子东西)"可以前置于主谓之间;(18)b 为复指型处置句,把宾语前置到介词"个(相当于普通话的'把')"前,并用"伊(它)"复指宾语。陈传佳(1996)指出,这些提宾句能表达不同的语气,(18)a 的提宾强调动词结果,(18)b 的复指型处置句是为了强调宾语[①],因而提宾有其语用目的。

(17)(语境:怎么,你找我有事儿吗?)

你^{53}# 放$^{213-42}$ 担$^{213-53}$ 物^5 落$^{5-2}$ 来$^{35-21}$。

你　放　　CL　　东西　下　来

"你放这/那担子东西下来。"

---

① 陈传佳(1996)并未解释为何(18)a 是"强调动词结果"、(18)b 是"为了强调宾语"。这里如果为其加上语境,句子表达的语用信息则更加清晰了(见文下附例)。(18)a 中只有"放落来(放下来)",后续才能有"担(挑)"这个动作;另外,我们可以从其句法结构中看到"[TP 你[T'T[VP 担物 i[V'[V' 放[VP2 落来][CIP eᵢ]]]]]]","担物"提到动词"放"前,宾语不在最后一个 NS 指派域内,因此,重音落在动词"放"上("放"保持词汇调),以此强调动词语义,这里韵律上的"重"是凸显语义的手段。(18)b 中通过添加标记"个伊(把它)",用代词"伊"复指前置宾语,凸显对宾语的处置。
　a. 弟弟:哇,担物件好重。(哇,这担子东西好重。)
　　妈妈:你担物放落来,我来担。(你这担子东西放下来,我来挑。)
　b. 弟弟:你睇,我会担只担物。(你看,我会挑这担子东西。)
　　妈妈:你担物个伊放落来,要等下乞你物掉去。(你这担子东西把它放下来,要不然等一下被你弄坏了。)

（18）a. 你^{53}＃担$^{213-53}$物^5＃放^{213}落$^{5-2}$来$^{35-21}$。

　　　　你　CL　东西　放　下　来

　　　　"你这／那担子东西放下来。"

　　b. 你^{53}＃担$^{213-53}$物^5＃个$^{55-1}$伊$^{33-33}$放^{213}落$^{5-2}$来$^{35-21}$。

　　　　你　CL　东西　把　它　放　下　来

　　　　"你这／那担子东西把它放下来。"

但我们发现（19）和（20）宽焦句中的动补结构带宾句如果宾语不前置则不合法。

（19）（语境：A问"外面怎么回事儿？怎么那么吵？"，B回答如下。）

　　a. ＊阿$^{33-33}$明^{55}＃拍$^{2-3}$拍$^{2-3}$死$^{53-24}$去$^{213-21}$只$^{2-2}$狗^{53}。

　　　　阿明　　打　打　死　Asp①　CL　狗

　　　　"＊阿明打死了这／那只狗。"

　　b. ？阿$^{33-33}$明^{55}＃青$^{33-33}$拍$^{2-3}$白$^{2-3}$拍$^{2-3}$只$^{2-3}$狗^{53}。

　　　　阿明　　[tshẽ]　打　[pɛʔ]　打　CL　狗

　　　　"？阿明一个劲儿地打这／那只狗。"

（20）（语境：A问"外面怎么回事儿？怎么那么吵？"，B回答如下。）

　　a. 阿$^{33-33}$明^{55}＃对$^{213-42}$只$^{2-3}$狗^{53}＃拍$^{2-3}$拍$^{2-3}$死^{53}去$^{213-21}$。

　　　　阿明　　把　CL　狗　打　打　死　Asp

　　　　"阿明把这／那只狗打死了。"

　　b. 阿$^{33-33}$明^{55}＃对$^{213-42}$只$^{2-3}$狗^{53}＃青$^{33-33}$拍$^{2-3}$白$^{2-3}$拍^2。

　　　　阿明　　把　CL　狗　[tshẽ]　打　[pɛʔ]　打

　　　　"阿明把这／那只狗一个劲儿地打。"

（19）a及（19）b分别是动词重叠后带补语以及动词重叠结构变体——"青V白V"后带宾语的句子，两句的宾语出现在动词后，可接受程度较低或不合法，而用介词"对"将宾语提前时〔如（20）a、b〕，句子合法。再如：

（21）（语境：A问"怎么回事儿？妹妹怎么哭了？"，B回答如下。）

　　＊伊^{33}＃物$^{5-2}$彩$^{55-11}$彩$^{55-11}$撮$^{2-3}$书^{33}。

　　　　他　弄乱　乱　CL　书

　　　　"＊他弄乱那堆书。"

————————

① "Asp"为"aspect"（体）的缩写。

（22）（语境：A问"怎么回事儿？妹妹怎么哭了？"，B回答如下。）

  a. 伊³³# 撮²⁻³ 书³³# 物⁵⁻² 到²¹³⁻⁵³ 舐⁵⁵⁻¹¹ 舐⁵⁵。

    他　　CL　书　弄　Part①　乱　乱

    "他那堆书弄得乱乱的。"

  b. 伊³³# 对²¹³⁻⁴² 撮²⁻³ 书³³# 物⁵⁻² 到²¹³⁻⁵³ 舐⁵⁵⁻¹¹ 舐⁵⁵。

    他　把　　CL　书　弄　Part　乱　乱

    "他把那堆书弄得乱乱的。"

同样，（21）为动补结构带宾语，该句子非法，只有将宾语提到动词前〔如（22）a〕或用介词"对"将宾语提前〔如（22）b〕才合法。

基于韵律句法学理论，我们认为上述现象与揭阳话的核心重音规则有关。核心重音由句中主要动词指派给其直接管辖的补述语。在（19）a、b及（21）的例句中，由于动补结构或动词本身过于复杂，其后如若再带定指宾语（定指宾语为韵律上较轻的成分），则会形成句子 NS 范围内"前重后轻"的韵律结构，违背了"前轻后重"的韵律要求，句子非法。因此韵律激活句法移位，直接提前或用介词"对"将（19）和（21）中韵律相对较轻的成分（有定宾语）提到谓语前，此时核心重音由动词指派给其后的补述语或落在该复杂动词上，这样才拯救了非法的句子，（20）a、b 的句法结构如（23）和（24）所示。

（23）

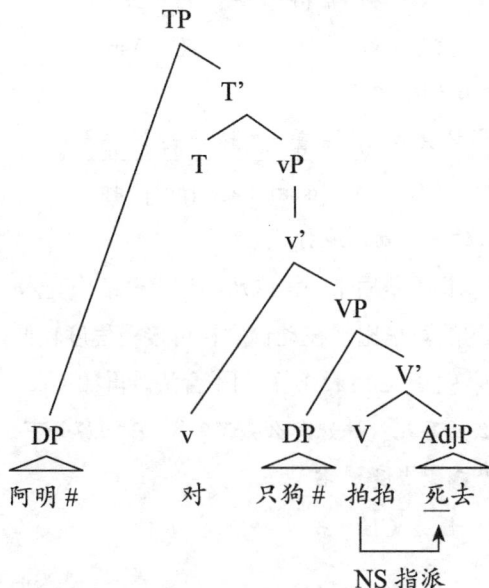

---

① "Part"是"particle"（小品词/助词）的缩写。

（24）

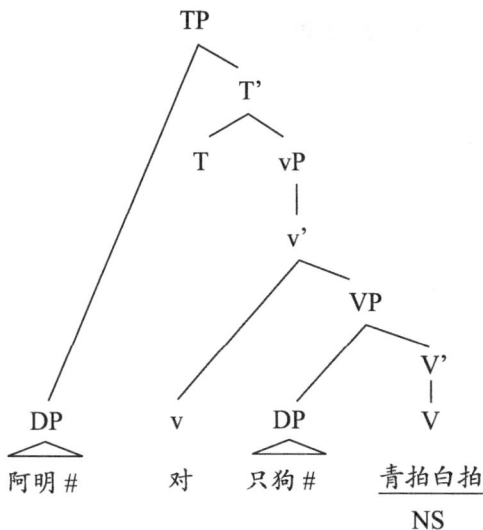

5. 结语

本文通过对比句法上同构的宽域焦点句与窄域焦点句的揭阳话变调模式，指出核心重音与保持词汇调的成分相关，并进一步论证核心重音落在句末动宾结构之内，由句末动词指派给其直接管辖的补述语。另外，我们考察了揭阳话"对"字句谓语动词不能挂单现象，原因在于动词前的"对＋DP"双分支结构短语与单支动词形成了前重后轻的韵律格局，违背了揭阳话"前轻后重"的韵律要求，因而被删除，此为韵律对句法的删除作用；当复杂动词或动词重叠后带补语，若句子再带定指宾语，该宾语需提到动词前，否则不合韵律要求，导致句子非法。宾语提前以拯救句法，此为韵律对句法（操作）的激活作用。

关于宽域焦点句双宾结构 [V IO DO]，如"我送同学本书"，谓语部分中的直接宾语（DO）"书"与间接宾语（IO）"同学"都保持词汇调，此时如何确定哪个成分承载核心重音？理论表明一个句子中有且仅有一个核心重音，因此同在谓语动词之后的两个宾语必然仅有一个承担核心重音，那么核心重音落在何处？ Li（1990）将普通话双宾结构中的[V IO]分析为一个复杂动词，DO为其宾语。据此，冯胜利（2009：92）认为双宾句的核心重音由该复杂动词整体指派给DO。揭阳话是否也可以如此分析？进一步推论，如果其中一个宾语位置为核心重音所在，尽管两个宾语都保持词汇调，但韵律表现一定会有其他差别，那么此处两个保持词汇调的成分的韵律属性有何不同？该问题仍是今后研究的课题之一。

参考文献

陈传佳 . 1996. 潮汕方言的宾语前置 . 韩山师范学院学报, (1): 98-104.

冯胜利 . 2000. 汉语韵律句法学 . 上海: 上海教育出版社 .

冯胜利 . 2009. 汉语的韵律、词法与句法 (修订本). 北京: 北京大学出版社 .

冯胜利 . 2013a. 汉语的核心重音 . 中国语学, (260): 6-24.

冯胜利 . 2013b. 汉语韵律句法学 (增订本). 北京: 商务印书馆 .

冯胜利, 王丽娟 . 2018. 汉语韵律语法教程 . 北京: 北京大学出版社 .

何元建 . 2011. 现代汉语生成语法 . 北京: 北京大学出版社 .

李艳惠, 冯胜利 . 2015. "一" 字省略的韵律条件 . 语言科学, (1): 1-12.

林伦伦, 陈小枫 . 1996. 广东闽方言语音研究 . 汕头: 汕头大学出版社 .

林晓燕 . 2020. 闽南方言揭阳话句重音的韵律研究 . 北京语言大学硕士学位论文 .

施其生 . 2011. 汕头方言连读变调的动态运行——兼论汉语方言连读变调的研究视角 . 中国语文, (4):
    334-345.

赵元任 . 1980/2002. 中国话的文法 (增订版). 丁邦新, 译 . 香港: 中文大学出版社 .

钟　奇 . 2007. 汉语方言的重音模式 . 新加坡国立大学博士学位论文 .

Behaghel O. 1909. Beziehungen zwischen Umfang und Reihenfolge von Satzgliedern. *Indogermanische Forschungen*, 25: 110-142.

Chen M Y (陈渊泉). 2001. *Tone Sandhi: Patterns Across Chinese Dialects* (汉语方言的连读变调模式). 北京: 外语教学与研究出版社 .

Cinque G. 1993. A null theory of phrase and compound stress. *Linguistic Inquiry*, 24.2: 239-297.

Duanmu S. 1993. Rime length, stress, and association domains. *Journal of East Asian Linguistics*, 2: 1-44.

Duanmu S. 1995. Metrical and tonal phonology of compounds in two Chinese dialects. *Language*, 71.2: 225-259.

Feng S L. 1995. *Prosodic Structure and Prosodically Constrained Syntax in Chinese*. Ph.D. dissertation, University of Pennsylvania.

Feng S L. 2003. Prosodically constrained postverbal PPs in mandarin Chinese. *Linguistics*, 41.6: 1085-1122.

Li Y-H A. 1990. *Order and Constituency in Mandarin Chinese*. Dordrecht: Kluver Academic Publishers.

Liberman M, Prince A. 1977. On stress and linguistic rhythm. *Linguistic Inquiry*, 8.2: 249-336.

Quirk R, Greenbaum S, Leech G, et al. 1972. *A Grammar of Contemporary English*. London: Longman.

Xu H L. 2007. Aspect of Chaozhou grammar: a synchronic description of the Jieyang variety. *Journal of Chinese Linguistics Monograph Series*, 22: 1-304.

Xu Y, Chen S W, Wang B. 2012. Prosodic focus with and without post-focus compression: a typological divide within the same language family? *The Linguistic Review*, 29: 131-147.

Zubizarreta M L. 1998. *Prosody, Focus, and Word Order*. Cambridge, Mass.: MIT Press.

The Syntactic Effect of the Nuclear Stress Rule of the Jieyang Dialect in Southern Fujian

Lin, Xiaoyan

Faculty of Linguistic Sciences, Beijing Language and Culture University

Abstract: Feng (2003) concluded that there are four types of nuclear stress rules (NSR) in different languages: Nuclear Stress Rule (Liberman & Prince 1977), Depth Stress Principle (Cinque,1993), Selectionally based NSR (Zubizarreta,1998) and Government-based NSR in Chinese (Feng,1995/2003). However, there are few studies on the NSR of Chinese Southern Fujian dialects.

Based on the theory of Prosodic Syntax, this work discusses the nuclear stress (NS) of the Jieyang dialect in Southern Fujian and the interactions between prosody and syntax. The findings are as follows:

Firstly, in the Jieyang dialect, the focus can be highlighted by tone sandhi, as shown in (1):

(1) a. $\underline{A^{33\text{-}33}\text{-}ma^{55}}$ # $kio^{213\text{-}53}$ $\underline{a^{33\text{-}33}\text{-}ti^{35}}$ # $k^hu^{213\text{-}53}$ $boi^{53\text{-}35}$ $\underline{tsui^{53}}$. [no focus]

　Mum　　　ask　younger brother go　　buy　water

　"Mum asked my younger brother to buy water."

　　b. $\underline{A^{33\text{-}33}\text{-}ma^{55}}$ # $kio^{213\text{-}53}$ $\underline{a^{33\text{-}33}\text{-}ti^{35}}$ $\underset{\sim}{k^hu^{213\text{-}21}}$ $\underset{\sim}{boi^{53\text{-}213}}$ $\underset{\sim}{tsui^{53\text{-}213}}$. [narrow focus]

　　Mum　　　ask　younger brother go　　buy　water

　　"Mum asked my younger brother to buy water (not asked me)."

(1)a is a non-focused sentence. The subject $a^{33\text{-}33}\text{-}ma^{55}$ (mum), the objects $a^{33\text{-}33}\text{-}ti^{35}$ (younger brother) and $tsui^{53}$ (water) keep their lexical tones (the underlined words), and other words need to change their inherent tones at the syntactic level. But in the narrow focus sentence (1)b, when $a^{33\text{-}33}\text{-}ti^{35}$ is the focus, the tone sandhi pattern before $a^{33\text{-}33}\text{-}ti^{35}$ is the same as (1)a, while the following elements change their tone sandhi patterns (the part with wavy line) into neutral tones. It can be seen that the focal information in Jieyang dialect can be highlighted by changing the pitch of the following elements, which is similar to the focus stress achieved through changing the intensity between the stressed one and the non-stressed one in Beijing Mandarin. As is shown in this research, the stress in the Jieyang dialect is closely related to tone sandhi, and the focal element is the one that keeps its lexical tone.

Secondly, based on the end-weight principle proposed by previous scholars (Behaghel, 1909; Quirk et al., 1972; Chao,1980), we exclude that the subject which maintains the lexical tone is the NS. It seems that the components that maintain the lexical tone are in the deepest embedded position of the structure. But we further exclude that the NS domain is in the PP after the main verb, which means that P can not assign the NS. Moreover, it is not allowed that two elements that keep their lexical tones appear after the main verb at the end of the non-focus sentence at the same time (ditransitive verbs are not included here, which need to be discussed separately). All the above facts can infer the NSR of the Jieyang dialect: The NSR in the Jieyang dialect is assigned by the main verb to its directly governed complement.

Finally, we discuss two syntactic phenomena constrained by prosody. The stress pattern of [w s] in NS domain in the Jieyang dialect requires: a. the main verb of *TUI* (equal to *BA* in Mandarin) sentence cannot show up alone in the end [shown in (2) and (3)]; b. when there is a complex verb or a verb with a complement in the sentence, if there is also an object in the sentence, then the object must be moved out of NS domain before the main verb in the S-structure [shown in (4) and (5)].

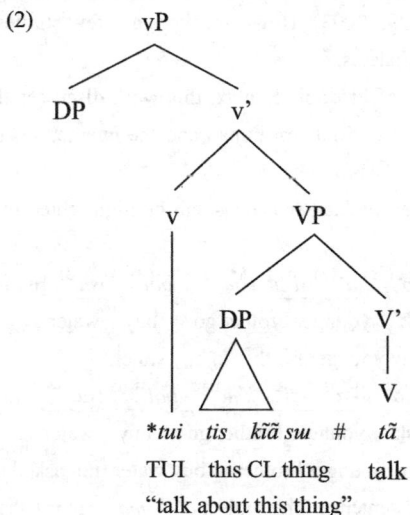

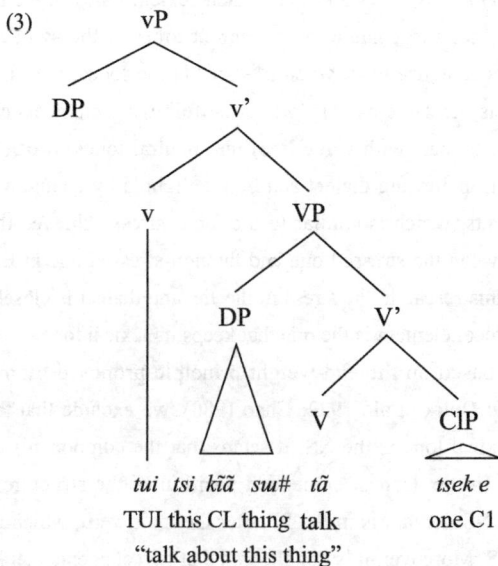

(2)

```
              vP
          /        \
        DP          v'
                 /      \
               v         VP
                       /     \
                     DP       V'
                     /\        |
                    /  \       V
```

*tui   tis   kĩã su   #   tã
TUI   this CL thing   talk
"talk about this thing"

(3)

```
              vP
          /        \
        DP          v'
                 /      \
               v         VP
                       /     \
                     DP       V'
                     /\      /    \
                    /  \    V      ClP
```

tui tsi kĩã su# tã   tsek e
TUI this CL thing talk   one Cl
"talk about this thing"

(4)

```
              * TP
            /    \
           /      T'
          /      /  \
         /      T    VP
        /            |
       /             V'
      /            /    \
     /            s      w
    DP           V'      DP
    △          /  \      △
 A-Maŋ#   pʰaʔpʰaʔ si kʰɯ   tsiaʔ kao
 A-Ming   beat beat die Part  CL  dog
```
"A-Ming beats that dog to death."

(5)

```
              vP
            /    \
          DP      v'
                /   \
               v     VP
               |    /   \
               |   DP    V'
               |   △    /  \
               |   |    V   ClP
               |   |    |    △
 tui  tsi kĩã  sɯ#  tã      tsek e
 TUI this CL thing talk    one Cl
```
"talk about this thing"

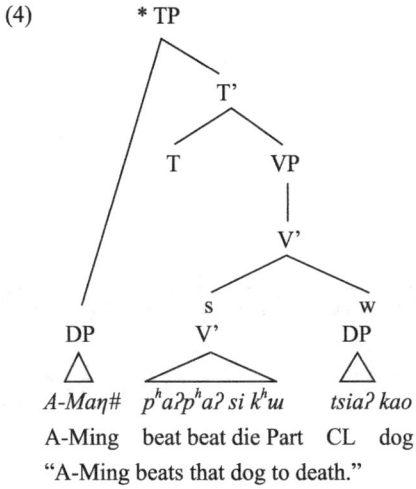

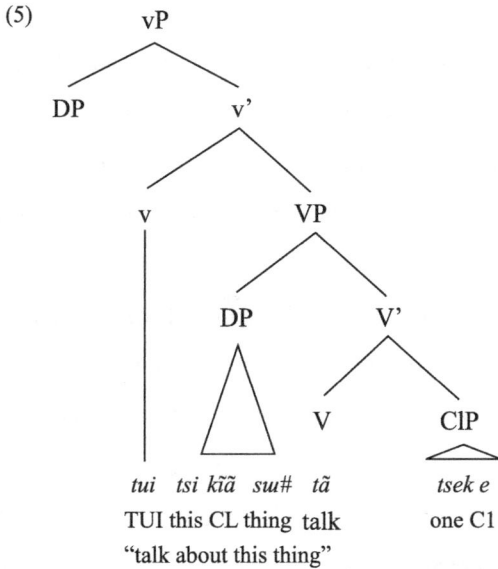

Keywords: Southern Min dialect; Jieyang dialect; NSR; prosody; syntax

林晓燕

北京语言大学语言科学院

linxiaoyan0807@163.com

Two Problems in Theories of Tone-melody Matching

D. Robert Ladd

Abstract: Recent work on how lexical tones are matched with musical melodies has shown that a satisfactory match generally requires the *pitch direction* between musical notes to be the same as the pitch direction between the corresponding tones. This principle applies in a number of unrelated tone languages in both Asia and Africa. The interaction of this pitch direction principle with other principles is often approached (at least implicitly) in terms of ranked violable constraints, and at least one study has made explicit use of the descriptive framework of Optimality Theory. Nevertheless, some empirical and theoretical issues remain poorly understood. This paper considers two such problems on the basis of recent studies of modern Cantonese popular music ("Cantopop"). First, it discusses so-called "oblique" matches, where either the tone sequence is unchanging while the musical sequence rises or falls, or the musical pitch stays level across a sequence of different tones. These have often been treated as near-matches, but investigation shows this to be empirically incorrect, with unclear implications for the idea of violable constraints. Second, the paper discusses the treatment of contour tones in determining a good match: contour tones are handled differently in different languages, and there is evidence that they may be intrinsically difficult to accommodate in a well-matched melody.

Keywords: Cantopop; text-setting; tone; contour tones

1. Introduction

The past few decades have seen considerable research on the principles that govern the correspondence between text and melody in songs in tone languages. It is now generally recognised that the tonal sequences in a song text and the note sequences in the accompanying musical melody should <u>match</u> in some way. The most important principle of a good match between the tones of a song text and the melody appears to involve the <u>direction of the pitch movement</u> from one note to the next: ideally, the musical pitch movement should be in the same direction as the direction of the natural tonal movement between the syllables sung on those notes. More particularly, rising melodic sequences should not accompany syllables in which the tonal sequence is falling (e.g. High tone followed by Mid tone), and rising tonal sequences should not be set to falling musical melodies. Like the artistic constraints involved in meter and rhyme, the prohibition on mismatched pitch direction is not absolute, but the empirical evidence that such a principle exists now comes from many unrelated tone languages, and the basic idea of avoiding such mismatches is now shared across most recent work on tone-melody matching.

One of the earliest studies in this current line of research on tone-melody matching is an exploratory paper by Chan (1987a), which dealt with Cantonese popular songs and film music (see also Chan, 1987b). Chan observed that in songs with multiple verses set to the same melody, the <u>sequence of syllable tones</u> on any given melodic line was nearly identical in each verse, even though the words were completely different. That is, it appears that a musical melody somehow dictates which Cantonese words can be used at specific places in the melody, just as a rhyme scheme dictates which words are available for use at the end of a line of rhyming verse. Chan proposed the basic pitch-direction rule summarized above and discussed various specific problems of detail. The relevance of pitch direction was confirmed experimentally for Cantonese by Wong & Diehl (2002), and has been demonstrated for other languages by Schellenberg (2009, 2012) and others. McPherson & Ryan (2018) present a formal analysis of the pitch-direction principle expressed in terms of the interacting violable constraints of Optimality Theory (e.g. both a preference for matching pitch direction and a prohibition against non-matching pitch direction); their work was based on folk songs in Tommo So (a Dogon language spoken in Mali). A summary review of the past few decades' work is given by Ladd & Kirby (2020).

By far the best-studied language in this line of research is Cantonese, in part because of its links to an active tradition of westernized pop music, so-called "Cantopop" (粤语流行音乐). This was the subject of a Hong Kong Ph.D. dissertation by Ho (何咏诗) (2010), which firmly established the systematic nature of Cantopop's tone-melody matching and investigated many of the details. Two more recent Master's dissertation projects at the University of Edinburgh, one (Lo, 2013) supervised by me and one (Lin, 2018) supervised by my colleague James Kirby, have confirmed and built on Ho's conclusions. My aim in this paper is to use the fairly well understood facts about tone-melody matching in Cantopop to shed light on two problems with current work on tone-melody matching in general.

2. Basic Empirical Findings on Tone-melody Matching in Cantopop

2.1 Explanation of Terminology and Methods

Empirical evaluation of the correspondence between tone and melody in recent work – not just work on Cantopop but all the research briefly summarized in the introduction – has generally been based on the description of bigrams: sequential pairs of musical notes and the accompanying syllables. This is illustrated in Figure 1, a line taken from the 2003 song "Next Station Tin Hau", by Twins:

站 在 大 丸 前 细 心　看 看 我 的 路

zaam22 zoi22 daai22 jyun35cin21 sai33 sam55 hon33 hon33 ngo23 dik5 lou22

Figure 1   Bigrams in a line from a Cantopop song (adapted from Lin, 2018)

The bigrams are labelled with capital letters A–K. For every bigram, the pitch direction of both the musical sequence and the tonal sequence can be described as rising, falling, or unchanging. The definition of these three possibilities, when applied to the musical sequence, is straightforward: for example, bigrams C and F are rising, bigrams D and G are falling, and bigrams A and H are unchanging. For the tonal sequence, in bigrams consisting of level tones, the pitch direction is also easy to define: for example, bigram F (consisting of a mid-level tone followed by a high-level tone) is rising, while bigram G is falling and bigrams A, B, and H are unchanging. For bigrams containing contour tones – like bigram D, with a high-rising tone followed by a low-falling tone, or bigram I, with a mid-level tone followed by a low-rising tone – the situation is somewhat more complex. We return to this question shortly, and the place of contour tones in tone-melody matching more generally is one of the two problems we consider in the second half of the paper (section 3.2).

Once we have defined both the musical and the tonal pitch direction in a given bigram, we can define three types of correspondence between the tones and the melody. Following Ladd and Kirby, we refer to these three as similar, contrary, and oblique. In a "similar" setting[①] both the musical sequence and the tonal sequence are identical – both rising, for example. In a "contrary" setting, the two sequences go in the opposite

①   The term *setting* here is based on the notion of "text-setting", the process of taking a given text (the song lyrics) and fitting them to a melody. This notion is not necessarily very accurate for describing tone-melody matching in many folk traditions [e.g. Lissoir (2016) on Tai Dam, Karlsson (2018) on Kammu], but it applies fairly well to composed music like Cantopop songs.

direction – one rising and the other falling. "Oblique" settings cover the remaining possibilities: either the musical sequence is unchanging and the tonal sequence rises or falls (oblique I), or the tonal sequence is unchanging and the accompanying melody rises or falls (oblique II). The terms are illustrated graphically in Figure 2.

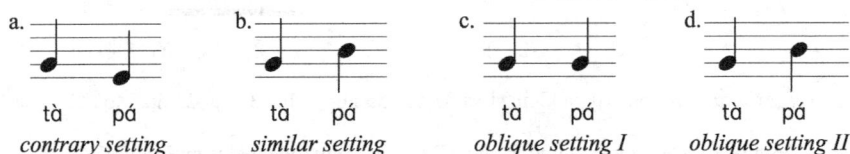

a. contrary setting   b. similar setting   c. oblique setting I   d. oblique setting II
(tà pá)   (tà pá)   (tà pá)   (tà pá)

Figure 2   Possible bigram types (Ladd & Kirby, 2020)

Ho, Schellenberg, and McPherson and Ryan all use the term parallel for Ladd and Kirby's "similar". Ho and Schellenberg treat oblique as "non-opposing"; McPherson and Ryan adopt Ladd and Kirby's term "oblique" but group it together with "parallel" as "non-contrary". In both cases the terminology conveys the idea that oblique is somehow neutral or intermediate between similar and contrary, a less serious violation of the expectation that the tonal sequence and the melodic sequence should match. This conception of "oblique" is the other of the two problems considered in the second half of the paper.

Given the categorization of pitch direction into three types (rising, falling, unchanging) and given the categorization of the tone-melody correspondence in any given bigram into three types (similar, contrary, oblique), quantitative data from a corpus of songs can be displayed in a 3×3 matrix, with the musical pitch direction on one axis and the tonal pitch direction on the other. The distribution of the bigram types in the nine cells of the 3×3 matrix is illustrated in Table 1.

Table 1   Matrix diagram summarizing bigram types

		Musical pitch direction		
		Rising	Falling	Unchanging
Tonal pitch direction	Rising	**similar**	contrary	• oblique
	Falling	contrary	**similar**	• oblique
	Unchanging	• oblique	• oblique	**similar**

With actual data presented in such a matrix, we can evaluate empirical predictions based on various principles governing tone-melody matching. For example, if a prohibition on contrary settings were the only determinant of a good tone-melody match, we would predict that bigrams in the two "contrary" cells of the matrix should be uncommon, but would have no real basis for predicting the proportion of bigrams in the other cells. On the other hand, if we assume that there is not only a constraint prohibiting contrary settings, but also a constraint preferring "similar" settings, we would predict that bigrams in the cells along the diagonal containing similar settings should be more frequent than those in other cells, as shown in Table 2:

Table 2   Matrix diagram displaying frequency predictions about bigram types

		Musical pitch direction		
		Rising	Falling	Unchanging
Tonal pitch direction	Rising	**frequent**	rare	• (unclear)
	Falling	rare	**frequent**	• (unclear)
	Unchanging	• (unclear)	• (unclear)	**frequent**

We would still have no clear prediction about the "oblique" cells of the matrix, but as we shall see in section 2.3, quantitative data from Cantopop seem to confirm that "oblique" is not a coherent category and that the two sub-types – those where the musical note on the two syllables is the same and those where the two tones are identical – can be clearly distinguished.

2.2   Cantonese tone and the problem of contour tones

Cantonese is generally analysed (e.g. Matthews & Yip, 2011) as having six tones: high level (55), high-rising (35), mid level (33), low-falling (21), low-rising (23), and low-level (22)[①]. The numbers in parentheses give the conventional phonetic description

---

① There are also three "checked tones" (入声), High, Mid, and Low, that occur only in syllables closed by a stop, but these are readily identified with the three level tones of the main six-tone set [i.e., T1 (阴平), T3 (阴去), and T6 (阳去)]. Note also that in present-day Hong Kong Cantonese there appears to be a merger in progress between T5 (阳上, 23) and T2 (阴上, 35) (e.g. Bauer et al., 2003).

of the tones in terms of the five-level system introduced by Chao (1930). The six tones are illustrated in Figure 3, which displays: (1) the traditional Western identifying numbers for each tone [T1 (tone 1), T2, etc.]; (2) the traditional Chinese designations; and (3) the conventionally assumed "Chao numbers" indicating the tone's beginning and ending pitch levels. Throughout the rest of the paper we will use all three methods of referring to specific tones.

With this background, let us return to the issue of how to define the pitch direction across bigrams involving contour tones (in Cantonese, T2, T5, and T4). Consider for example a bigram in which both syllables bear T4 (阳平 , 21). Taking the Chao pitch levels as a rough phonetic description of the pitch direction on each tone, we can describe the tone sequence across the bigram is something like the following:

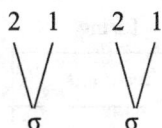

$$
\begin{array}{cc}
2\ 1 & 2\ 1 \\
\diagdown\diagup & \diagdown\diagup \\
\sigma & \sigma
\end{array}
$$

We can imagine a variety of principles that might define a good musical match to this tone sequence. For example, perhaps a good match would prescribe rising musical pitch across the bigram, corresponding to the rise from level 1 to level 2 across the syllable boundary. Or perhaps the musical pitch should be falling, to express the overall fall in pitch from level 2 at the beginning of the bigram to level 1 at the end. Or perhaps the musical pitch should remain unchanging, because the tones on each syllable are phonologically the same.

Tone	Level	Pitch pattern	Level
T1 （阴平）	5	1	5
T2 （阴上）	4	2	4
T3 （阴去）	3	3	3
T5 （阳上）		5	
T6 （阳去）	2	6	2
T4 （阳平）	1	4	1

Figure 3 Cantonese tones

As it happens, Chan's original description of tone-melody matching addressed this problem and suggested that, in Cantonese, what counts in evaluating the pitch direction from one tone to the next is the **endpoint** – the final pitch level – of each tone. Roughly speaking, a falling tone that ends low counts as low, and a rising tone that ends high counts as high. This also seems to be true of some other Asian tone languages as well [e.g. Kirby & Ladd (2016) on Vietnamese], though in some languages [e.g. Thai; see Ketkaew & Pittayaporn (2014)] the situation may be considerably more complex. Even within Chinese, recent work by Zhang & Cross (2021) on folksongs in Chaozhou (Teochew, 潮州) shows that for text-setting purposes tones must be grouped into three categories (High, Mid and Low), but that the endpoint principle fails to group them correctly. For Cantonese, however, Ho's thesis amply confirms that the end pitch (Ho sometimes uses the term *tonal target*) is the key to dealing with contour tones.

Concretely, the endpoint principle means that the tonal pitch direction in a tonal bigram consisting of T1 (阴平 , 55) and tone T2 (阴上 , 35) counts as "unchanging", because both tones end at level 5; the same is true of a bigram consisting of T3 (阴去 , 33) and T5 (阳上 , 23), where both tones end at level 3. By the same logic, a bigram consisting of T1 (阴平, 55) followed by T3 (阴去, 33) and a bigram consisting of T2 (阴上 , 35) followed by T5 (阳上 , 23) both involve falling pitch direction, from level 5 (at the end of the first tone of the bigram) to level 3 (at the end of the second).

For purposes of their experiment Wong and Diehl settled on a three-way distinction between High, Mid and Low endpoints, grouping both T6 (22) and T4 (21) together as Low. Ho's subsequent work showed clearly that we get a more accurate picture of tone-melody matching in Cantopop if we assume that T6 (阳去, 22) counts as Low and T4 (阳平 , 21) counts as Extra-Low. I return to this issue in section 3.2; to avoid the potentially confusing use of both Chao's pitch level numbers and Cantonese tone numbers, I will adopt the terms High, Mid, Low, and Extra-Low throughout the paper for referring to tone endpoint levels.

2.3   Quantitative Studies of Tone-melody Matching in Cantopop

In this section I summarise the data from two relatively recent studies of Cantopop songs. Both are based on Master's dissertation projects at the University of Edinburgh, one (Lo, 2013) supervised by me and one (Lin, 2018) supervised by my colleague James Kirby. (Kirby has subsequently done further work on Lin's data and throughout the paper I refer to the "Kirby/Lin corpus".) Lo's corpus was based on 11 songs and a total of 2,665 bigrams; the Kirby/Lin corpus was based on 8 songs and a total of 1,720 bigrams. Lin's study focused on a comparison between Cantonese and Mandarin versions of the same songs, but with respect to Cantonese very similar methodology was used in both studies. Songs were transcribed and the bigrams classified in the ways described in section 2.1; the classification of tonal bigrams treats T4 as Extra-Low, as just described. Both studies reveal a very similar picture that is in line with Ho's conclusions, but I focus on the two Edinburgh studies in order to illustrate my points with quantitative data. In this short section I treat the two datasets together, whereas the discussion in section 3 is based primarily on the Kirby/Lin corpus, as it is the only one for which I have access to a complete file of raw data.

Table 3 presents the numbers from both studies combined into a single dataset. The total number of bigrams in each cell is given in section (a), while section (b) presents the same numbers as percentages of the total of 4,385 bigrams. Section (c) shows the proportions row-by-row (so that each row sums to 100%), while section (d) shows the proportions column-by-column (so that each column sums to 100%). This allows us to consider the treatment of the three types of tonal pitch direction [section (c)] and the three types of musical pitch direction [section (d)] separately.

Table 3   Distribution of bigram types in the combined Lo/Lin Cantopop data

(a)

		Musical pitch direction		
		Rising	Falling	Unchanging
Tonal pitch direction	Rising	**1,410**	98	• 65
	Falling	154	**1,279**	• 80
	Unchanging	•• 190	•• 375	**734**

(b)

		Musical pitch direction		
		Rising	Falling	Unchanging
Tonal pitch direction	Rising	*32.2%*	*2.2%*	• *1.5%*
	Falling	*3.5%*	*29.2%*	• *1.8%*
	Unchanging	•• *4.3%*	•• *8.6%*	*16.7%*

(c)

		Musical pitch direction			
		Rise	Fall	Unchg	
Tonal pitch direction	Rise	**89.6%**	6.2%	• 4.1%	100%
	Fall	10.2%	**84.5%**	• 5.3%	100%
	Unchg	•• 14.6%	•• 28.9%	**56.5%**	100%

(d)

		Musical pitch direction		
		Rise	Fall	Unchg
Tonal pitch direction	Rise	**80.4%**	5.6%	• 7.4%
	Fall	8.8%	**73.0%**	• 9.1%
	Unchg	•• 10.8%	•• 21.4%	**83.5%**
		100%	100%	100%

It can be seen immediately from Table 3 (b) that "contrary" settings (shown in the two shaded cells of the matrix) are very uncommon, while at the same time Table 3 (d) shows that "similar" settings (those in the three cells along the diagonal, with heavy black borders) constitute more than three-quarters of the whole corpus. This clearly suggests that tone-melody matching in Cantopop involves both a prohibition on contrary settings and a preference for similar settings, and that these constraints may interact in some way. In the context of the current research reviewed in the introduction, this is hardly a surprising conclusion, but it is striking to see just how large the quantitative differences are between prohibited and preferred bigrams. Moreover, this finding appears to confirm the view (e.g. Ho, 2010: 36ff.; Schellenberg, 2013) that tone-melody matching in Cantonese is quite strict compared to many languages. As just noted, the larger purpose of Lin (2018) study was to make an explicit comparison between Cantonese and Mandarin, and her results show clearly that Cantonese is much stricter in this respect than standard Mandarin.

Somewhat more surprisingly, it can also be seen that there is a clear difference between the two different types of "oblique" settings illustrated in Figure 1 above. These are shown in Table 3 in the cells marked with the symbols · (I) and · · (II). From sections (a) and (b) we can see that "Oblique II" bigrams, where the tone remains the same but the musical pitch is either rising or falling, are far more common in the corpus than "Oblique I", where the tonal pitch direction is rising or falling but the musical pitch stays the same. The bottom row of Table 3 (c) shows that "Oblique II" settings are relatively common with unchanging tonal sequences, although it is clear that "similar" settings (where unchanging musical pitch mirrors the unchanging tone) are preferred in these cases as well. By contrast, the upper two rows of Table 3 (c) show that in rising or falling tonal sequences, oblique I settings are less common even than contrary settings. This suggests that the category "oblique" may be somewhat incoherent.

3. Two Problems

The remainder of the paper is devoted to more detailed discussion of two specific problems that the approach sketched so far brings to light. These are the apparent incoherence of the category "oblique", just mentioned, and the question of how to determine pitch direction across bigrams that include contour tones.

3.1 Oblique Settings

The Cantopop evidence just reviewed seems to show clearly that the two subtypes of oblique are not equivalent. It can be seen from the first two rows of Table 3 (b) that oblique I bigrams – where the tonal sequence is rising or falling but the musical sequence remains unchanging – are less frequent than "contrary" settings, where the tonal and musical sequences go in opposite directions. Ho (2010: 60) reports exactly the same finding, and states that what we are calling an oblique I bigram "always represents a perceived mismatch". If the only constraints on tone-melody matching involve the closeness of the match between the music and the text, this finding is unexpected.

The difference can be easily explained if we assume the existence of a strictly musical constraint that disfavors same-note sequences (or, looked at the other way, a constraint that prefers musical melodies that keep moving). This constraint is "strictly musical" in the sense that it applies only to a feature of the melody, not to how closely tone and melody match; it is thus comparable to McPherson and Ryan's proposal that in Tommo So songs rising musical bigrams are disfavored. In terms of a ranked-constraint approach like Optimality Theory, this musical constraint would be outranked only by the preference for "similar" settings: unchanging musical sequences are allowed in the case of unchanging tonal sequences, where they yield a "similar" bigram, but not otherwise. Looking only at the rightmost column of Table 3 (d) above, we see that roughly five-sixths of all repeated-note musical sequences in the dataset involve unchanging tonal sequences and therefore "similar" bigrams.

The suggestion that moving melodies are preferred is also consistent with the distribution of oblique II bigrams. From the bottom row of Table 3 (c) above, we see that scarcely more than half of the unchanging tone sequences are set to unchanging musical sequences, even though such a setting would be "similar" (and therefore, on a simple account, preferred). Here again, the preference for similar settings seems to interact with an independent preference for moving melodies. In fact, a more detailed breakdown of the oblique II data in the Kirby/Lin corpus suggests that we are dealing with the special treatment of a particular sequence. Specifically, any "unchanging" tonal sequence involving either of the two "High" tones (i.e., the sequences T1+T1, T2+T2, T1+T2, and T2+T1) shows a moderate preference for a <u>falling</u> musical setting over the expected unchanging or same-note sequence. All other unchanging tonal sequences, as expected by the general preference for "similar" settings, show a preference for unchanging or same-note musical sequences. This difference is presented graphically in

Figure 4[①]. The explanation for this special treatment of High tonal sequences is hardly clear, but one might speculate that the tendency to "declination" of F0 during spoken phrases and utterances may make it more natural to set a High-High sequence to a slightly falling musical melody. The same phenomenon is noted by Ho (2010: 65f.), who also suggests the same speculative explanation.

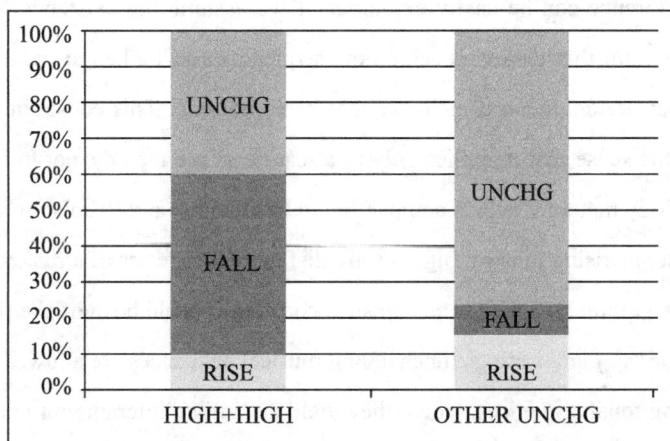

Figure 4　Special treatment of High+High tonal sequences

In any case, the evidence just reviewed suggests that there are problems with any descriptive framework for tone-melody matching that takes the category "oblique" to be on a par with the categories "contrary" and "similar". The clear differences between what we have called "oblique I" and "oblique II" certainly argue for distinguishing those two types from one another. More importantly, the fact that contrary settings are more frequent than oblique I settings seems to point to a more general problem with the way the notion of constraint violation is used to account for the details of tone-melody matching.

Specifically, as Proto (2016) has pointed out, "oblique" settings are treated in most work as if they were neutral in some way, neither a complete match nor a complete

---

① Ho (2010: 63ff.) finds a complementary tendency for unchanging Extra-Low tonal sequences [sequences consisting of T4 (阳平 , 21) syllables] to be set to a *rising* musical melody. The Kirby/ Lin data hint at the same conclusion, but there are too few cases to be confident, which is why I have grouped T4+T4 sequences with Mid+Mid and Low+Low bigrams in Figure 4.

mismatch; we have already mentioned this in connection with the implications of Schellenberg's term "non-opposing" (which Proto also uses) and McPherson and Ryan's term "non-contrary". This idea is a consequence of conceptualizing the principles of tone-melody matching in terms of interacting but contradictory violable constraints: if the two key constraints are a prohibition on contrary settings and a requirement for similar settings, then oblique settings should be preferable to contrary settings, because a "contrary" bigram violates *both* the prohibition on contrary settings and the requirement for similar settings, whereas an "oblique" bigram (either oblique I or oblique II) violates only the latter but not the former. But since the Cantopop data shows that oblique I settings are actually *less* frequent than contrary settings and that oblique I and oblique II are not comparable, it is plainly misleading to regard "oblique" as simply a less serious mismatch than "contrary". At present it is hardly clear how to refine the approach so that it better fits actual song data, but Proto's critique directs our attention to the need for some sort of rethinking.

3.2   Setting Contour Tones

So far I have simply adopted Chan's "endpoint principle" for categorizing pitch direction across tonal sequences involving contour tones, and have simply stated that Ho's application of this principle to Cantonese (distinguishing between "Low" and "Extra-Low" endpoints) is superior to Wong and Diehl's version that lumps together tones 6 (阳去 , 22) and 4 (阳平 , 21) as "Low". In this section I first present the evidence for Ho's analysis and then discuss further evidence for the general correctness of the endpoint principle itself. Finally, I discuss a few specific cases that suggest that the endpoint principle may nevertheless coexist with special treatment of certain specific tones or combinations of tones. All the data are taken from the Kirby/Lin corpus.

The evidence for Ho's analysis can be found in a quantitative comparison of T4+T6 bigrams and T6+T4 bigrams. If the endpoint principle is correct and if T6 (阳去 , 22) ends Low but T4 (阳平 , 21) ends Extra-Low, we should expect that T4+T6 bigrams should preferentially be set to rising musical melodies while T6+T4 bigrams should prefer falling melodies. This is exactly what we see in the Kirby/Lin corpus. Altogether, the corpus contains 90 T4+T6 bigrams and 68 T6+T4 bigrams. The vast majority of the T4+T6 tonal sequences are set to a rising musical sequence, whereas the majority of the T6+T4 tonal sequences are set to a falling musical sequence. The comparison is summarized graphically in Figure 5. It is clear that the two types of bigrams are treated differently.

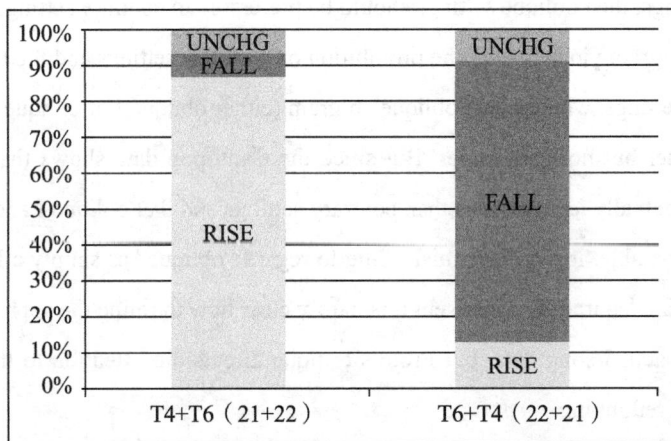

Figure 5　Different patterns of setting tonal sequences T4+T6 and T6+T4 in the Kirby/Lin corpus

A more basic test of the validity of the endpoint principle is to compare bigrams consisting only of level tones with bigrams involving contour tones. If the endpoint principle is correct, there should be no quantitative difference between the two types of bigram. For example, we can compare the level-tone bigram T1 (阴平, 55) + T3 (阴去, 33), which involves only High level and Mid level, with bigrams that also include T2 (阴上, 35) and T5 (阳上, 23). According to the endpoint principle, T2 and T5 should be treated as High and Mid, respectively. We should therefore expect that the musical settings of bigrams with T2 and T5 should be indistinguishable from those involving T1 and T3. Ho (2010: 47) makes this same point.

Three sets of such comparisons[①] are displayed in Table 4. In each section of Table 4, the data from the bigram type that consists only of level tones is shaded; the other

①　The fourth possible comparison, namely unchanging High+High sequences, is not included, because of the fact (shown graphically in Figure 4) that these sequences are treated as a special case for tone-melody matching.

three types of bigrams (level+contour, contour+level, and contour+contour) follow in the three immediately following rows. Clear evidence for the validity of the endpoint principle is seen in the fact that – with a few exceptions that I return to below – there is no obvious overall difference between bigrams involving only the High and Mid level tones (the shaded top rows of each section of Table 4) and those involving contour tones. The percentages of bigrams in the boldface columns of the table – where the musical sequence matches the tonal sequence – appear roughly comparable.

Table 4   Comparison of bigrams composed only of level tone (shaded rows) with bigrams including at least one contour tone

Tonal pitch direction	Musical pitch direction			
a. Falling tonal sequences (High-Mid)	Falling	Rising	Unchanging	Total
T1 (High level) + T3 (Mid level)	**76 (84%)**	11	3	90
T1 (High level) + T5 (Rising to Mid)	**41 (77%)**	9	3	53
T2 (Rising to High) + T3 (Mid level)	**31 (91%)**	1	2	34
T2 (Rising to High) + T5 (Rising to Mid)	**29 (81%)**	3	4	36
b. Rising tonal sequences (Mid-High)	Falling	Rising	Unchanging	Total
T3 (Mid level) + T1 (High level)	7	**54 (76%)**	10	71
T5 (Rising to Mid) + T1 (High level)	11	**43 (70%)**	7	61
T3 (Mid level) + T2 (Rising to High)	7	**22 (71%)**	2	31
T5 (Rising to Mid) + T2 (Rising to High)	2	**24 (92%)**	0	26
c. Unchanging tonal sequences (Mid)	Falling	Rising	Unchanging	Total
T3 (Mid level) + T3 (Mid level)	4	6	**46 (82%)**	56
T5 (Rising to Mid) + T3 (Mid level)	3	12	**19 (56%)**	34
T3 (Mid level) + T5 (Rising to Mid)	6	9	**27 (64%)**	42
T5 (Rising to Mid) + T5 (Rising to Mid)	3	1	**14 (78%)**	18

More generally, Table 4 displays the overwhelming evidence – already seen in Table 3 – that Cantopop prefers "similar" settings, not merely avoiding tone-melody mismatches, but actively seeking matches. The pattern is seen clearly in the difference between the columns in boldface and those in normal font: falling tonal sequences tend to be set to falling musical sequences, rising tonal sequences to rising musical sequences, and unchanging tonal sequences to unchanging musical sequences. There appear to be minor differences depending on the pitch direction, but the overall preference for matching is not in doubt.

At the same time, though, in sections (b) and (c) of Table 4 we find a few cells (highlighted by heavy black borders) that may involve special cases. Perhaps the most notable of these involves the rising sequence T5+T2. This sequence is matched by a musical rise in more than 90% of cases, compared to only 70%–75% for the other Mid+High tonal sequences. Why might this be special? Phonetically, T5+T2 is the only one of the four Mid+High sequences in which the *tonal* pitch rise is continuous across the two syllables: perhaps this phonetic property makes the rising musical setting especially appropriate. Similar factors may explain the less consistent patterns seen with the unchanging tonal sequences in the third section of the table: sequences of completely identical tones (level tones T3+T3 or contour tones T5+T5) are matched by unchanging musical sequences about 80% of the time, but the two types of mixed sequences in the table are much more variable and are musically matched in only about 60% of bigrams. It therefore seems important to emphasize that the broad validity of the matching principles does not preclude the existence of special cases. As McPherson and Ryan put it, "a single aggregate rate of tone-tune association calculated across a whole corpus...obscures a great deal of complexity". In the same vein, Ho (2010: 55) suggests sardonically that finding 80% of "similar" bigrams in matrix-style diagrams like those in Table 3 above "is significant enough to satisfy most linguists' curiosity" and states clearly that it is a mistake to assume that the remaining 20% are simply irregular.

Finally, despite the existence of the endpoint principle, there is reason to suspect that contour tones may be inherently difficult to accommodate to a musical melody in an aesthetically satisfying way. We have just seen that the tonal sequence T5+T2 is set to a rising musical melody in over 90% of cases, unlike all other instances of Mid+High sequences where proportions are closer to 70%. A different kind of evidence suggests another reason to think that contour tones may pose a more general problem for songwriters: it appears that words with the high rising tone T2 (阴上 , 35) may be actively avoided.

Table 5   Token frequency of the tones in the Kirby/Lin corpus compared to baseline Cantonese
data from Leung et al. (2004)

Tone	Token frequency (Leung et al.)		Token frequency (Lin/Kirby)	
	Number	Percent	Number	Percent
T1 阴平	30,145	21.36%	401	23.31%
T2 阴上	23,346	16.54%	178	10.35%
T3 阴去	27,002	19.13%	319	18.55%
T4 阳平	15,898	11.26%	231	13.43%
T5 阳上	15,098	10.70%	215	12.50%
T6 阳去	29,660	21.01%	376	21.86%
Total	141,149	100.00%	1,720	100.00%

This can be seen by examining the relative frequency of the individual tones in the corpus as a whole. Previous quantitative work by Leung et al. (2004), which reported both type frequency and token frequency of the six tones in a large (>141,000 syllables) corpus of Cantonese text, gives us a baseline for estimating their expected relative frequency in the Kirby/Lin corpus. This is shown in Table 5. It can be seen from the two shaded cells that the proportion of syllables with T2 (阴上 , 35) in the Kirby/Lin corpus is less than two-thirds of what would be expected on the basis of the Leung et al. frequency data, while the proportions of all the other tones are roughly the same or greater. This suggests that it is somehow awkward or unsatisfying to set the high-rising contour of T2 to a single note in a musical melody[1]. Such a situation is entirely comparable to the constraints on lexical choice posed by rhyme and meter: for example,

---

[1]   This speculation is consistent with the findings of Schellenberg & Gick (2020), who show that Cantonese amateur singers generally show "microtonal" variation in singing syllables with a rising tone on a single musical note.

the English word *vacuum* cannot be used at the end of a line of rhyming verse because no other word rhymes with it, and words like *automobile* or *seventy-six* are difficult to accommodate in the iambic meter of much traditional English poetry. Although the Kirby/Lin corpus is too small for serious statistical evaluation, Table 5 shows how quantitative studies may at least allow systematic observations on topics that seem at first glance to be purely a matter of aesthetic judgement. A qualitative study exploring the judgements of Cantopop songwriters might confirm or disprove the speculation that they actively avoid using words with Tone 2.

4. Prospect

The discussion in this paper has illustrated in some detail how the simple quantitative approach to data reduction developed in recent work succeeds in capturing important aspects of the principles of tone-melody matching. Whether or not these principles are then expressed explicitly in terms of an Optimality Theory grammar or in some other way, it seems clear that text-setting practice in tone languages is based in some way on the interaction of violable constraints. However, my goal in this paper has been to draw attention to two problems that may require refinements to our way of thinking about the problem. The actual way oblique settings are used in Cantopop seems to make clear that it is inaccurate to think of "oblique" as simply a neutral way of avoiding a more serious constraint violation. Similarly, the treatment of contour tones in text-setting seems to show that a simple principle such as the endpoint principle will cover a large proportion of the data but that the residue of exceptions and problems should encourage us to take a closer look for special cases and sub-regularities, and perhaps even to accept that some tones and tone sequences are simply awkward to set to music and may be avoided for that reason.

I am not suggesting, of course, that contour tones and oblique settings are the only problems in current work; there are other foundational issues that this paper could have discussed in the same way. In particular, it seems likely that the **interval** between the two notes in a musical bigram is important in evaluating its effect on the match between tone and melody. The role of interval is discussed by Carter-Ényì (2016) in his analysis of tone-melody matching in Yoruba music, and McPherson and Ryan's Optimality Theory analysis incorporates different constraints based on the size of the interval between the two notes of a bigram. Specifically, they suggest that a large musical rise or fall makes a tone-melody mismatch worse than a mismatch involving a small interval. By contrast, Ho (2010: 76-80) emphasizes the possibility that specific tonal sequences actually favour specific musical intervals, and shows that mismatches can be made worse both by intervals that are too large and by intervals that are too small: roughly speaking, the phonetic interval between the tone endpoints in a bigram must somehow be matched by the musical interval between the corresponding notes. It is not immediately obvious how such cases might be accommodated in a strict Optimality Theory analysis. In any case, interval needs to be more thoroughly taken into account in future work.

Nevertheless, the basic approach reviewed here seems to offer a wealth of tractable research questions for the future. Among other things, this represents a real opportunity for Chinese scholars. For example, the recent paper by Zhang & Cross (2021) on Chaozhou folksongs, mentioned earlier, reports clear findings within the general framework discussed here; one of the specific questions that they are able to address is the role of complex tone sandhi (变调) in tone-melody matching. As a Southern Fujian variety (闽南语), Chaozhou syllables exhibit large differences between citation forms and words spoken in phrasal context. Zhang and Cross show clearly that the tonal sequence in a bigram needs to be defined in terms of the surface sandhi tones, not the underlying citation tones. Although this finding is intuitively not surprising, Zhang and Cross's work gives us clear empirical validation of the intuition, based on a clear theoretical and methodological approach. The rich variety of tonal systems and of musical traditions in Chinese thus provides a natural laboratory for comparing different systems and a unique opportunity to deepen our understanding of tone-melody matching.

Acknowledgments

I thank James Kirby for providing me with access to the data on which Lin (2018) is based. A preliminary version of this paper was presented at a one-day workshop on music and language at the University of Massachusetts, Amherst, in May 2019. Thanks to James Kirby and Gao Jiayin (高佳音) for much useful discussion.

References

Bauer R S, Cheung K H, Cheung P M. 2003. Variation and merger of the rising tones in Hong Kong Cantonese. *Language Variation and Change*, 15: 211-225.

Carter-Ényi A. 2016. *Contour Levels: An Abstraction of Pitch Space Based on African Tone Systems*. Ph.D. dissertation, The Ohio State University.

Chan M K M. 1987a. Tone and melody in Cantonese. *Proceedings of the Thirteenth Annual Meeting of the Berkeley Linguistics Society*: 26-37.

Chan M K M. 1987b. Tone and melody interaction in Cantonese and Mandarin songs. *University of California Working Papers in Phonetics*, 68: 132-169.

Chao Y R (赵元任). 1930. A system of "tone letters". *Le Maître Phonétique*, 30: 24-27.

Ho W S V (何咏诗). 2010. *A Phonological Study of the Tone-melody Correspondence in Cantonese Pop Music*. Ph.D. dissertation, University of Hong Kong.

Karlsson A. 2018. Coordination between lexical tones and melody in traditional Kammu singing. *Journal of the Phonetic Society of Japan*, 22.3: 30-41.

Ketkaew C, Pittayaporn P. 2014. Mapping between lexical tones and musical notes in Thai pop songs. *Proceedings of the 28th Pacific Asia Conference on Language, Information and Computation* (PACLIC 28): 160-169.

Ketkaew C, Pittayaporn P. 2015. Do note values affect parallelism between lexical tones and musical notes in Thai pop songs?. *Proceedings of the 18th International Congress of Phonetic Sciences*.

Kirby J, Ladd D R. 2016. Tone-melody correspondence in Vietnamese popular song. *Proceedings of the 5th International Symposium on Tonal Aspects of Languages* (TAL-2016): 48-51.

Ladd D R, Kirby J. 2020. Tone-melody matching in tone language singing. In: Gussenhoven C, Chen A J. *The Oxford Handbook of Language Prosody*. Oxford: Oxford University Press, 676-687.

Leung M-T, Law S-P, Fung S-Y. 2004. Type and token frequencies of phonological units in Hong Kong Cantonese. *Behavior Research Methods, Instruments, & Computers*, 36.3: 500-505.

Lin R Q. 2018. *A Comparison of Tonal Text-setting in Mandarin and Cantonese Popular Songs*. MSc dissertation, Edinburgh: University of Edinburgh.

Lissoir M P. 2016. *Le khap Tai Dam, Catégorisation et Modèles Musicaux*. Ph.D. dissertation, Université Libre de Bruxelles and Université Sorbonne Nouvelle.

Lo A T C. 2013. *Correspondences Between Lexical Tone and Music Transitions in Cantonese Pop Songs: A*

Quantitative and Analytic Approach. MA dissertation, University of Edinburgh.

Matthews S, Yip V. 2011. *Cantonese: A Comprehensive Grammar* (2nd ed.). London & New York: Routledge.

McPherson L E, Ryan K M. 2018. Tone-tune association in Tommo So (Dogon) folk songs. *Language*, 94.1: 119-156.

Proto T. 2016. Methods of analysis for tonal text-setting. The case study of Fe' Fe' Bamileke. *Tonal Aspects of Language (TAL) 2016*, 162-166.

Schellenberg M. 2009. Singing in a tone language: Shona. In: Akinloye O, Lioba M. *Selected Proceedings of the 39th Annual Conference on African Linguistics*, 137-144.

Schellenberg M. 2012. Does language determine music in tone languages?. *Ethnomusicology*, 56.2: 266-278.

Schellenberg M. 2013. *The Realization of Tone in Singing in Cantonese and Mandarin*. Ph.D. dissertation, University of British Columbia.

Schellenberg M, Gick B. 2020. Microtonal variation in sung Cantonese. *Phonetica*, 77.2: 83-106.

Wong P C M (黄俊文), Diehl R L. 2002. How can the lyrics of a song in a tone language be understood?. *Psychology of Music*, 30: 202-209.

Zhang X (张曦), Cross I. 2021. Analysing the relationship between tone and melody in Chaozhou songs. *Journal of New Music Research*, 50.4: 299-311.

声调与旋律匹配理论中的两个问题

D. 罗伯特·拉德

爱丁堡大学

摘　要　近期关于词汇声调与音乐旋律如何匹配的研究表明，通常情况下音符之间的音高方向要与其对应声调的音高方向相同才是合适的匹配。这一原则同时适用于亚洲和非洲的本身并无谱系关系的声调语言。该原则和其他原则之间的相互作用通常是基于一些可排序的制约条件组成的序列，并且至少有一项研究已经明确采用了优选论的操作框架。然而，对一些实证和理论问题的理解还有待完善。本文基于近期关于现代粤语流行音乐的研究，旨在讨论如下两个问题：其一，讨论所谓的"倾斜"(oblique) 匹配问题，即音调音高在音乐旋律上升或下降时保持不变，或者不同旋律音高在不同的声调上保持同一音高水平。这通常被看作是相近匹配，研究表明这种匹配在经验层面上是不正确的，但目前并不能清楚地说明该匹配违背了哪些限制条件。其二，本文还讨论轮廓声调如何决定一个合适的匹配——轮廓声调在不同语言中的处理方式不同，且有研究表明，轮廓声调本质上很难和音乐旋律完美匹配。

关键词　粤语流行音乐　文本配置　声调　轮廓声调

D. Robert Ladd

University of Edinburgh

D.R.Ladd@ed.ac.uk

Chinese Prosodic Transcription (CHIPROT) and the Prediction of Prosodic Structure

Hana Třísková (廖敏)

Abstract: This paper introduces a new prosodic transcription called CHIPROT (based on *Hanyu Pinyin*), primarily designed for L2 teaching purposes. It is a tool for transcribing Chinese utterances and dialogues of colloquial style delivered at a natural tempo.[①] CHIPROT may also be used to indicate the prominence patterns of short phrases (2–3 syllables) called "minimodules", or "phonetic chunks", which draw on the notion of formulaic language. The features labelled by CHIPROT are (1) the degree of prominence of particular syllables (*ma*, *mā*, ***mā***, ***MĀ***), and (2) phrasing (prosodic phrases and prosodic words). CHIPROT was initially inspired by the system of Professor O. Švarný (1920–2011). However, it is based on a different phonological analysis of Chinese stress, whose crucial notions are *a normal syllable* and *a weakened syllable*. The current paper argues that some features of prosodic structure (particularly

---

① In this article, I use the term Chinese for Standard Chinese of *putonghua* type, or Mandarin.

syllable weakening) can be predicted, and that these predictions can be built into the transcription procedure. CHIPROT is graphically simple and highly intuitive. It has been tested in pedagogic practice. Final version, presented in this article, has already been systematically applied in a recently published textbook (Třísková, 2021). CHIPROT can be used by teachers and compilers of pedagogic materials and may also be useful for linguists engaged in research on connected speech.

Keywords: Mandarin; Standard Chinese; phonetics and phonology; prosody; prosodic transcription; teaching Chinese as a second language

1. Rationale

When considering the sound structure of this or that language, all literate laymen probably know about the existence of vowels and consonants. However, they may have a rather vague idea about features that stretch *over* vowels and consonants. Usually, they are not acquainted with the term "prosody", let alone the term "suprasegmental features". Learning that prosody comprises properties such as stress, pauses, intonation, rhythm, tempo or loudness, they still tend to think that prosodic features are less important than vowels and consonants, which make up the words and are reflected in the script. Unfortunately, the same mostly holds for L2 teachers. Chinese language teachers are no exception: their main suprasegmental concerns are the four lexical tones, tone sandhi, the neutral tone (轻声), and disyllabic tone combinations.[①] Explanations of the features of connected speech are limited. The same holds for textbooks.

---

① Important topics proposed for teaching Chinese pronunciation are suggested in Třísková (2017a) in English, and Třísková (2017b) in Chinese.

Although audio files are included as an integral part of most current textbooks, clarification of various prosodic phenomena students may hear there (e.g. undershooting of tonal targets) is mostly missing. In addition, except in early lessons (the number depends on the particular textbook), sentences are usually presented in Chinese characters, while *Hanyu Pinyin* is placed elsewhere. In classroom teaching, teachers are usually satisfied if students read the sentences character by character, with full tones ("scripted speech"). Their main pedagogic goal is proper character recognition, good initials, finals, and tones. Thus, the phonetic form of the resulting utterance sounds as a sequence of isolated words mechanically aligned side by side like beads on a string, deprived of the utterance-level prosody.

However, utterances in natural L1 speech are more than strings of fully pronounced words. It is not advisable to neglect prosody in L2 (Chinese) teaching, as prosodic features have vital functions in oral communication. One result of neglecting prosodic features may be that students speak like robots. Their speech often has no rhythm, wrongly placed breaks, no changes of syllable prominence, erroneous intonation patterns, no reflection of information structure, etc. To help students speak more naturally from the early stages of learning, we can:

1. Give them **basic instruction on the prosodic features** of spoken Chinese.

2. Provide the characters hand in hand with *Hanyu Pinyin* **notation of sentences** wherever needed and for as long as needed.

3. Furnish *Hanyu Pinyin* with certain graphic marks rendering major prosodic features: stress, and grouping (phrasing). This may be called **prosodic transcription**.

In this paper, I will introduce my proposal for prosodic transcription, called **CHIPROT** (Chinese Prosodic Transcription), which was primarily designed for language teaching purposes. Its tentative versions were presented in Hong Kong in June 2018 (my talk at the Chinese University of Hong Kong) and in Beijing in May 2019 [my talks at the Institute of Linguistics of the Chinese Academy of Social Sciences, at Beijing Language and Culture University (hereafter referred to as "BLCU"), and at Capital Normal University]. The final version of CHIPROT was introduced at two online conferences in 2021 (ICPG-7 invited speech, and CASLAR-6 workshop).[①]

2. Initial Remarks About CHIPROT

2.1 Sources of Inspiration

Previous systems of prosodic annotation developed for the Chinese language include Mandarin ToBI and Chinese ToBI (C-ToBI). The ToBI (Tones and Break Indices) system was originally developed by Janet Pierrehumbert and Mary Beckman in the early 1990s to transcribe intonation, accent, and prosodic boundaries in American English. It was conceived within the Autosegmental-Metrical Phonology framework (Silverman et al., 1992; Beckman & Ayers, 1994). Later on, ToBI systems were designed for other languages. Research on the Chinese ToBI systems was carried out at the Ohio State University (Mary Beckman, Marjorie Chan). **Mandarin ToBI** was proposed in 1999 (Peng et al., 2005: 230, 250). Yet another system, **C-ToBI** (Chinese ToBI), was developed in the Institute of Linguistics of the Chinese Academy of Social Sciences. The first version appeared in 1996, the third in 2002; see Li (2002) and Li & Zu et al. (2007).

However, to the best of my knowledge, no attempt has yet been made to develop a comprehensive system for practical Chinese language teaching. The only exception seems to be the prosodic transcription of **Professor Oldřich Švarný** (史瓦尔尼 , 1920–2011), Czech linguist, phonetician, and my teacher. Švarný developed a rather sophisticated non-electronic transcription system over the course of several decades. He introduced his concept in two articles (Švarný, 1991a, b; Švarný's articles published in English and German can be found in the volume Uher & Slaměníková, 2019). Švarný's transcription system is based on *Hanyu Pinyin*. It annotates two major prosodic features: degree of stress for particular syllables (six degrees altogether), and phrasing (prosodic phrases and prosodic words). Švarný's prosodic analysis and his transcription system

---

① ICPG-7 is the 7th International Conference on Prosodic Grammar, organized by Faculty of Linguistic Sciences, BLCU, April 17–18, 2021; CASLAR-6 is the 6th International Conference on Chinese as a Second Language Research, organised by the George Washington University, Washington D.C., USA, July 30–August 1, 2021.

were applied in two large non-electronic corpora (subsequently digitized). Both corpora were recorded by a native Beijing speaker and prosodically annotated later on. They represent a rather unique source of material to date.

The larger corpus is related to a voluminous dictionary of Chinese morphemes, titled *A Learning Dictionary of Modern Chinese* (in Czech; Švarný, 1998–2000). Next to grammatical analysis of individual morphemes, it comprises about 16,000 example sentences illustrating the usage of particular morphemes in context. The sentences were recorded over the course of several months in 1969 (Švarný employed a single speaker: Beijing-born Mrs. Tang Yunling Rusková 唐云凌). The recordings were prosodically annotated by Švarný over the following six years (the work was finished in 1976).

(74)

1. jiǎ: nǐ-yǒu-qián ׀jiè-gei-wo-ma? yǐ: ׀yǒu „ nǐ-yào ׀duōshao?

2. nǐ-׀yàoshi yǒu-nǐ-׀gēge name-cōngming jiu-hǎo-le.

3. zhèi-zhang-zhuōz yǒu-׀èr-chǐ kuǎn. (zhè-zhang-zhuōz ׀èr-chǐ kuǎn.)

4. jiǎ: zhèr-you / dǎzì׀jǐ-ma? (v,׀dǎzìjǐ-ma?) yǐ: ׀yǒu „ zai-shūzhuōr-׀dǐxia-ne.

4a. jiǎ: ׀wánli you-shénme ? yǐ: ׀méi-shenme. jiù-shi yǒu-yi-diǎnr ׀tǔr.

5. yǒu-ren-shuō nǐ-׀bìng-le „ nǐ-zěnme zai-׀zhèr-ne?

6. /yǒu-d-rén, (you-xiē-rén,) ׀bù-xǐhuan chǐ-yú.

7. ׀zhǐ, you-yǐ-miànr-׀guāng „ yǐ-miànr-׀máo.

Figure 1   Sample of Švarný's transcription: seven example sentences illustrating the use of the
verb *yǒu* 有 (*A Learning Dictionary of Modern Chinese*, 1998–2000: 71). Note that this
version of Švarný's transcription is slightly different from the version shown in Figure 2.

A smaller and newer corpus forms part of a university textbook, *Grammar of Spoken Chinese in Examples* (in Czech; Švarný et al., 1991–1993). The textbook comprises 260 paragraphs treating particular phenomena of Chinese grammar. These phenomena are illustrated by several thousand example sentences. The sentences were recorded in 1990–1991 (by Mrs. Tang Yunling Rusková again) and subsequently prosodically annotated.

§2,4 1.pokrač. <u>Sloveso /yǒu/ ve významu mít</u>　　　　YD 3

1.laǒshî̊ you kěběnr, xuésheng yě̱ you kěbenr.　2.xuésheng yǒu̱ běnz,
lǎoshī yě̱ you benz.　3.wǒmeṉ shî xuésheng, wǒmeṉ yǒu kěběnr.　4.wǒ̱
-you yǔyî̱, ta yě̱ you yǔyī.　5. lǎoshī you̱ zîxîngchē, xuésheng yě̱ you
zîxîngchē.　6.gōngreṉ you qîchē. nóngmin yě̱ you qîchē.　7. ⌈wǒmeṉ you
máobî̱, (nebo: wǒmen you̱ máobî̱,) nîmeṉ you gāngbî̱, tāmeṉ you qiānbî̱.
8. ⌈xuésheng̱ you máobî̱, (nebo: xuésheng you̱ máobî̱,) yě̱ you qiānbî̱.
(ex.č.7, přízvukování slov /máobî̱/, /gāngbî̱/ mimo kontrastní srovnání:
/zhe⁼shi máobî̱./ a stejně tak:/zhe⁼shi gāngbî̱./)

Figure 2　Sample of Švarný's transcription: example sentences illustrating the use of the verb
yǒu 有 "to have" (*Grammar of Spoken Chinese in Examples,* Švarný et al., 1991–1993: 46)

Švarný's transcription system served as a major source of inspiration for CHIPROT.
My analysis of syllable prominence is conceived differently, though (see below). Also,
the graphic form of the two systems is different. Švarný was severely limited by his use
of a typewriter, while CHIPROT may take advantage of electronic fonts and graphics.
While developing CHIPROT, I used Švarný's second corpus (Švarný et al., 1991–1993).
I compared his transcripts of numerous sentences with my own transcripts. As noted
above, the corpus was recorded by a single native speaker. Mrs. Tang Yunling, being a
rather lively and spontaneous person, recorded the sentences in quite an easy, natural
manner far from slow classroom speech. However, she had lived in Prague, outside of
her native country, for a large part of her life. This fact certainly had a bearing on her
pronunciation, which may have become fossilized in some respects over the years. Thus,
I also had to validate the wider applicability of CHIPROT using other speech materials. I
have transcribed a number of dialogues from several textbooks: *HSK Standard Course 1*
(Jiang, 2014), *Integrated Chinese* (Liu et al., 2017), and the Czech *Textbook of Chinese
Conversation* (Uher et al. 2007, 2016). I selected the samples carefully, choosing
natural tempo audio recordings and avoiding slow classroom speech. The results
indicate that CHIPROT can be used to transcribe current colloquial Mandarin without
any problems.

2.2   CHIPROT Design and Purpose

CHIPROT marks two prosodic features: **degree of prominence of particular syllables**, and **prosodic phrasing**. Intonation is not annotated, since it would overburden the transcription. My concept works with only two basic intonation patterns: falling and non-falling (Třísková, 2021). These are generally predictable from grammar (falling pattern for finished statements, question-word questions, alternative questions, and A-not-A questions; non-falling pattern for non-final prosodic phrases, particle *ma* 吗 questions, and grammatically unmarked questions. A double question mark can be possibly used in the last two cases, e.g. Nǐ-qù-ma?? 你去吗? Nǐ-qù?? 你去? Tone sandhi is reflected in CHIPROT, e.g. *Ní-**hǎo*** (你好).

Example of CHIPROT:

这辆汽车是我们的第一辆汽车。 "This car is our first car."

plain *Hanyu Pinyin*:   *Zhè liàng qìchē shì wǒmende dì yī liàng qìchē.*

CHIPROT transcription: ***Zhè**-liàng **qìchē** // shì-wǒmende dì-**YÍ**-liàng qìchē.*

CHIPROT prosodic transcription was designed to be as iconic, user-friendly, and intuitive as possible, thus requiring no complicated instructions for readers. However, in order to decipher the graphics and read the utterances adequately, readers require preliminary basic tuition on prosodic features.[1] This comprises, for example, explaining:

• The means of manifestation of **syllable prominence** (such as expanding/ compressing pitch range, lengthening/shortening syllable duration, and segmental reductions in unstressed syllables) and their interplay with the four tones.

• The means of manifestation of **prosodic boundaries**, besides silent pause (especially the final lengthening at the end of prosodic phrases and finished utterances).

• Basic **intonation patterns** (falling and non-falling) and their interplay with the four tones.

After receiving such instruction, students may be able to read transcribed utterances with relative ease as they listen to the audio (or even without the audio later

---

① Of course, solid knowledge of the basics, such as proper pronunciation of disyllabic tone combinations, or proper pronunciation of T0, is tacitly expected.

on). Transcribed utterances, in combination with audio recordings, can serve as a good basis for practice and for subsequent work on removing errors with the help of a teacher. Thus, natural speech production can be learned. More advanced students can use the same resources to practice speech perception (听力): they may listen to the audio recordings and attempt to transcribe the utterances themselves, using CHIPROT. Such practice may help them become aware of various prosodic features of connected speech they had not previously noticed.

My major ambition is to offer CHIPROT to **teachers and compilers of pedagogic materials**. They can use it to transcribe common colloquial sentences/dialogues according to the audio recordings. Of course, mastering the transcription procedure inevitably comprises getting acquainted with the prosodic features of connected Chinese, and with the essential principles of CHIPROT. Attaining a certain degree of practical experience with transcription is yet another necessary condition for a satisfactory outcome.

2.3　CHIPROT Utilization to Date

The CHIPROT system has been tested in teaching practice for several years. Since 2017, I have been using it in my courses on Chinese prosody (Charles University in Prague) for second-semester students. Introducing the system at this level seems to be most appropriate: students already know the basics (the initials, the finals, the tones, basic vocabulary and grammar, simple sentences and phrases). At the same time, they have not developed fossilized errors. After finishing the course I always distribute a questionnaire asking students to verbalize their impressions. Students' feedback on the course in general and CHIPROT in particular has been very positive[①].

Further, CHIPROT has already been systematically applied in structured teaching material. I used it to transcribe about 80 example sentences and short dialogues in the textbook *Speak Chinese with Ease: Prosody of Colloquial Chinese* (Třísková, 2021,

---

① The feedback from the year 2023: "CHIPROT is intuitive. It makes sense and gives me an insight into the principles." (P.M.) "For me CHIPROT is an unbeatable transcription. It is easy, logical and intelligible." (P.T.) "I am fully satisfied with CHIPROT. It is better than Pinyin." (L.J.) "CHIPROT is great, it definitely eases reading." (A.M.K.)

in print in Czech; the English translation is in progress; the forthcoming textbook was introduced at the CASLAR-6 conference in 2021). These sentences and dialogues with audio recordings, illustrating various prosodic phenomena, were selected from the above-mentioned textbook *Grammar of Spoken Chinese in Examples* (Švarný et al., 1991–1993). Švarný's prosodically annotated corpus is a rich resource offering examples of prosodic phenomena in many different contexts. However, it is structured according to *grammatical* topics. Thus, the examples of particular *prosodic* phenomena had to be laboriously retrieved in the corpus.

In what follows I will describe the CHIPROT annotation conventions used to mark syllable prominence and prosodic units.

3. Syllable Prominence

CHIPROT assumes four degrees of syllable prominence. The theoretical basis of my prominence concept can be found in Třísková (2020). The crucial notions are *a normal syllable*, and *a weakened syllable*. That is, I view the **weakening of normal syllables** as a major issue in examining Chinese stress. Note that except for the highest degree (emphasis/contrastive stress), I do without the term "stress" in my prominence scale. However, for convenience, I use the common term "stressed syllable" when speaking of a phonetically salient (relatively prominent) syllable. Similarly, I use the term "unstressed syllable" for non-prominent, phonetically weak syllables. After all, stress is a relative matter. As Feng Shengli points out in his ICPG-7 paper:

> Stress is not a sound, it is a relationship (重音不是 "音"，重音是关系)… Stress ("重") only exists in relation to non-stress ("轻")…If we are looking for stress, we should not look for a stressed item, but for a relative prominence (如果找重音，不是看哪儿重，而是看哪儿有 "相对凸显" 的关系). As for whether this relationship is reached by enhancing [a particular syllable], or by other means, it is secondary (至于该关系是用 "加重" 或其他手段来表现，则是第二位的) (Feng, 2021: 7).

Feng is speaking of "other means" of expressing relative prominence. We may infer that **syllable weakening** may be the most important of these other means. For instance, an iambic pattern may be attained *either* by keeping the first syllable fully pronounced and enhancing the second syllable, *or* by weakening the first syllable and keeping the second syllable fully pronounced (without enhancing its prominence). We may add that the second solution is "cheaper" in terms of articulatory effort and thus may be preferred by speakers. Feng's approach to stress is perfectly in line with my own.

What is a meaningful number of stress degrees? **Švarný** assumed six categories, which might be too many. His categories were in a way abstract constructs arising from the combination of two features: 1. Degree of tone fullness; 2. Presence/absence of stress; see Třísková (2011).

C-ToBI and Mandarin ToBI suggest four degrees of stress. **Mandarin ToBI** accepts the following "stress levels" in the stress tier (Peng et al., 2005: 255):

S3: syllable with fully realized lexical tone

S2: syllable with substantial tone reduction, e.g. undershooting of tonal target with duration reduction

S1: syllable that has lost its lexical tonal specification, e.g. in a weakly-stressed position

S0: syllable with lexical neutral tone, i.e., inherently unstressed syllable

Like C-ToBI and Mandarin ToBI, **CHIPROT** also proposes four degrees of prominence. However, they are conceived differently (see section 3.1). The additional "top-prominence" syllable is more prominent than S3. On the other hand, S2 and S1 are collapsed into the "weakened syllable" degree. The reasons for collapsing weak-tone syllables and neutralized syllables are explained in section 3.5.

3.1 Degrees of Syllable Prominence and Their Graphic Form

CHIPROT is based on *Hanyu Pinyin*. For expressing syllable prominence it gets along with mere two graphic distinctions: bold vs. non-bold letters, and lower-case vs. upper-case letters. As regards the fonts, note that the current form of CHIPROT uses italics. Giving *Hanyu Pinyin* in italics is a common practice in texts printed in languages, which use the Latin alphabet. This practice helps readers identify *Hanyu Pinyin* words at first sight and distinguish them from the surrounding text. However, Chinese textbooks and pedagogic materials do not follow this custom. They are accustomed to using some sort of sans-serif typeface.

The four degrees of syllable prominence are marked as follows:[①]

MĀ **top-prominence syllable** (the most prominent syllable of a prosodic phrase/ utterance; see section 3.6)

tentative Chinese term: 强音节

mā **normal syllable** (ordinary syllable with full tone; see section 3.3)

tentative Chinese term: 常音节

mā **weakened syllable** (the tone is either weakened, or even completely neutralized; see section 3.5)

tentative Chinese term: 弱音节

ma **toneless syllable** (morpheme without a lexical tone; see section 3.4)

tentative Chinese term: 无调音节 / 无调语素

3.2   Marking Syllable Prominence: Main Principles

• A minority of Chinese morphemes are **toneless**, i.e., they do not have a lexical tone (*de* 的, *le* 了, *ba* 吧, etc.). I call them 无调语素. They are "unstressed" by default, as they have no lexical tone which would give them the potential to become "stressed".

• An absolute majority of Chinese morphemes are **tonal**, i.e., they have a lexical tone. I call them 有调语素. Lexical tone gives them the potential to become prominent, "stressed". This potential may or may not be exploited in connected speech. Tonal morphemes may either realize as **normal** syllables, as **weakened** syllables, or as **enhanced** syllables.

• **Chinese tonal morphemes** generally strive to be realized with full, perceptible tones in connected speech, because tones distinguish lexical meanings of morphemes.

• Quite a few tonal morphemes/syllables may become **weakened** in connected speech (弱音节). Their tone is either **weak** yet still perceivable (弱调音节) or completely

---

① Most of the Chinese terms appearing below emerged from extensive discussions with Professor Cao Wen at BLCU in October 2011.

neutralized (失调音节). Syllable weakening does not happen without a reason.

• Syllables which do not have any perceivable tone are called **atonic syllables** (不带调音节). Their pitch is dependent on the tone of the preceding tonal syllable (see, e.g. Lee & Zee, 2014: 375). Atonic syllables comprise neutralized syllables (which have lost their tone in connected speech), and toneless morphemes/syllables (which never had a lexical tone). In Švarný's corpus around 30% of syllables were atonic. About half of them were toneless syllables and the other half were neutralized syllables (Švarný, 1991a: 210).

• In connected speech some tonal morphemes/syllables may be **prosodically enhanced**, becoming rather prominent (强音节). Usually, there is only one such syllable in the utterance/prosodic phrase. The word which carries it is called **a nucleus** in the present study. Quite often these cases can be predicted – from grammar, information structure, pragmatics, etc.

Predictions of the prominence degree of particular syllables can be **built in the transcription procedure** as the first step, making the process faster and more theoretically justified. Thus, a draft of a transcript can be prepared even before listening to the audio. This draft may serve as a basis for further corrections of the transcript, based on careful listening and examination of the utterance by means of software for speech analysis such as PRAAT.

Below we take a closer look at particular degrees of prominence: normal syllables (section 3.3), toneless syllables (section 3.4), weakened syllables (section 3.5), and top-prominence syllables (section 3.6).

3.3 Normal Syllables (*mā*)

I call syllables realized with ordinary full tone **normal syllables** 常音节 . Cf. Chao Yuan Ren's "normal stress" 正常重音 (Chao, 1968: 35). See also Třísková (2020: 82-83). Normal syllables are not overly prominent ("stressed"). They just carry full distinguishable tone. In CHIPROT, normal syllables (常音节) are printed in bold, carrying a tone mark (*mā*). They may be viewed as a **default form of tonal morphemes**. As a starting point, we may assume that all tonal morphemes would be realized as fully pronounced normal syllables in connected speech (pedagogic practice often stops at this point). In turn, the first step of the transcription procedure is the representation of all tonal syllables in bold type, and of course with a tone mark. For instance, in this sentence the only syllable which must not be in bold is the toneless lexical suffix *zi* 子 :

Zhuōzi shàng yǒu sān běn shū. 桌子上有三本书。

"There are three books on the table."

Sometimes it is hard to find any difference in prominence in neighbouring tonal syllables, as may be the case for the word *huāpíngr* 花瓶儿 "vase" in the following utterance:

Bǎ-huāpíngr // fàng-zài ZHUŌzi-shàng. 把花瓶儿放在桌子上。

"Put the vase on the table."

Yet this does not pose a problem, because the adjacency of normal syllables is regarded as acceptable/common/natural. It is not viewed as some sort of stress clash. Thus, CHIPROT liberates the transcriber from the enforced pursuit of stressed syllables in cases where phonetic material does not offer clear support for such an evaluation.

3.4   Toneless Syllables (*ma*)

Chinese has a number of **toneless morphemes** which do not have a lexical tone (无调语素). This group is fully predictable from the lexicon – the syllable carries no tone mark in dictionaries. In CHIPROT, toneless syllables are printed in non-bold type, carrying no tone mark (*ma*). Toneless morphemes are "unstressed" by default – their weak realization is basically predictable. Sometimes they may be **prolonged in final position**, i.e., at the end of a prosodic phrase or utterance (the well-known phenomenon of phrase-final lengthening is more or less universal in languages). Their loudness may also be non-negligible. They may even display pitch movement. Thus, such syllables may sometimes sound rather conspicuous. However, the roots of *this* sort of conspicuousness do not lie in prominence ("stress") structure. Rather, such syllables serve as carriers of emotional or pragmatic meanings.

We shall distinguish two major groups of toneless items: monosyllabic toneless function words, and second syllables in some types of disyllabic words.

3.4.1　Monosyllabic Toneless Function Words (the Clitics)

structural particles: *de* 的, *de* 得, *de* 地

verb aspect particles: *le* 了, *zhe* 着, *guo* 过

sentence-final particles: *ma* 吗, *ne* 呢, *a* 啊, *le* 了

Particles are always "unstressed" (although they may become rather conspicuous at the end of an utterance). They are always tightly attached to the preceding word. I borrow the general term "clitics" for this group of Chinese function words.

3.4.2　The Second Syllable in T+T0 Disyllabic Words

While the majority of disyllabic Chinese words have both syllables tonal (e.g. *xuéxiào* 学校 "school"), there are also words whose second syllable is inherently toneless, thus carrying no tone mark in dictionaries, e.g. *fu* 腐 in the word *dòufu* 豆腐 "bean curd". The normative dictionary *Xiandai Hanyu Cidian* (abbreviated XHC) prints these words with a dot between the syllables and no lexical tone mark on the second syllable: dòu·fu.

This group of words is far from homogeneous. Below are the major cases:

- words with lexical suffixes, e.g. *zi* 子 as in *háizi* 孩子 "child", *tou* 头 as in *gútou* 骨头 "bone", *me* 么 as in *shénme* 什么 "what", *men* 们 as in *rénmen* 人们.

- names of relatives created by reduplication: *māma* 妈妈 "mom", *gēge* 哥哥 "elder brother"

- words with disyllabic morphemes (rare): *pútao* 葡萄 "grapes", *bóli* 玻璃 "glass"

- other nouns, verbs, and adjectives: *shìqing* 事情 "matter", *péngyou* 朋友 "friend", *míngbai* 明白 "to realize", *gàosu* 告诉 "to tell", *róngyi* 容易 "easy", *piàoliang* 漂亮 "beautiful"

In some cases, minimal pairs can be found (Li, 1981):

对头　*duìtou* "enemy" (XHC duì·tou)　*duìtóu* "correct" (XHC duìtóu)

东西　*dōngxi* "thing" (XHC dōng·xi)　*dōngxī* "east and west" (XHC dōngxī)

地道　*dìdao* "genuine" (XHC dì·dao)　*dìdào* "tunnel" (XHC dìdào)

Note that I do not place in the T+T0 group those cases which *cannot* be retrieved in the XHC dictionary with a toneless second syllable. If a disyllabic item is not present in XHC, I keep a tone mark on the second syllable. I view it as a weakened syllable.

Examples are:

- reduplicated of monosyllabic nouns: ***tiāntiān*** 天天 "every day"
- reduplicated of monosyllabic verbs: ***kànkàn*** 看看 "take a look" (see section 3.5.4)
- verbs with direction complements: ***zuòxià*** 坐下 "sit down" (see section 3.5.5)
- verbs with some resultative complements: ***kànjiàn*** 看见 "spot" (see section 3.5.6)
- verbs with complements expressing a short action: ***zuòyíhuìr*** 坐一会儿 "sit for a while"

3.5   Weakened Syllables (*mǎ*), Commonly Weakened Morphemes

Besides toneless words/morphemes/syllables, connected speech delivered at a natural tempo contains quite a few **underlyingly tonal syllables** which become weakened to a greater or lesser degree in particular contexts (弱音节). They are shorter and their tone becomes **less conspicuous** (as a result of a compressed pitch range and short duration), or sometimes even **completely neutralized**. The segments of weakened syllables may have their articulatory targets undershot, and some segments can even completely disappear in rapid casual speech. The overall number of weakened syllables in an utterance may vary according to speech style, communication situation, speech rate, the individual speaker, his/her dialectal background, etc. The largest occurrence of weakened syllables can be observed in fast colloquial speech used in everyday communication in Beijing-type Mandarin.

Note that in weakened syllables **I do mark the underlying lexical tone**, even if the syllable becomes completely neutralized – for instance, in ***kànkàn*** 看看, ***dǎkāi*** 打开, ***zhèlǐ*** 这里, ***huílái*** 回来, ***tīngbùdǒng*** 听不懂, ***qiǎokèlì*** 巧克力. There are several reasons for this:

1. The tone may reappear in other contexts (e.g. ***dǎkāi*** 打开 vs. ***dǎbùkāi*** 打不开).

2. There is no need for the transcriber to decide whether the tone is "still there" or "completely gone". In fact, this is not so important – it may be regarded only as a sort of phonetic detail in most cases. After all, there is no clear border between a weakened tone and a neutralized tone. As stated above, the degree of phonetic reduction is a continuum. On the other hand, what really matters is the presence or absence of the lexical tone –

this is a fundamental phonological feature reflected in dictionaries.

3. Students may appreciate the information about the underlying tone.[①]

In general, **phonetic weakening is a result of semantic weakening** (Liang, 2003). Both phonetic and semantic weakening form a continuum. Let us look at the **weakening continuum** now.

• At one extreme point of the weakening continuum there are morphemes that became purely formal in the course of time, losing their original meaning completely (e.g. the structural particle *de* 的, or the lexical suffix *zi* 子). Such extreme semantic weakening finally resulted in **permanent loss of tone**. Permanent loss of meaning/tone is thus a product of language change. The morpheme was gradually turned into a toneless morpheme, entering the lexicon as such.

• Next there are morphemes/words which have an underlying lexical tone, yet are **obligatorily** pronounced as atonic in specific grammatical contexts. An example is the negative *bù* 不 in potential forms of verbs – for example, ***tīngbùdǒng*** 听不懂 "be unable to understand". *Bù* 不 has a lexical tone; however, it must be pronounced as atonic in this context. Another case is the second syllable in reduplicated monosyllabic verbs. An example of this is ***kànkàn*** 看看 "take a look". The second item should be pronounced as atonic, although it still has an underlying T4.

• In some cases, we may observe "only" **a strong inclination** to weak pronunciation in particular contexts, yet weakening is not obligatory (see below, commonly weakened morphemes). If such morphemes/words are weak, they may or may not be completely atonic. Typical examples are monosyllabic personal pronouns, such as *tā* 他. The syntactic function of such pronouns also matters, increasing the multifariousness of the weakening continuum. If *tā* 他 functions as a *subject*, standing at the beginning of the utterance, it may often be weakened, yet it keeps at least the remnants of T1. Consider, for example, the sentence: *Tā bù rènshi wǒ.* 他不认识我。 "He does not know me." On the other hand, if *tā* 他 functions as an object, it will be prone to completely atonic pronunciation:

---

① I admit that the presence of tone mark on fully neutralized syllables may sometimes be confusing. Yet I decided that the above arguments for the use of tone mark on such syllables are sufficiently compelling.

Wǒ bù rènshi tā. 我不认识他。"I do not know him." There may be contexts where *tā* 他 restores its full tone or even becomes emphasized: *Bù shì wǒ, shì **tā**!* 不是我，是他! "It is not me, it is **him**!"

- At the other extreme of the weakening continuum there are content words. They weaken their meaning/tone(s) **only occasionally**. This happens, for instance, when the word is repeated and has no substantial semantic importance in the given context. Yet such a word tends to keep remnants of tone(s), resisting complete neutralization (though that may certainly happen in fast, sloppy speech). Content words are least prone to prosodic weakening, representing the least conspicuous and least frequent/stable/predictable cases.

In some Chinese monosyllabic words/morphemes with lexical tone, the inclination to become weakened in connected speech is higher than in other words/morphemes. They may be weakened rather **frequently** (in some cases even obligatorily), yet most of them may occasionally gain prominence and even become strikingly prominent. I will tentatively call these items **commonly weakened morphemes (CWMs)**.[①]

Speaking of "commonly weakened morphemes", the meaning of the word "commonly" needs to be explained. Importantly, the sources/motivations for this "common" weakening are not accidental or arbitrary. Weakening is mostly **rule-governed** (Třísková, 2020). Thus, many cases of weakening can be predicted – from grammar, phonology, lexicon, information structure, or pragmatics.

The members of the CWM group share one important feature: a general inclination to become weakened. This entitles us to establish them as a specific group worth investigating. Nevertheless, the CWM group is **rather heterogeneous**. The members of the group display different grammatical properties, including different degrees of freeness-boundness. Clearly, the same phonetic surface form (weak/neutralized tone) may have different sources, rooted in different linguistic levels. We may also observe a *different degree* of inclination to become weakened (this may even hold for members of

---

① Chinese morphemes (*yǔsù* 语素) can be either free, representing a monosyllabic word, or bound, being a part of a compound word. Similarly, CWM can either be an independent word (such as *tā* 他 "he"), or a bound morpheme (such as *xiān* in ***xīn**xiān* 新鲜 "fresh").

the same subgroup, such as the cliticoids; see section 3.5.1).

Phonetically, the CWM group (monosyllabic tonal function words in particular) is rather complicated, as the morpheme/word in question may comprise at least **two possible phonetic forms**: strong and weak (cf. English "words with weak forms", see Třísková, 2016: 131; 2017c). This has pedagogic consequences – namely, that students have to master both forms. These phonetic forms may sound quite different. A fully pronounced *tā* 他 with noticeable aspiration, an open vowel, long syllable duration, and a clear, high T1 ([tʰaː]¹) sounds quite dissimilar from a weakened *tā* 他 with slight or even no aspiration, a centralized vowel, short syllable duration, and a neutralized tone ([tə]).

The CWM group definitely deserves attention (Třísková, 2016; 2017c; 2020), as the low degree of prominence of its members is rather common. What is more, the prosodic behavior of these items displays a good deal of predictability. Thus, a deeper investigation of the CWM group inventory and the properties of individual members may help us understand some important principles of natural speech rhythm in colloquial Mandarin. Importantly, predictions can also be built into the CHIPROT transcription procedure. This is precisely the reason why I deal with the CWM group in detail in this article.

An overview of the main cases/subgroups of commonly weakened items follows below. There are **14 groups altogether**, addressed in sections 3.5.1 to 3.5.14. I proceed from the level of morphemes and words to the levels of phrase and finished utterance.

3.5.1 Monosyllabic Tonal Function Words (the Cliticoids)

Monosyllabic tonal function words tend to become weakened in connected speech. However, they may occasionally gain prominence if emphasized. For example, the adverb *dōu* 都 "all" may be weakened, if it only has a formal meaning, while in other contexts it may retain its full semantic content, being rather prominent. Compare:

Lián TĀ-dōu lái-le. 连他都来了。 *dōu* [ɖɔ] "Even **he** came." (construction *lián-dōu*)
Tāmen DŌU lái-le. 他们都来了。 *dōu* [ɖoʊ] "**All** of them came." (emphasized *dōu*)

I call this group of words **the cliticoids** 类附着词 (this term was coined in Třísková, 2016: 134; 2017c: 34; 2020: 94). They are:

- **three personal pronouns** *wǒ* 我 "I", *nǐ* 你 "you", *tā* 他 "he" / 她 "she"
- **classifiers, measure words:** *gè* 个, *běn* 本, *jiān* 件, *tiáo* 条; *xiē* 些 …
- **monosyllabic prepositions:** *zài* 在, *gěi* 给, *dào* 到, *bǎ* 把 …
- **monosyllabic postpositions:** *shàng* 上, *xià* 下, *lǐ* 里
- **the verbs** *shì* 是, *zài* 在, **existential** *yǒu* 有
- **monosyllabic conjunctions:** *gēn* 跟, *hé* 和 …
- **formal adverbs:** *jiù* 就, *hěn* 很, *dōu* 都, *yě* 也
- **monosyllabic modal verbs:** *huì* 会, *xiǎng* 想, *yào* 要 …
- **the verbs** *lái* 来, *qù* 去 **with another verb**

Note that not all monosyllabic tonal function words belong to the cliticoids (e.g. *zhè* 这 "this"). Further, there are some Chinese function words which are disyllabic (e.g. the personal pronoun *wǒmen* 我们 "we", the postposition *lǐmiàn* 里面 "inside", the conjunction *kěshi* 可是 "but"). These also do not belong to the cliticoids.

The last group – the verbs *lái* 来, *qù* 去 – has been newly added to the group of the cliticoids (Třísková, 2020: 95 only lists 8 groups). These verbs may be used with another verb (before or after it), meaning "to go to", "to be about to", "in order to". In this case, they regularly become weakened. They often do not need to be translated at all, being mainly formal. For instance:

***Wǒmen-liǎ** lái-**TǍO**lùn-tǎolùn-ba*. 我们俩来讨论讨论吧。
"Let us discuss it."

***Wǒ-yòng** hǎo-**HUÀ** qù-**quàn**-tā //, tā-yě-bù-**TĪNG**. 我用好话去劝他，他也不听。
"I used nice words to persuade him, but he still would not listen."

*Tā-dào-**pù**zi mǎi-**RÒU**-qù-le*. 他到铺子买肉去了。
"He went to the store to buy meat."

As mentioned above, the group of cliticoids is **not homogeneous**. The degree of semantic weakness, or "functionalness", is not identical in all cliticoids. Consequently, the degree of willingness to become weakened is not identical either. Take the classifier *gè* 个 for example. Its affiliation to the category of function words could hardly be questioned. It may be emphasized only rarely. On the other hand, modal verbs, the adverbs such as *dōu* 都, etc., may retain some degree of prominence more often. Their affiliation to the cliticoid group may perhaps raise some questions. For the present classification, the major criterion is consistent fading of the semantic content of the item (and subsequent phonetic weakening) in many/most contexts.

3.5.2　Two Neighboring Monosyllabic Tonal Function Words

Sometimes two cliticoids (monosyllabic tonal function words) occur together. This often happens at the beginning of a sentence. The examples are:

bǎ-tā	把他	"him"
gěi-tā	给他	"to him"
tā-zài	他在	"he at"
nǐ-jiù	你就	"you then"
jiù-shì	就是	"then is"
tā-hěn	他很	"he very"

Usually, both items form a disyllabic prosodic word. The first FW (function word) receives weak prominence, while the second FW is completely atonic. The result is an **inconspicuous trochee**, where the first item is just slightly prominent. I neglect this in transcription in order not to overburden the CHIPROT graphics, writing both items as non-bold (and of course with a tone mark). For instance, *bǎ-tā* 把他 in the following utterance:

*Bǎ-tā jiào-dào **Wǒ**-zhèr-lái*. 把他叫到我这儿来。

"Call him to me."

Only if the first item sounds clearly prominent, I put it in bold:

***Bǎ**-tā jiào-dào **Wǒ**-zhèr-lái*.

Note that in some prosodic words of this type the first FW has **no grammatical relationship** with the second FW, e.g. *tā-hěn* 他很 "he very". How can such a prosodic word be formed? The requirements of rhythm may sometimes override the grammar, causing a word to break away from its grammatical mate and **"desert"** to the preceding monosyllabic word, saving it from standing alone. Monosyllabic prosodic words are generally undesirable. Further, similar length prosodic words is more welcome than extremes, i.e., very short or very long prosodic words. Thus, 1+3 is conveniently turned into 2+2 in the following utterance:

Tā-hěn CŌNGming. 他很聪明。

"He is (very) clever."

3.5.3   Words Favoring the Trochee Pattern

The majority of the Chinese lexicon consists of disyllabic words. Consequently, accentuation of disyllabic words represents a major issue in the process of evaluating the prominence of particular syllables of speech flow. A small part of the disyllabic lexicon is comprised of words with a toneless second syllable, which have a stable trochee pattern (e.g. *háizi* 孩子 "child"; see section 3.4.2). However, the majority of the Chinese lexicon is comprised of **words with two tonal syllables** (e.g. *huǒchē* 火车 "train"). For general discussion about their accentuation, see section 3.5.13. In the present section we shall be concerned just with one specific group.

Some Chinese disyllabic words with two tonal syllables inherently favor **the trochee pattern** in most contexts, even prepausally (Wang & Chu, 2008). The pronunciation of the second syllable is most often completely atonic (that is, the pattern is 重轻, while 重中 is less common). There may be several dozen such words. The normative dictionary *Xiandai Hanyu Cidian* (XHC) marks them by a dot between the two syllables and a tone mark on the second syllable:

	XHC:		my system:	
做法	zuò · fǎ		*zuòfǎ*	"method"
这里	zhè · lǐ		*zhèlǐ*	"here"
新鲜	xīn · xiān		*xīnxiān*	"fresh"
因为	yīn · wèi		*yīnwèi*	"because"
底细	dǐ · xì		*dǐxì*	"details"
刚刚	gāng · gāng		*gānggāng*	"just"
力量	lì · liàng		*lìliàng*	"strength"

Note that Beijing speakers *regularly* pronounce such words with the neutral tone on the second syllable, see the dictionary *Beijinghua Qingsheng Cihui* (Zhang, 1957). For words with a *stable* neutral tone on the second syllable (dòu.fu 豆腐) see section 3.4.2.

There are many other words which may actually belong to this group, although XHC does not recognize them as such. That is, they are printed *without* a dot between both syllables, e.g. cuòwù 错误 "mistake", sùdù 速度 "speed", yuànwàng 愿望 "wish" (Wang, 2016: 32, Třísková, 2020: 93).

3.5.4 Second Syllable in Many 3–4 Syllabic Words

Accentuation of 3–4 syllabic words (which represent a rather small proportion of the Chinese lexicon) is relatively stable. In most of them, the second syllable is pronounced in the neutral tone. The last syllable tends to be the most prominent.

- ***huǒchēzhàn***   火车站   "train station"
- ***shuǐmòhuà***   水墨画   "ink painting"
- ***búxiùgāng***   不锈钢   "stainless steel"
- ***qiǎokèlì***   巧克力   "chocolate"
- ***Xīshuāngbǎnnà***   西双版纳   "the region Xishuangbanna"
- ***zīběnzhǔyì***   资本主义   "capitalism"

3.5.5 Second Syllable in Reduplicated Monosyllabic Verbs

Both monosyllabic and disyllabic Chinese verbs may be reduplicated to express a short, finished action. If a monosyllabic verb is reduplicated, the second syllable should be pronounced in the neutral tone:

- ***kànkàn***   看看   "take a look"
- ***shuōshuō***   说说   "talk about"
- ***tīngtīng***   听听   "listen"
- ***chángcháng***   尝尝   "taste"

The numeral *yī* 一 "one" may be inserted between both components: ***kànyīkàn*** 看一看. The pronunciation of *yī* is also atonic.

3.5.6 Directional Complements

Directional complements attached to a Chinese verb describe the direction of an action (up, down, away from the speaker, towards the speaker, etc.). The complement may either be monosyllabic (e.g. *lái* 来 in *huílái* 回来) or disyllabic (e.g. *chūlái* 出来 in *kànchūlái* 看出来). Directional complements should be pronounced in the neutral tone. This holds both for monosyllabic and disyllabic directional complements:

- *huí*lái 回来 "come back here"
- *huí*qù 回去 "go back"
- *kū*qǐlái 哭起来 "start crying"
- *zǒu*chūqù 走出去 "walk out"
- *kàn*chūlái 看出来 "figure out"

If a verb with a directional complement is turned into a potential form, the complement gains prominence. (see section 3.5.8).

3.5.7   Some Resultative Complements

Chinese resultative complements indicate the result of an action. Most resultative complements retain the original meaning of the morpheme, being fully pronounced, e.g. *hǎo* 好 (*zuòhǎo* 做好 "to accomplish successfully"), *wán* 完 (*shuōwán* 说完 "to finish speaking"), *cuò* 错 (*xiěcuò* 写错 "to write wrongly"), *bǎo* 饱 (*chībǎo* 吃饱 "to eat until full"). However, some resultative complements are exceptions to this rule. They have already become formalized and should be pronounced in the neutral tone: *jiàn* 见, *zhù* 住, *dào* 到, *zháo* 着, *diào* 掉, *sǐ* 死, *kāi* 开 (Lin, 1957: 71).

- *kàn*jiàn 看见 "see, notice"
- *jì*zhù 记住 "remember"
- *xiǎng*dào 想到 "give a thought"
- *shuì*zháo 睡着 "fall asleep"
- *chī*diào 吃掉 "eat completely"
- *qì*sǐ 气死 "be angry to death"
- *dǎ*kāi 打开 "open"

If a verb with a resultative complement is turned into a potential form, the complement is always prominent (see section 3.5.8).

3.5.8   The Negative bù 不 in Potential Forms of Verbs

In verbs with directional or resultative complements (e.g. *chūlái* 出来 "to come out") the negative *bù* 不 may be inserted between the verb and the complement, indicating the impossibility of accomplishing the action (*chūbùlái* 出不来 "be unable to come out"). The negative *bù* 不 should be pronounced in the neutral tone. On the other hand, directional/resultative complement becomes fully pronounced, restoring its original tone (e.g. *chūlái* vs. *chūbùlái*).

- *kànbújiàn*　看不见　"be unable to see"
- *zǒubúdòng*　走不动　"be unable to walk"
- *nábúzhù*　拿不住　"be unable to grasp"
- *dǎbùkāi*　打不开　"be unable to open"
- *chībùliǎo*　吃不了　"be unable to eat everything"

If the toneless structural particle *de* 得 is inserted instead of *bù* 不, the meaning is reversed: "to be able to accomplish the action". The prominence pattern remains the same as above:

- *kàndejiàn*　看得见　"be able to see"
- *dǎdekāi*　打得开　"be able to open"

3.5.9　Question Words Used as Indefinite or Relative Pronouns

Question words such as *shénme* 什么 "what", *shéi* 谁 "who", *shéide* 谁的 "whose", *wèishénme* 为什么 "why", etc., if used in their original questioning function, are usually the most salient item in the utterance (see section 3.6.5). However, they may be used as **indefinite pronouns** or **relative pronouns** in other contexts. In this case they become weakened, although they may retain some degree of prominence and the remnants of tone (or sometimes even full tone).

For instance, the question word *shénme* 什么 "what" can be used as an indefinite pronoun "anything, something":

Ní-MǍI-shénme //, wǒ-CHĪ-shénme. 你买什么，我吃什么。

"I will eat anything you buy."

The question word *jǐ* 几 "how many" may be used in the meaning "a couple of":

Wǒmen jiā-lǐ zhí-yǒu jǐ-zhī-YÁNG //, MÉI-yǒu-niú. 我们家里只有几只羊，没有牛。

"Our family only has a couple of sheep, we do not have cows."

The question word *duōshǎo* 多少 "how many/much" can be used in a negative sentence, meaning "not much":

Wǒmen-MÉI-yǒu duōshao-qián. 我们没有多少钱。

"We do not have much money."

3.5.10   Other Tonal Morphemes Which Tend to Become Weakened

There may be yet other cases of tonal morphemes/words which tend to become weakened in connected speech, for instance:

- the prefix *dì* 第 (*dì-yī* 第一 "the first", *dì-èr* 第二 "the second"...)
- *yīxià* 一下 "at once" after the verb (*kànyīxià* 看一下 "take a glance")
- ...*de shíhou* 的时候 "when" (*tā lái de shíhou* 他来的时候 "when he came")

3.5.11   The Negative *bù* 不 in A-not-A Questions

A-not-A questions (see section 3.6.4) represent one type of Chinese question. The verb/adjective is repeated, while the negative *bù* 不 is placed between the two items. If the verb/adjective is **monosyllabic**, the negative *bù* 不 should be pronounced in the neutral tone. The whole structure forms one prosodic word:

- ***lái-bù-lái?***   来不来?   "come or not?"
- ***chī-bù-chī?***   吃不吃?   "eat or not?"
- ***qù-bú-qù?***   去不去?   "go or not?"
- ***kàn-bú-kàn?***   看不看?   "look or not?"
- ***hǎo-bù-hǎo?***   好不好?   "good or not?"

Note that if the verb is **disyllabic**, the rhythmic pattern changes: the negative *bù* 不 assumes a certain prominence, standing as the first item of a new prosodic word. Repeated verb is rather weak – for instance, *Nǐ-**XǏ**huan **bù**-xǐhuan?* 你喜欢不喜欢? "Do you like it or not?" See section 3.6.4.

3.5.12   Monosyllabic Verbs Followed by an Object

A monosyllabic verb may become weakened if it is followed by an object:

xiě 写 "write"

*Nǐ-hái-xiě bó**KÈ**-ma?* 你还写博客吗?

"Do you still update your blog?"

3.5.13   The Second Syllable in Non-final Disyllabic Tonal Words

Before dealing with this topic let us make some general remarks about accentuation patterns in Chinese disyllabic tonal words. Examining "word stress" (词重音) in Chinese words consisting of two tonal syllables (such as *huǒchē* 火车 "train"), linguists have not reached any considerable consensus so far. I assume two underlying patterns (Třísková, 2020: 92):

1. **the spondee pattern** ("equal-stress pattern", 重重, 等重, 轻重不分), with **the iamb pattern** (中重, 右重) as a variant. Note that I do not recognize any need to establish the iamb as an independent pattern. I view the difference between the spondee and the iamb as a phonetic detail. The iamb pattern is mostly induced by the prepausal position (i.e., a post-lexical factor).

2. **the trochee pattern** (重轻, 左重), regardless of the degree of second syllable weakening (it may be either atonic or weakened, yet it is atonic in most cases).

This solution is quite similar to the analysis of disyllabic stress patterns in Beijing Mandarin presented in Wang & Feng (2006). They describe two patterns: 左重 (trochee) and 右重 (iamb). While the 左重 (trochee) pattern always has a weaker second syllable, in the 右重 (iamb) pattern the weaker first syllable is not a rule (that is, both syllables may sometimes have equal prominence). Regarding lexical stress, the authors recognize **only one underlying pattern: trochee**, or 左重, which includes 轻声词 and 带调 左重词 . All other disyllabic words are argued not to have lexical stress at all (不是 左重的双音节词没有词重音). They may either be realized as 右重 (iamb) or have both syllables of equal prominence (其左右音节可以看作轻重不分或差不多). The authors finally conclude: "[Only] the trochee pattern can be viewed as lexical stress; all other stress patterns are induced by factors coming from elsewhere than the lexicon." (左重为词汇重音, 非左重形式由词汇以外因素决定) Most recently, Feng Shengli (Feng, 2021: 7) has proposed "a new definition of lexical stress in colloquial speech style", taking into account speech style and word frequency, which influence the actual surface stress pattern of a word. He claims that it is impossible to find a solution for Chinese lexical stress without taking these factors into account. Feng challenges current theories of lexical stress, seeing problems in the very understanding of what "stress" as such is. Feng points out again that stress is a relationship (重音是关系而不是音体). He wonders whether the Chinese colloquial speech style has word stress at all.

Regarding the distribution of the realization/surface patterns of disyllabic tonal words, I generally distinguish two major situations:

– Some words **favor the trochee pattern**. These were treated in section 3.5.3.

– The majority of Chinese disyllabic tonal words may have more or less **variable accentuation**. Disyllabic words with two tonal syllables often keep full tones on both syllables in connected speech. Sometimes it is hard to tell which syllable is more prominent. To put it another way, the word assumes a **spondee** pattern (等重, 重重). Occasionally, the second syllable may be more prominent, the word thus assuming the **iambic** pattern (中重, 右重). This may happen especially before a pause, as a result of final lengthening. **The spondee (/iamb) pattern** may be viewed as a **default pattern** of disyllabic tonal words (except for those treated in section 3.5.3, such as 做法 zuò · fǎ "method").

Yet in some situations this pattern **may be modified**. Under the pressure of rhythm and syntactic/information structure, the second syllable may be pronounced with a weak or even neutral tone, the whole word assuming the **trochee** pattern (重轻).

yīgòng 一共 "altogether"

Yígòng DUŌshao-qián? 一共多少钱?

"How much is the total?"

Weakening of the second syllable is dependent on both context and inherent properties of the word, such as its inner morphological structure. Speech style and frequency of the word in speech matter as well (Feng, 2021). The more common and colloquial the word, the stronger the inclination to resort to the trochee pattern. The more preserved or perceived the original meaning of the morphemes, and the more formal the speech style, the stronger the inclination to keep the default spondee pattern with full pronunciation of both morphemes (or, in other words, the lower the inclination to weaken the second syllable). For instance, in the word *zhīdào* 知道 "to know" the original meaning of both morphemes ("to know" and "way") is hardly perceived nowadays. The pronunciation of the second morpheme is most often atonic. XHC writes the word as zhī · dào.[1]

———————

[1]   Note that if the verb *zhīdào* 知道 is preceded by the negative *bù* 不, the pattern is changed: *zhīdào*, but ***bú-zhīdào***.

The context, as said above, is an important factor determining the actual word accentuation. If the word is in prepausal position and/or focused, it tends to keep the original full prominence of the second syllable. On the other hand, we can observe that when the word in question is *not* followed by a break – that is, if "something follows" – weakening of the second syllable often occurs, though definitely not always (Wang & Chu, 2008: 143). Let us give a few more examples of non-final disyllabic tonal words realized as trochees:

hángkōng 航空 "aviation"

Shì-HÁNGkōng-xìn-ma? 是航空信吗?

"Is it an airmail letter?"

jīdàn 鸡蛋 "eggs"

Jīdàn HÉN-hǎochī. 鸡蛋很好吃。

"The eggs are (very) tasty."

fàngxīn 放心 "relieved"

Wǒ-fàngxīn-DUŌ-le. 我放心多了。

"I was greatly relieved."

This phenomenon is, among other things, undoubtedly related to syntax, as prosodic structure and syntactic structure are to a large extent interrelated. As Feng (2019a, 2019b) points out, the interaction between syntax and prosody is bidirectional: prosody not only constrains syntactic structures, but also activates syntactic operations. These phenomena are also treated in the textbook (Feng & Wang, 2018). Concerning the relationship between grammar and prosody, see also Lin (1962) and Švarný & Uher (2014).

It must be pointed out that Chinese disyllabic tonal words are not equally ready to surrender to such pressures and shift to a trochee pattern. The phenomenon of **variable stress patterns in disyllabic words** was analysed by Oldřich Švarný back in the 1970s (Švarný, 1974). Švarný's description of such variability was based on a large corpus of utterances (Švarný, 1998–2000; see section 2.1). He collected numerous tokens of the same word type, examining their prominence patterns in various contexts.[①] By means of descriptive statistics he established **seven "accentuation types" of disyllabic words**, based on their degree of willingness to weaken the second syllable, i.e., their inclination for the trochee pattern.[②] For instance, the word *dòufu* 豆腐 "bean curd" belongs to the extreme type (1) with a 100% inclination for trochee (1). The word *zuòfǎ* 做法 "method" is the next type (2), with a strong inclination to trochee (2). The following four types (3, 4, 5, 6) display different degrees of variability. The last type (7) includes words such as *lǎoshī* 老师 "teacher", whose willingness to be realized as a trochee is very low. Note that Švarný was concerned with "non-stress" in disyllabic words, instead of "stress"; cf. the notion of " 以轻显重 ", mentioned in Feng (2021: 14).

Švarný did not explore the conditions and contexts of second syllable weakening in detail. He only observed the tendency for iambs to occur at the end of a rhythmic unit, and for trochees to occur at the beginning or inside a rhythmic unit (Švarný, 1998–2000: xxxviii). This topic is examined, for example, in Wang & Chu (2008). Elucidating the conditions for weakening of the second syllable in disyllabic words in connected speech is a task which remains for future research. In any case, Švarný's early analysis of accentuation patterns in disyllabic words was fairly ahead of its time. The current analysis of Feng seems to have much in common with Švarný: "The typical form of lexical stress in colloquial speech style is atonic or weak pronunciation [of the second syllable]; these two have nothing to do with 'stress' or 'enhancement'" (口语词重音的典型形式是 "轻声" 或 "轻读"，二者均非 "重音" 或 "加重") (Feng, 2021: 7). Important treatments of lexical stress can be found for instance in Kratochvil (1974); Yin (1982); Wang et al. (2003).

As we know, the issue of "word stress" in Chinese remains unresolved to date. Variability of accentuation in disyllabic words may be viewed as proof of the **non-existence of word stress in Chinese** across the lexicon (Třísková, 2020: 87–94).

---

① Note that Švarný never used a computer.
② The number of accentuation types was later reduced to five in the textbook Švarný (1991–1993) (vol. I., p. 176).

3.5.14 Contextual Weakening of Full Words

A content (autosemantic/lexical/full) word may become phonetically weakened in speech if it is not semantically important in the given context. Such sort of weakening is related to information structure and pragmatics.

- Content word may become weakened if repeated:

  qìchē 汽车 "the car"

  Zhè-liàng qìchē // shì-wǒmende dì-YÍ-liàng qìchē. 这辆汽车是我们的第一辆汽车。

  "This car is our first car."

- Content words following the focus tend to be weakened (post-focus weakening):

  lái 来 "to come"

  Tāmen DŌU-lái-le. 他们都来了。

  "All of them came."

This phenomenon may seem quite natural and not hard to understand. It can be found in many languages. However, it turns out that it is rather difficult to grasp **in pedagogical practice**. Students may be reluctant to weaken tones in content words, even though the information structure requires it. They tend to believe that the meaning of the whole utterance could be damaged if the tones are not conspicuous enough. In fact, the opposite is true: if the content word is not weakened in a particular context, the utterance may sound awkward. While the meanings of single words are clear, the communicative meaning of the whole message may be blurred or even hard to comprehend. The second occurrence of the word *qìchē* 汽车 (the first sentence) may serve as an example. If it is pronounced just as fully as the first *qìchē*, the utterance sounds odd.

3.6 Top-prominence Syllable (*MĀ*)

The most prominent syllable of an utterance/prosodic phrase usually belongs to a content word. Function words bear such prominence less frequently. Theoretically, only *tonal* function words can be "stressed" in Chinese. In our analysis, the word which carries the most prominent syllable is called **the nucleus**.

Can the most prominent syllable in an utterance/prosodic phrase **be predicted?** I shall treat the following situations: default nucleus, emphasis, particle *ma* 吗 questions, A-not-A questions, question-word questions, and alternative questions.

3.6.1   Default Nucleus

In so-called "neutral" speech[①] without any special emphasis (broad focus), the greatest prominence seems to rest on the last full word of the utterance:

Huǒchē-shàng **rén**-hěn **DUŌ**. 火车上人很多。

"There are a lot of people in the train."

Xiáojiě //, wǒ-yào **jì-fēng-XÌN**. 小姐，我要寄封信。

"Miss, I want to send a letter."

Default nucleus may not be particularly salient. In this case *duō* and *xìn* may suffice, instead of **DUŌ** and **XÌN**.

3.6.2   Emphasis

Emphasized words bear the greatest prominence in the utterance or prosodic phrase. Emphasis is fully determined by the will of the speaker and can be found basically anywhere in the utterance. The items following the emphasized word tend to be weakened (post-focus weakening).

When two items are contrasted (contrastive stress), both items are usually emphasized:

Tā-**xǐhuan** chī-**YÚ** //, **bù**-**xǐhuan** chī-**RÒU**. 他喜欢吃鱼，不喜欢吃肉。

"He likes to eat **fish**, does not like to eat **meat**."

Negatives, such as *bù* 不 , *méi* 没 , *bié* 别 , are often emphasized:

Wǒmen-**MÉI**yǒu duōshao-qián. 我们没有多少钱。

"We do not have much money."

Non-neutral, emotionally charged words often attract emphasis, e.g. *piān* 偏 "provocatively":

- *Nǐ*-**BIÉ**-kàn! 你别看！ "Do not look at it!"

- *Wǒ*-**PIĀN**-kàn! 我偏看！ "I'm looking whether you like it or not!"

A function word may occasionally be emphasized if it is tonal. One example is the

---

① In fact, no such thing as "neutral" speech exists in real life. I use this common term only for the sake of convenience.

personal pronoun *tā* 他 :

– *SHÉI bù-xǐhuan chī-ròu*? 谁不喜欢吃肉? "Who does not like to eat meat?"

– *TĀ bù-xǐhuan chī-ròu*. 他不喜欢吃肉。 "**He** does not like to eat meat."

Note that in emotionally charged, expressive speech there may be more emphasized items in one prosodic phrase. Yet this situation is not so common.

3.6.3 Particle *ma* 吗 Questions (Polarity Questions)

Polarity questions are those which offer a choice between two possibilities, expecting either a positive or a negative answer. Because the answer is typically (though not always) either YES or NO, they are often called **yes/no questions**. In Chinese, polarity questions are those comprising the particle *ma* 吗. Grammatically unmarked questions also belong here. In such questions, the most salient item is quite naturally **the item the speaker is asking about**. This item will probably carry the nucleus. For instance:

Nǐ-shēnti HǍO-ma? 你身体好吗?

"How are you?" (Are you in good health?)

Shì-HÁNGkōng-xìn-ma? 是航空信吗?

"Is it an airmail letter?"

3.6.4 A-not-A Questions (Affirmative-negative Questions)

A-not-A questions use the affirmative and negative forms of the predicate.

If the verb/adjective is **monosyllabic**, the first item is the most prominent, while the pronunciation of the negative *bù* 不 occurring between both items is atonic. The three items form a prosodic word:

Tāng RÈ-bú-rè? 汤热不热?

"Is the soup hot or not?"

If the verb/adjective is **disyllabic**, the rhythmic pattern changes: the negative *bù* 不 assumes a certain prominence, standing as the first item of a new prosodic word. Repeated verb is rather weak:

Nǐ-XǏhuan bù-xǐhuan? 你喜欢不喜欢?

"Do you like it or not?"

3.6.5   Question-word Questions

Question-word questions, as the name suggests, contain a question word: **who, where, when**, etc. Thus, they are frequently called "wh-questions" in English. When asking such questions, the speaker is seeking some specific information.

The question word is usually the most prominent item of the utterance:

Tā-SHÉNme-shíhou-lái? 他什么时候来?

"**When** shall he come?"

However, in some contexts, the speaker may emphasize the item he/she is asking about. This is the case in the following question:

XIĀNGJIĀO zěnme-mài? 香蕉怎么卖?

"How much are **bananas**?"

Bananas may be placed on a vendor's stall among other fruits and vegetables. While asking about the price is expected in such a situation, clear identification of the item "bananas" is crucial for the speaker to get the right answer. Note that *both* syllables in the word *xiāngjiāo* are marked as top-prominence syllables. The adjacency of such syllables (like the adjacency of normal syllables) is perfectly acceptable.

3.6.6   Alternative Questions

The speaker offers the hearer two alternatives to choose from using the conjunction *háishi* 还是 "or". Usually, both items are equally prominent:

Nǐ-zhù-ZHÈR //, háishi-NÀR? 你住这儿，还是那儿?

"Do you live **here**, or **there**?"

When the choice is between the positive and negative forms of the same thing, the first item is more salient than the second. The negative, e.g. *bù* 不, becomes prominent:

Nǐ-rènwei zhè-HǍO //, háishi BÙ-hǎo? 你认为这好，还是不好?

"Do you think this is **good**, or **not** good?"

If the items to choose from are whole phrases composed of several words/ morphemes, the salient syllables are chosen according to the actual objects of choice:

Tā-shì MĚIguó-rén //, háishi YĪNGguó-rén? 他是美国人，还是英国人?

"Is he American, or English?"

4. Phrasing (Prosodic Units)

Regarding prosodic units, Mandarin ToBI and Chinese ToBI have quite complicated prosodic hierarchies.

Mandarin ToBI assumes the following prosodic units: minor prosodic phrase, major prosodic phrase, breath group, and prosodic group. The break indices are: 0 (reduced syllable boundary), 1 (normal syllable boundary), 2 (minor-phrase boundary), 3 (major-phrase boundary), 4 (breath group boundary), and 5 (prosodic group boundary).

Chinese ToBI assumes the following prosodic units: prosodic word (PW), minor prosodic phrase (MIP), major prosodic phrase (MAP), and intonation group (IG).

CHIPROT (like Švarný) assumes prosodic units of three levels:

prosodic word: words forming one PW are connected by a dash (-)

prosodic phrase: the boundary of a non-final PPh is marked by a double slash (//)

finished utterance: the boundary is marked by a sentence-final punctuation mark (.?!)

4.1 Prosodic Word

A prosodic word (PW) is usually, though not always, composed of several lexical items. Most often they are grammatically related to each other. However, in rapid speech a function word may "desert" to the preceding prosodic word (see section 3.5.2). Below I will review the major structural types of prosodic words.

4.1.1 Single Word

Prosodic words composed of a single word are rather rare. Especially if the word is monosyllabic (and/or a function word), it seldom stands as a prosodic word. Disyllabic content words are better able to stand as prosodic words:

Zhè-shì Yǐzi. 这是椅子。

This is a chair.

4.1.2 Content Word with Attached Function Word(s)

Most commonly, a prosodic word is formed by a content word with function word(s) attached to it (before, after, or both). In the utterance below we can find two

FWs attached to some content words: the preposition *bǎ* 把 (a proclitic), and the post-verbally placed preposition *zài* 在 (an enclitic):

> *Bǎ-xíngli cún-zài huǒchēZHÀN.* 把行李存在火车站。

"Store your luggage at the train station."

A function word contained in a prosodic word does not always have a grammatical relationship with its neighbor (see section 3.5.2). For instance, the adverb *jiù* 就 in the following example grammatically belongs to the following verb:

> *Wó-ZǍO-jiù kànguo Hóng-Lóu-Mèng.* 我早就看过《红楼梦》。

"I read (the novel) *Dream of the Red Chamber* a long time ago."

Note that **"unstressed" function words cannot stand alone.** In connected speech they have to join some other word to form a prosodic word together. This phenomenon has important pedagogical consequences.

4.1.3 Two Content Words

Many prosodic words comprise **two content words,** such as *xué* 学 "learn" and *zhōngwén* 中文 "Chinese" in the following example:

> *NĚIxiē xuésheng xué-zhōngwén?* 哪些学生学中文？

"Which students learn Chinese?"

Sometimes function word(s) may be added, e.g. the personal pronouns *tā* 他 "he", *wǒ* 我 "I" in the following example (the second prosodic phrase):

> *Wǒ-ZHĪdào // tā-bù-xǐhuan-wǒ.* 我知道他不喜欢我。

"I know that he does not like me."

Sometimes function word(s) may be inserted between two content words. This is the case of the unstressed word *jǐ* 几 meaning "couple of" in the following example:

> *Zhè-běnr cídián-lǐ // SHÁO-jǐ-yè.* 这本儿词典里少几页。

"There are a few pages missing in this dictionary."

4.1.4 Two Function Words

Some prosodic words are composed of only two function words (usually standing at the beginning of an utterance or prosodic phrase). These cases have already been treated in section 3.5.2.

4.1.5 In-between Structures

Some structures (morphemic sequences) cannot be found in a dictionary, so there are reasons to deprive them of the status of an independent word. Yet the relationship of their components may be extremely tight, so they stand as one PW. Major examples are reduplicated monosyllabic verbs/adjectives, and also verbs with directional, resultative, and other complements, including potential forms of verbs. These structures should enter a prosodic word as a whole, without falling apart (e.g. *lái-de-zǎo* 来得早 "to come early").

Note that if the complement is *not* monosyllabic, it is joined more loosely and can stand as a separate prosodic word:

*Zhè-zhǒng **diǎnxin** // **zuò-de BÙ-hǎo-chī**.* 这种点心做得不好吃。

"This dessert is not tasty."

4.1.6 Words with Particles

Verb aspect particles *le* 了, *zhe* 着, *guo* 过, **structural particles** *de* 得, *de* 的, *de* 地, and **sentence-final particles** such as *ma* 吗, *ne* 呢, *le* 了, *ba* 吧 are toneless. They are always tightly attached to the preceding word, forming a prosodic word. An example is the particle *ma* 吗 in the following utterance:

*Zhè-shì **Nǐ**de-ma?* 这是你的吗?

"Is this yours?"

4.1.7 Idioms

Various types of idioms, stereotyped phrases, frequent collocations, etc., usually form one prosodic word. For instance:

***Ài** //, **Wáng-lǎoshī** //, **háo-jiǔ-bú-JIÀN**!* 哎，王老师，好久不见!

"Oh, teacher Wang, we have not seen each other for a long time!"

4.1.8 A-not-A Questions

An A-not-A question forms a prosodic word if the item asked about is monosyllabic:

Tāng RÈ-bú-rè? 汤热不热?

"Is the soup hot or not?"

If the verb/adjective is **disyllabic**, the patterning is different (see section 3.6.4).

4.2   Prosodic Phrase

Prosodic words join to form larger units: prosodic phrases (PPh). A prosodic phrase may sometimes contain just one prosodic word. More often there are two or three (rarely more) prosodic words in one prosodic phrase. In this section, we shall be concerned with **non-final prosodic phrases** (such a phrase is not the last one in the utterance). PPh boundary may occur after a non-final clause (4.2.1), after a prepositional phrase (4.2.2), after a longer noun phrase standing utterance-initially (4.2.3), after particular items in enumerations, and (less frequently) after a predicate followed by a longer noun phrase. A hearer can detect the boundary using several signals, usually occurring in combination: non-falling intonation pattern, slight final lengthening, and less often a silent pause. Note that there may or may not be a comma in the orthography (e.g. a longer noun phrase standing as a subject is not followed by a comma).

4.2.1   Non-final Clause

Zhèr-yǒu YǏzi //, nàr-yǒu ZHUŌzi. 这儿有椅子，那儿有桌子。

"Here is a chair, and there is a table."

4.2.2   Prepositional Phrase

Bǎ-huāpíngr // fàng-zài ZHUŌzi-shàng. 把花瓶儿放在桌子上。

"Put the vase on the table."

4.2.3   Preverbal Noun Phrase

A subject, time/place determination, or utterance-initially placed object may be followed by a notable prosodic boundary if it is longer.

Nèi-jí-běnr SHŪ // wǒ-dōu kànWÁN-le. 那几本书我都看完了。

"I have read these books already."

4.3   Finished Utterance

A prosodic boundary occurring at the end of finished utterances is indicated by **sentence-final punctuation**. The acoustic signals of the boundary are more conspicuous than for non-final prosodic phrases:

– a falling intonation pattern for statements, question-word questions, alternative questions, and A-not-A questions; a non-falling intonation pattern for particle *ma* 吗 questions and grammatically unmarked questions

– noticeable final lengthening

– a silent pause (more likely than after a non-final prosodic phrase)

5. CHIPROT Cookbook

In previous paragraphs, I have tried to demonstrate that many features of prosodic structure can be predicted. In this section, I will attempt to describe the CHIPROT transcription procedure involving certain predictions. I have chosen four sentences, (A), (B), (C), and (D), as examples to clarify the procedure. It has five steps (or six if we include step /0/). Steps /2/, /3/, and /4/ are predictions.

Step /0/

The sentence is jotted down or already available in plain *Hanyu Pinyin* (in italics). Tonal syllables carry tone marks, toneless syllables carry no tone mark: *mā, ma*.

(A) *Zhuōzi shàng yǒu sān běn shū.* 桌子上有三本书。

"There are three books on the table."

(B) *Shì hángkōng xìn ma?* 是航空信吗？

"Is it an airmail letter?"

(C) *Nǐ mǎi shénme, wǒ chī shénme.* 你买什么，我吃什么。

"I will eat anything you buy."

(D) *Bǎ tā jiào dào wǒ zhèr lái.* 把他叫到我这儿来。

"Call him to me."

Step /1/

All tonal syllables will be put in bold type (they of course carry a tone mark): ***mā***. This can be easily done by putting the whole sentence in bold type and then **unbolding toneless syllables** (see section 3.4). Regularly there are very few or even no toneless syllables in a sentence.

(A) *Zhuōzi shàng yǒu sān běn shū*. 桌子上有三本书。

The only toneless syllable is the lexical suffix *zi* 子.

(B) *Shì hángkōng xìn ma*? 是航空信吗？

The only toneless syllable is the question particle *ma* 吗.

(C) *Ní mǎi shénme, wǒ chī shénme*. 你买什么，我吃什么。

There are two toneless syllables: two occurrences of the suffix *me* 么.

(D) *Bǎ tā jiào dào wǒ zhèr lái*. 把他叫到我这儿来。

There is no toneless syllable in this sentence.

Step /2/

Tonal words/morphemes that are predicted to be **weakened** will be **unbolded**: *mā*. Many of them will be cliticoids (see section 3.5.1). Note that normal syllables may neighbor each other (see section 3.3).

(A) *Zhuōzi shàng yǒu sān běn shū*. 桌子上有三本书。

The following items can be predicted as weakened: the postposition *shàng* 上, the verb *yǒu* 有, and the classifier *běn* 本. All of them belong to the cliticoids.

(B) *Shì hángkōng xìn ma*? 是航空信吗？

Only one item can be predicted as weakened at this point: the verb *shì* 是, belonging to the cliticoids. In the phrase *hángkōng xìn* 航空信 "airmail letter" we have to wait for step /4/ to decide on the prominence of particular syllables. The reason is that the weakening/enhancement of some syllables may be rooted in the information structure.

(C) *Ní mǎi shénme, wǒ chī shénme*. 你买什么，我吃什么。

The following items can be predicted as weakened: the personal pronouns *nǐ* 你, *wǒ* 我 (the cliticoids) and the question word *shénme* 什么 used as a relative pronoun (3.5.9).

(D) *Bǎ tā jiào dào wǒ zhèr lái*. 把他叫到我这儿来。

The following items can be predicted as weakened: the preposition *bǎ* 把, the personal pronoun *tā* 他, the preposition *dào* 到, and the personal pronoun *wǒ* 我. All of them belong to the cliticoids. The word *zhèr* 这儿 is a place word, thus we keep it as a normal syllable at this point. The verb *lái* 来 functions as a directional complement here, being just a formal indicator of the direction towards the speaker. Thus, it will be predicted as weak.

Step /3/

mark **phrasing** (prosodic words/phrases) -, //

The words which would presumably be tightly bound in speech, forming a **prosodic word**, will be connected by a dash, e.g. *sān-běn-shū* 三本书. Remember that toneless and weakened items cannot stand alone. The most frequent weak, unstressed items are the clitics (3.4.1) and cliticoids (3.5.1).

Short utterances usually stand as a single **prosodic phrase**. Its boundary is already marked by a sentence-final punctuation mark. Longer utterances may be composed of two or, less commonly, three or more prosodic phrases. The boundary of the non-final prosodic phrase will be marked by a double slash (//). With respect to decisions about prosodic boundaries of non-final prosodic phrases, the relevant factors to consider were outlined in section 4.2.

(A) ***Zhuōzi-shàng-yǒu sān-běn-shū***. 桌子上有三本书。

The weak postposition *shàng* 上 must be tightly attached to the preceding noun. The verb *yǒu* 有 has a close grammatical relationship with the following noun phrase *sān běn shū* 三本书. However, in rapid speech *yǒu* 有 will most probably "desert" to the preceding word *zhuōzi* 桌子 under the pressure of rhythm, forming a prosodic word with it. The noun phrase *sān běn shū* 三本书 forms a rather typical prosodic word composed of a numeral, a classifier, and a noun.

(B) ***Shì-hángkōng-xìn-ma***? 是航空信吗？

The copula *shì* 是 is usually "unstressed", thus it cannot stand alone. In this sentence, it would join the following noun phrase, *hángkōng xìn* 航空信, as a proclitic. *Shì* could certainly be prominent if it is emphasized by the speaker (then it could possibly even stand alone as a prosodic word). However, this is hard to determine without knowing the previous context and hearing the audio, so at this point we presume *shì* is a weak proclitic. The toneless question particle *ma* 吗 has no other choice but to be attached to the preceding word. The resulting prosodic word, forming a prosodic phrase and a finished utterance at the same time, is rather long (five syllables). This long prosodic word could fall apart into two prosodic words if the speaker hesitates and inserts a break after the verb *shì* 是. This may manifest in perceptible lengthening and (in the case of a strong hesitation) by a silent pause. If *shì* is emphasized, it could also possibly stand alone as a prosodic word, as mentioned above.

(C) *Ní-**mǎi**-shénme //, wǒ-**chī**-shénme.* 你买什么，我吃什么。

This utterance is composed of two clauses, and thus most probably of two prosodic phrases divided by a break. The prosodic boundary would be manifested by a final lengthening of the syllable *me* 么, and possibly by a silent pause. The personal pronouns *nǐ* 你, *wǒ* 我 will be tightly attached to their verbs as proclitics.

(D) *Bǎ-tā **jiào**-dào wǒ-**zhèr**-lái.* 把他叫到我这儿来。

Two cliticoids *bǎ* 把, *tā* 他 at the beginning of the utterance will most probably form a disyllabic prosodic word. The preposition *dào* 到 is placed after the verb in this sentence. Its pronunciation is typically atonic in such a position, tightly joining the preceding verb as an enclitic. The expression *wǒ zhèr* 我这儿 is a set phrase "here where I am", thus both items must be tightly joined. The last item *lái* 来 is formal and weak, so it joins the preceding item.

Step /4/

We look for the items which are presumably the most prominent in the utterance: the words carrying emphasis, contrastive stress, default nucleus, etc. (3.6). Pertinent syllables will be capitalized: *MĀ*.

(A) *Zhuōzi-shàng-yǒu sān-běn-**SHŪ**.* 桌子上有三本书。

If there is no concrete context suggesting that the speaker wishes to emphasize some particular word (e.g. *zhuōzi* 桌子, *shàng* 上, *sān* 三), this utterance will have a default nucleus on the last content word *shū* 书.

(B) *Shì-**HÁNG**kōng-xìn-ma?* 是航空信吗?

In this particle *ma* 吗 question, the speaker is obviously wondering whether this letter will be sent by airmail or as ordinary mail (*píngxìn* 平信). Thus, in the phrase *hángkōng xìn* 航空信 "airmail letter" we can expect the word *hángkōng* 航空 to be the most prominent. Because it is not prepausal, its accentuation pattern will probably be a trochee (3.5.13). The word *xìn* 信 is not semantically important in the given context and will undergo post-focus weakening.

(C) *Ní-**MǍI**-shénme* //, *wǒ-**CHĪ**-shénme.* 你买什么，我吃什么。

The two verbs *mǎi* 买 "buy" and *chī* 吃 "eat" are semantically the most important, thus they will probably be the most prominent items of the utterance. Both relative pronouns *shénme* 什么 (3.5.9) can be expected not just to be weakened, but even to be completely atonic here (post-focus weakening).

(D) *Bǎ-tā **jiào**-dào **WǑ**-zhèr-lái.* 把他叫到我这儿来。

The listener is urged to take somebody to the speaker. Thus the most important word in this imperative sentence is clearly the personal pronoun *wǒ* 我 in the expression *wǒ zhèr* 我这儿 "here where I am". The morpheme *zhèr* 这儿 and the morpheme *lái* 来 are only supplementary and formal. Their weak, atonic pronunciation is supported by their post-focal position.

Step /5/

Listen to the audio and **make corrections**. I have tried to show that some/many prosodic features can be predicted without hearing the audio recordings because they are rule-governed to a large extent. However, our predictions may certainly be imperfect. Speech tempo, speech style, individual habits of the speaker, specific information structure or pragmatic context, etc. may influence the surface prosodic form and make some of our predictions wrong. Careful listening to the audio is thus the last step, which gives the transcript the final touch. While evaluating the prominence of particular syllables or phrasing in listening, there may still be some questionable points. In such cases speech analysis software (such as PRAAT) would be needed to support our final assessments. There may be some unclear cases, but they should not be frequent.

6. Minimodules

I have shown how the CHIPROT transcription can be used to transcribe whole utterances. It may also be used to indicate the prominence structure of commonly used short phrases such as:

shù-shàng	树上	trochee	●·
ní-hǎo	你好	iamb	·●
zhè-běn-shū	这本书	cretic	●·●
gěi-bàba	给爸爸	amphibrach	·●·
wūzi-lǐ	屋子里	dactyl	●··
zài-Běijīng	在北京	bacchius	·●●
xuéxiào-lǐ	学校里	antibacchius	●●·

I call these brief, two- or three-syllable sequences **minimodules**, or **phonetic chunks**. They draw on the notion of formulaic language (Třísková, 2017c) and can be efficiently used in pedagogic practice. The labels for prominence patterns are borrowed from verse meter of Ancient Greek poetry. Note that minimodules do not need to employ the highest degree of prominence (*MĀ*), since most of them are not finished utterances.

7. Conclusion

The CHIPROT transcription was, above all, designed as a pedagogic tool. It may aid those who are studying Chinese as a second/foreign language and struggling with the prosodic form of the utterances. The aim is to help learners speak with more ease, fluency, and naturalness. **Language teachers** may test CHIPROT here or there. They may find it useful to exploit some of its features while preparing teaching materials and handouts. **Students** can experiment with CHIPROT. They may, for example, find it useful to draw up some transcripts related to particular lessons (the annotation procedure is relatively easy, user-friendly, and computer-friendly; the system does not contain any unusual graphic marks, complicated conventions, etc.). However, my long-term objective is to encourage **writers of pedagogic materials** to incorporate CHIPROT into their texts. This would, of course, take a good deal of prosodic knowledge and practical transcription skill. Indeed, this is the process I have been through myself, discovering various flaws, drawbacks, and traps in the system and improving it step by step.

Linguists engaged in research on connected speech may also find CHIPROT useful. It may help them discover major prosodic rules and tendencies while analysing the prosodic form of Chinese utterances anchored in real communication contexts – instead of artificial, fabricated sentences pronounced in isolation. As the transcription procedure can be executed in several clear steps, it may perhaps even be automated to some extent. The necessary software, if designed, could be used to process larger sets of speech data such as spoken language corpora.

CHIPROT certainly may have its shortcomings or points which escaped my notice. Yet I trust that its final version represents a rather consistent, theory-based, and robust system. Its occasional blind spots or lurking problems may be successfully solved in the course of time. Feedback from future users of the CHIPROT system may greatly help to polish it. Any comments or criticisms would certainly be welcome.

References

Beckman M E, Ayers G M. 1994. *Guidelines for ToBI Labeling*. Ohio State University. http://www.speech. cs.cmu.edu/tobi/ToBI.0.html.

Chao Y R (赵元任). 1968. *A Grammar of Spoken Chinese*. Berkeley and Los Angeles: University of California Press.

Feng S L (冯胜利). 2019a. *Prosodic Syntax in Chinese: History and Changes*. New York: Routledge.

Feng S L (冯胜利). 2019b. *Prosodic Syntax in Chinese: Theory and Facts*. New York: Routledge.

Feng S L (冯胜利). 2021. 韵律体语法与汉语的词重音 (Prosody of stylistic-register grammar and lexical stress in Chinese). Paper presented at the 7th International Conference on Prosodic Grammar (ICPG-7), Tianjin.

Feng S L (冯胜利), Wang L J (王丽娟). 2018. 汉语韵律语法教程 (*A Course of Prosodic Grammar*). Beijing: Peking University Press.

Jiang L P (姜丽萍). 2014. HSK 标准教程 1 (*HSK Standard Course 1*). Beijing: Beijing Language and Culture University Press.

Kratochvil P. 1974. Stress shift mechanism and its role in Peking dialect. *Modern Asian Studies*, 8.4: 433-458.

Lee W-S, Zee E. 2014. Chinese phonetics. In: Huang C-T J, Li Y-H A, Simpson A. *The Handbook of Chinese Linguistics*. Oxford: Wiley Blackwell, 369-399.

Li A J (李爱军). 2002. Chinese prosody and prosodic labeling of spontaneous speech. *Proceedings of Speech Prosody*, Aix-en-Provence, 39-46.

Li A J, Zu Y Q. 2007. Corpus design and annotation for speech synthesis and recognition. In: Lee C H, et al. *Advances in Chinese Spoken Language Processing*. Hong Kong: World Scientific, 263-268.

Li W M (厉为民). 1981. 试论轻声和重音 (Discussion on the neutral tone and stress). 中国语文 (*Studies of the Chinese Language*), 1: 35-40.

Li Z Q (李智强). 2018. 汉语语音系的与教学研究 (*Studies in Acquisition and Teaching of Mandarin Chinese Phonetics*). Beijing: Beijing Language and Culture University Press.

Liang L (梁磊). 2003. 声调与重音——汉语轻声的再认识 (Tone and stress: the Chinese neutral tone revisited). 第六届全国现代语音学学术会议论文集 (上) (*Proceedings of the 6th National Conference on Modern Phonetics, 1*). Tianjin: Nankai University: 192-197.

Lin T (林焘). 1957. 现代汉语补足语里的轻音现象所反映出来的语法和语义问题 (Grammatical and semantic problems related to the non-stress phenomenon in modern Chinese complements). 北京大学学报 (人文科学) (*Journal of Peking University; Philosophy and Social Sciences*), 9: 61-74.

Lin T (林焘). 1962. 现代汉语轻音和句法结构的关系 (The relationship between non-stress and grammatical structure in Modern Chinese). 中国语文 (*Studies of the Chinese Language*), 7: 301-311.

Liu Y H, et al. 2017. *Integrated Chinese* (4th ed.). Boston: Cheng & Tsui Company.

Peng S-H, Chan M K M, Tseng C-Y, et al. 2005. Towards a Pan-Mandarin system for prosodic transcription. In: Jun S-A. *Prosodic Typology: The Phonology of Intonation and Phrasing*. Oxford: Oxford University Press, 230-270.

Silverman K, Beckman M, Pitrelli J, et al. 1992. ToBI: a standard for labeling English prosody. *Proceedings of the 1992 International Conference on Spoken Language Processing (ICSLP 92)*, 867-870.

Švarný O. 1974. Variability of tone prominence in Chinese (Pekinese). *Asian and African Languages in Social Context*. Dissertationes Orientales (34). Praha: Academia, 127-186.

Švarný O. 1991a. The functioning of the prosodic features in Chinese (Pekinese). *Archiv Orientální*, 59.2: 208-216.

Švarný O. 1991b. Prosodic features in Chinese (Pekinese): prosodic transcription and statistical tables. *Archiv Orientální*, 59.3: 234-254.

Švarný O. 1998-2000. *Učební Slovník Jazyka Čínského*, I-IV (*A Learning Dictionary of Modern Chinese*, I-IV). Olomouc: Palacký University.

Švarný O, et al. 1991-1993. *Gramatika Hovorové Čínštiny v Příkladech*, I-IV (*A Grammar of Spoken Chinese in Examples*, I-IV). Bratislava: Komenský University.

Švarný O, Uher D. 2014. *Prozodická Gramatika Čínštiny* (*A Prosodic Grammar of Chinese*). Olomouc: Palacký University.

Třísková H. 2011. Prozodická transkripce čínštiny O. Švarného: čtyři historické verze (O. Švarný´s prosodic trancription of Chinese: four subsequent versions). *Nový Orient*, 66.4: 45-50.

Třísková H. 2016. De-stressed words in Mandarin: drawing parallel with English. In: Tao H Y. *Integrating Chinese Linguistic Research and Language Teaching and Learning*. Amsterdam/Philadelphia: John Benjamins Publishing Company, 121-144.

Třísková H. 2017a. Acquiring and teaching Chinese pronunciation. In: Kecskes I. *Explorations into Chinese as a Second Language.* Cham: Springer International Publishing, 3-30.

Třísková H. 2017b. 普通话语音教学探究 (A Journey through the teaching of the sounds of Standard Chinese). In: College of Arts, Capital Normal University (首都师范大学文学院). 燕京论坛 2014 (*Yanjing Forum 2014*). Beijing: Social Sciences Academic Press, 243-279.

Třísková H. 2017c. De-stress in Mandarin: clitics, cliticoids, and phonetic chunks. In: Kecskes I, Sun C F. *Key Issues in Chinese as a Second Language Research.* New York & London: Routledge, 29-56.

Třísková H. 2020. Is the glass half-full, or half-empty? The alternative concept of stress in Mandarin Chinese (玻璃杯半满抑或半空？汉语重音的另类观). 韵律语法研究 (*Studies in Prosodic Grammar*) (第四辑), 2019 (2): 64-105. Beijing: Beijing Language and Culture University Press.

Třísková H. 2021. *Mluvte čínsky hezky: prozodie hovorové čínštiny (Speak Chinese with Ease: Prosody of Colloquial Chinese).* Praha: Academia Publishing House.

Uher D, et al. 2007. *Učebnice čínské konverzace I (Textbook of Chinese Conversation I).* Praha: Leda.

Uher D, et al. 2016. *Učebnice čínské konverzace II (Textbook of Chinese Conversation II).* Praha: Leda.

Uher D, Slamčníková T. 2019. *Oldřich Švarný: Prosodia Linguae Sinensis.* Special issue of the journal *Far East*, 9.1: 74-106. Available at https://kas.upol.cz/fileadmin/userdata/FF/katedry/kas/vav/dalny_vychod/archiv/Dalny_vychod_IX_1_2019_e_verze.pdf.

Wang Y J (王韫佳). 2016. 轻声规范和教学琐议 (A Discussion of the Standardization and Teaching of the Neutral Tone). 国际汉语教学研究 (*Journal of International Chinese Teaching*), 2: 26-35.

Wang Y J (王韫佳), Chu M (初敏). 2008. 关于普通话词重音的若干问题 (Some problems related to lexical stress in putonghua). 中国语音学报 (*Chinese Journal of Phonetics*), 1: 141-147. Beijing: The Commercial Press.

Wang Y J (王韫佳), Chu M (初敏), He L (贺琳), et al. 2003. 连续话语中双音节韵律词的重音感知 (The perception of stress in disyllabic prosodic words in connected Chinese). 声学学报 (*Acta Acoustica*), 28.6: 534-539.

Wang Z J (王志洁), Feng S L (冯胜利). 2006. 声调对比法与北京话双音组的重音类型 (Tonal contrast and disyllabic stress patterns in Beijing Mandarin). 语言科学 (*Linguistic Sciences*), 5.1: 3-22.

Yin Z Y (殷作炎). 1982. 关于普通话双音常用词轻重音的初步考察 (A preliminary study on stress patterns of common disyllabic words in putonghua). 中国语文 (*Studies of the Chinese Language*), 3: 168-173.

Zhang X R (张洵如). 1957. 北京话轻声词汇 (*A Dictionary of Neutral-tone Words in Pekinese*). Beijing: Zhonghua Book Company.

汉语韵律标注（CHIPROT）与韵律结构的预测

廖　敏

捷克科学院东方研究所

摘　要　本文介绍了一种称为 CHIPROT 的新的韵律标注方式（基于汉语拼音），它最初是为第二语言教学而设计的。它是一种用于标注自然语速口语体的普通话话语的工具。CHIPROT 也可用于标注"小模块"或语音块（2～3 个音节组成的短语）的突显模式。"小模块"借鉴了公式化语言（formulaic language）的概念。CHIPROT 标注有以下特征：1. 区分各个音节的突显程度（*ma*、*mā*、***mā***、***MĀ***）；2. 分节法（韵律词和韵律短语）。该系统的构设是在史瓦尔尼（Švarný）教授的系统及 Mandarin ToBI、C-ToBI 的启发下，基于对汉语轻重音的不同语音分析而完成的。CHIPROT 的核心概念是"常音节"和"弱音节"。笔者认为，韵律结构的许多特征（尤其是音节弱化）是可以预测的，这些预测可以用于标注过程中。CHIPROT 图形具有标志性和直观性。它已在教学实践中得到检验。本文介绍的最终版本已应用于最近出版的教科书中。不仅教师和教材编写者发现 CHIPROT 很好用，而且从事连续语音研究的语言学家也会发现它很有用。

关键词　汉语　普通话　语音学与音位学　韵律　韵律描写　汉语作为第二语言教学

Hana Třísková

Oriental Institute, the Czech Academy of Sciences, Prague

triskova@orient.cas.cz

第七期当代语音学与音系学高级研修班重音研究专题名家答问集锦

1. Ladd 教授答问集锦

1.1 第一段答问环节

问题 1：**Leben**[①] 曾提出，分析声调时最好将声调模式（如旋律）指派给语素而非载调单位（**Tone-bearing Unit，TBU**）。我想这一说法更适用于非洲语言的声调。请问您怎么看待这个观点？

Ladd（以下简称 L）：我认为这样并不存在什么矛盾。我认为讨论英语中的 "声调语素"（tonal morpheme）非常有意义。比如 "上升—下降—上升调" 在大多数情况下显然表达的是一种令人惊讶的疑问。因此，当我们说 "Sue!?" 和 "A driving instructor!?" 时，该声调序列可以称为声调语素。我对此没有任何异议，但事实是，声调语素的各个部分与音段字符串之间的系联方式存在明显的规律性。因此我和 Leben 的观点没有任何矛盾。很显然，非洲语言的每个声调系联在每个载调单位上，但我认为英语也是如此。关键是要弄清楚句调语素这一概念的深层含义是什么。之所以存在分歧是因为句调类型学总是在谈这个（语言）和那个（语言）相同或者不同：对声调语言来说很容易，如果 "父（fù）" 和 "服（fú）" 不同，我们就很容易得出 "二者是不同语素" 的结论；但对英语或任何其他的纯句调语言来说，我们很难说 "这是一种形式，那是另一种形式"。但正如我开始所提到的，Leben 的 "声调语素" 观与我说的 "声调是音系的一部分，需要对其进行逻辑分析" 之间基本没有矛盾。

---

① Leben W R. 1973. *Suprasegmental Phonology*. Ph.D. dissertation, MIT.

问题 2：语法调（grammatical tone）属于句调还是声调？

L：对我来说，语法调显然是声调。从某种意义上说，语法调表示的并非句子层面的含义，比如非洲语言的动词形式中用声调表时态、情态等。你可能会觉得这些更像是句子层面的范畴，只是被整合到了词的形态变化中。这种分析不合理，我认为应当将其视为对声调的运用，但这确实显示出类型学问题的复杂性。

问题 3：能否请您详细说明一下"语言学音高（linguistic pitch）"和"语言音高（language pitch）"之间的区别？

L：我不太确定二者有何区别。我理解中的语言学意义上的音高，是借助语音手段实现语言学目的或交际目的的。如果单纯看功能，很难说这样的语言看起来更像声调语言还是句调语言。但这究竟是句子层面的意义还是语法意义？我认为"语言学音高"和"语言音高"并非只是术语上的区分。

问题 4：汉语的曲折调与非洲语言的曲折声调有所不同。很多人将汉语的曲折调分析为两三个平调的组合，但我认为这两种曲折调还是应该彼此独立来看，对吗？

L：对此我没有什么具体立场。当初基于非洲语言研究发展出自主音段音系学时，由于这种形式化手段非常适合分析非洲语言，很多人希望将其应用到汉语、泰语等语言的曲折声调分析上。我们以"Ayò is coming"为例，显然"Ayò lo"上的高调与"Ayò"上的低调来源不同，其中一个具有标记主语位置上名词短语末尾的语法功能，另一个是人名"Ayò"的词汇调。就非洲语言而言，我们不会把那些语音变化当作一个独立的东西，而是将其看作一个由低音和高音组成的序列。无论你是否想把这种分析方法应用到汉语或泰语等语言，我们都不可能说"这部分是低调，那部分是高调"。这种分歧一直都有。无论如何，非洲语言音节上的音高变化的确是两个声调作用的结果，这种分析无懈可击。但是对东亚语言来说就非常牵强了，这样分析仍然缺乏理据。因此，我并非绝对将这两种声调视为彼此独立的系统，但必须说明的是，东亚语言和非洲语言的声调情况完全不同。

问题 5：可否请您举例说明，如何在自主音段理论框架下分析汉语的词调和句调边界？

L：句调边界处有助词，基本都是轻声助词，然后在上面附加我所说的句调性的边界调（intonational edge tone）。汉语可能出现句末没有助词的情况，比如

Chang在1958年发表的一篇有关成都方言音系的文章中谈到的例子①。但我的意思是，汉语中大量的句子特别是疑问句的句末都有助词，边界调就附着在句末。不过也许你可以想出一些疑问句，这些例子通过句调表达疑问却没有句末助词，我们可以看看末尾音节的音高会发生什么变化，这就是 Chang 讨论的现象。

问题 6：形态类型是否是影响语言韵律类型的一个因素？

L：类型学的问题在于很多人不相信类型学是一个有用的研究对象，但形态确实存在于一些语言中。有些语言的形态极其复杂，而有些语言基本没有形态。韵律类型也是如此，有些语言使用音高，有些语言不用。因此我们能从类型学研究中学习到多少东西，这是个好问题。我认为做类型学研究，是一种有用的练习。但它可能无法告知我们所有的答案，只能给出可能的范围是什么。然而对那些坚信无论哪种语言都有某种普遍特征的人来说，类型之间存在差异可能是个问题。但我认为，形态类型和韵律类型可能会以某种方式相互作用，比如形态的存在可能会影响语法调的使用。举例来说，非洲语言的声调形态及其实现方式可能就与其形态类型有关，东亚语言中没有类似现象，因为东亚语言没那么多形态变化。就你的问题而言，这不是一个非常令人满意的答案，但值得讨论。

问题 7：请问有没有什么范式或模型，可以用来研究诸如汉语普通话等语言的声调和句调的调型互动？

L：有。事实上许毅的模型就是这样的，问题是这个模型对所有语言都进行类似汉语的处理。因此，对汉语来说许毅的模型是个好模型，是基于他对汉语声调、句调的研究而开发的。许毅认为这个模型可以以某种方式延伸应用到所有语言，我觉得行不通。他的基本思想是每个音节都有声调赋值，而声调赋值本身会受强调句调或句法层面其他基本特征（非词汇特征或语法特征）的影响，这些想法是可行的。他的研究重点是构建语音模型。

问题 8：从音系学层面来看，在什么情况下我们就必须将某个声调序列（例如汉语的"第一声＋第三声"）分析为一个相对凸显结构（例如"高低调"或是"扬抑格"）？

L：无论我们能否讨论汉语的相对凸显，这都是一个我很想了解的问题。大家可以做这方面的研究，因为你们有关于相对凸显的母语直感，可以判断汉语双

---

① Chang N-C T. 1958. Tones and intonation in the Chengtu dialect (Szechuan, China). *Phonetica*, 2: 59-85.

音词的抑扬和扬抑。汉语普通话中有成千上万的双音词。传统的汉语语言学理论区分"字"和"词"，但从实际应用角度而言，这些双音节的"词"才是独立词。因此我们可以去思考哪些是抑扬格、哪些是扬抑格，在座的各位都有母语语感，我对此知之甚少。

1.2　第二段答问环节

问题 1：音段和超音段是两个不同的方面，但也有交集。关于二者的交集部分，学界是否有一个特定的名称或定义？

L： 我认为，这种区分不太有用，因为音段和超音段概念可以说是欧洲语言的功能，但欧洲语言使用音高的方式与声调语言不同。因此，他们认为，先是有一串音段，然后才是其他（如超音段的）东西，这对说欧洲语言的人而言是非常自然的。但对汉语尤其是中古以来的汉语而言，显然音高和元音音质的组合方式更为复杂。因此我们无须担心音段和超音段的区别，这很可能是基于欧洲语言而进行的区分。

问题 2：重音是否必须固定在韵律结构（如音节或更大的单位）中？

L： 我认为重音本身不是独立的，而是韵律结构的一个方面。重音语言的韵律结构同样有其核心结构，即一强一弱的对比。

问题 3：除了轻声音节之外，汉语中如何定义"音节重量"呢？是通过音高还是连读变调模式？

L： 有些语言并不区分音节重量，可能汉语就是这样。我认为，不存在如何定义"音节重量"的问题，除非你认为音节重量是人类语言的普遍属性。这些东西可能并没有人们想象的那么普遍。

问题 4：请问，重读是元音重读还是音节重读？

L： 我不知道，可以把重音看成是在元音上，但我认为把它看成是整个音节如何融入一个相对凸显的结构可能更合理。（译者按：当谈论某个结构节律的相对凸显时，用音节可能更容易理解。）

问题 5：是什么原则使得"强—弱"成为一个单位或基本结构？

L： 我没有一种更概括的理论来解释。层次结构的概念在语言学中被广泛运用，特别是在句法和形态中，我的建议是它也适用于音系。

1.3　第三段答问环节

问题 1：这是不是说明重音在某种程度上也是心理语言学的结构体？

L：这当然也是看问题的一种角度。我想问的是，如何在心理语言学和语音学之间划清界限？在某种意义上，它们都是心理语言学。问题是，在我们的母语中，重音是我们从韵律结构的组合方式中推导出来的，就好比我们推导句法关系一样。当我们听自己的母语时，因为母语中存在着句法上的歧义结构，所以我们听到的可能是这种或那种结构；重音也可能存在歧义性，即可以听到这种或另一种组合方式。但重音不仅仅是指某个音节比别的音节更强，重音是必须根据语言中的音系和韵律结构来感知的东西。你可以说重音在某种程度上是心理语言学的结构体。我想我的说法会有些不同，相同的是你不能单纯根据某个音节的特定语音属性就认为该音节是重读音节。你还必须意识到，我们感知重音的方式与我们感知语言结构的其他抽象方面（包括句法歧义）的方式相同。这不是一个简单的关系。这也是为什么我认为"将词重音和句重音看成同一现象的一部分"这一观点是合理的。

问题 2：句重音的范域与相应的句法范域有关系吗？比如在罗马尼亚语这两个句子①中，可以说第一句的句重音在 VP 而第二句的句重音在 PP 或 DP 吗？

L：这是个好问题。总的来说，韵律范域和句法范域之间存在着较为紧密的对应关系，这是一个独立的研究领域。在我看来，很多研究都是基于句法的，并没有太多研究关注我们所谈论的关于韵律方面的一些问题。毫无疑问，句法与韵律结构的现象有着密切的关系，但具体是什么关系则很难描述。正如我所说的，因为大多数关于这个问题的研究对韵律结构的语音方面都不是很感兴趣。我不同意他们的一些观点，韵律范域和句法范域之间肯定存在着某种关系。

问题 3：可以假设人们对自己母语有一种感知重音的方式，而对外语有另一种感知重音的方式吗？

L：在二语语音习得的各个方面，你在第一语言学到的东西会影响你能在第

---

① o　　sǎ venim la voi?
将来时 我们 - 来　到 你
"我们到你家来好吗？"
版本 1：我们到你家来好不好？
版本 2：我们到你家来（还是别的地方）？

二语言中学到的东西。显然，很多人对第二语言的掌握程度非常高。一般来说，对于二语习得者，由于受到母语的影响，肯定有些东西比其他东西更难改变。所以，学习第二语言的时候，暂时先不管那些难以改变的东西，可能学得更容易一些。我认为感知重音的能力或许真的很难习得，特别是感知如希腊语与俄语中的一些带有低调的重音。我只能说这么多。但是我对"第一语言和第二语言存在绝对的界限"这一说法存疑。有些东西容易改变，而另一些东西比较难改变。但是我可以告诉你，在使用上述报告中的例子测试欧洲人时，他们都没能正确地感知重音。因此，从语言学研究中的实践角度来看，田野调查报告里关于重音位置的内容可能是错误的，或者至少很大可能是错误的。我们不应该将关于其他语言重音的田野调查的结论当作绝对正确的。因此，在重音方面肯定存在很多经验性的问题，而人们并没有过多地考虑这些问题。

1.4　第四段答问环节

问题 1：在音高或语调研究中如何定义 **H/L**？

L：这确实是人们长期以来一直在思考或感到困惑的问题，但就音高而言，关键在于不同的人有不同的嗓音。最明显的是，成年男性、成年女性和儿童的嗓音不同。正因如此，语音的高和低只是相对的概念。它必须是相对于说话者的音高范域而言的，这一有趣的问题与言语感知、言语心理学和语音学有关。不知为何，我们总是可以识别出一个给定的音高是如何与说话者的音域相关联的。明显的例子是，如果我试着用中文说"吃"，你能识别出我的声调是正确的，因为那已经接近我的最高音域了。但是，如果女性发出相同的音高（大概 150 赫兹），就会听起来很低。我们是如何做到这一点的？这是一个非常有趣的语音问题，但不是语言学问题。从语言学的角度看，如果一种语言具有平调，我们就有可能根据词汇的不同来研究声调的高低。例如，在约鲁巴语（Yorùbá）中，有一个带有两个中调的词和一个带有两个低调的词：

（1）īgbā　[mid – mid (M-M)] "200"

　　　ìgbà　[low – low (L-L)] "time"[①]

---

① 示例出处：Caldwell-Harris C L, Lancaster A, Ladd D R, et al. 2015. Factors influencing sensitivity to lexical tone in an artificial language: implications for second language learning. *Studies in Second Language Acquisition*, 37: 335-357.

如果我们把这两个词放在一起听，很容易听出"ī gbā"的音高比"ì gbà"高。在像约鲁巴语这样的声调语言中，人们听辨声调时不必把词放在一起。在某种程度上，我们可以听出"ì gbà"的音高在说话人调域的底部，而"ī gbā"在音域中部，而且并不存在一个高调的"í gbá"（假如真的有这样的词，我们也能够听辨出来）。不管怎么说，这在语音学中是个非常有趣的问题。从语言学角度来看，在声调语言中，基于词义的不同我们可以分辨清楚；在没有词调的语言中，会发生什么呢？两位荷兰研究者（Collier 和 't Hart）在语调音系学方面做了很多有趣的研究。他们指出："音高变化最基本的层面是较高音高与较低音高之间的差异"，"口语旋律的特点是音高在较高与较低之间的不断交替变换"。[①] 他们认为，音会在一些位置上升到一个较高水平，然后会在另一些位置下降到一个较低水平，比如荷兰语或英语。他们认为，我们可以从音系的角度来讨论语调，它只是音高层面高与低的区别。但最初的问题（"我们对此如何定义？"）在很多方面都遇到了困难。现在，如果我们假设对语调的音系描述是基于音高的高与低，并且如果我们把高与低看作自主音段（auto-segments），那么我们的任务即是去确定：音高层面的高与低出现在音段序列的哪个位置？什么语音因素决定这些高与低的实际音高等级？自 40 年前从自主音段的角度对语调进行分析以来，众多学者对这类问题做了很多研究。但回到最初的问题，这也绝对是谈论音高时的一个基本问题。这涉及言语感知和心理学层面，是普遍性的语言学问题，回答这些问题需要涉及具体的语音因素。所有这些都需要研究，而且确有不少学者正在从这个角度对语调进行探索。

问题 2：元音和音节哪一个承载重音？

L：我认为，简单来说，重音模式是附加在音节之上的，且通常是根据音节来计算的。但是我们探讨重音模式的时候往往都会说承重元音，其原因在于以下两点。首先从语音上看，元音可能是音节中仅有的声带发声的部分。例如英语中的音节"pop"，我们唯一能听到音高重音和音强的部分就在其中的元音上。所以很多重音的语音线索在声带发声时才能被听到，而且元音也可能是仅有的声带发声的部分。其次从音系上看，我们会把元音当作音节的核心，所以如果"重音"

---

① Collier R, 't Hart J. 1981. *Cursus Nederlandse Intonatie*. Louvain: Acco/De Horstink. 英文翻译参见：Ladd D R. 2008. *Intonational Phonology* (2nd ed.). Cambridge: Cambridge University Press.

指的是韵律结构中的核心位置，它就会落在元音上。

如果重音是音系上的中心，其音系和层级结构示例如下 [①]：

（2）

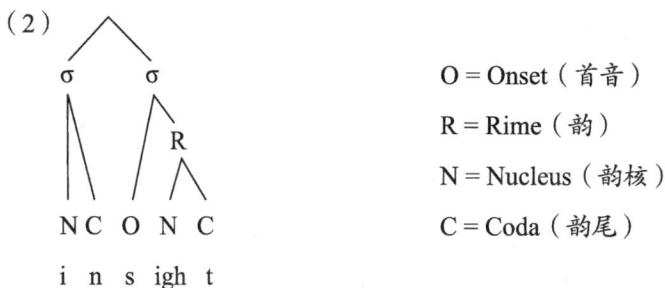

```
          σ       σ
          |      / \
          |     /   R
          |    |   / \
          N C  O  N   C
          i n  s igh  t
```

O = Onset（首音）
R = Rime（韵）
N = Nucleus（韵核）
C = Coda（韵尾）

在（2）中，"insight" 一词的第一个音节是这个成分的中心。对于 "insight" 这样一个有两个音节的词，我们会说其中一个音节强而另一个音节弱，强音节就是这个成分的中心，即重音音节。这是对重音现象的抽象定义。现在，如果我们以这种方式思考音系结构，我们将会得出一个很深的层级结构，其中每个音节的结构都相同。以音节 "sight" 为例，英语中的传统术语称为 "onset"（音首）和 "rhyme"（韵腹）。"音首" 和 "韵腹" 大致与汉语中的 "声母" 和 "韵母" 相对应。在韵腹中，有韵核和韵尾。在上面的例子中，我们可以说音首和韵腹是弱—强关系，且韵腹是音节的中心。具体来说，韵腹中的韵核是音节的中心。示例如下 [②]：

（3）

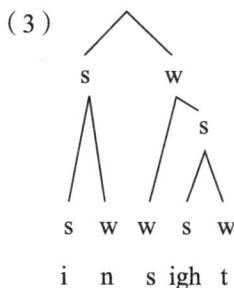

```
          s        w
         / \      / \
        /   \    /   s
        |    |   |  / \
        s    w   w s   w
        i    n   s igh  t
```

我们可以说在音节层面上有一个强音节和一个弱音节。但是在其中的重音音节中，我们也可以把元音看作最强的成分或者是音节成分的中心。也就是说，即使从音系的角度来看，我们可能也会考虑使用重音元音的说法而不是重音音节。但我认为，简单来说，重音系统基本上以音节为基础，因此使用重音音节的说法可能更准确。当然学者们之前使用重音元音的说法也是有原因的。

①② 示例出处：Ladd D R. 1986. Intonational phrasing: the case for recursive prosodic structure. *Phonology Yearbook*, 3: 311-340.

问题3：除了轻声音节外，汉语的"音节重量"如何定义？是根据声调的音高还是变调模式？

L：前几天我没怎么讲到音节重量的问题，现在也不打算讲。整个音节结构问题本身就是一个话题。需要注意的是，音节重量的定义会因语言的不同而不同。一个音节在一种语言中被认为是重音节，但在另一种语言中可能会被认为是轻音节。或者在一些语言中可能有三种不同程度的音节重量：轻音节、重音节和超重音节。或者音节重量在一些语言中可能不重要，有很多语言只将"CV"作为音节，而音节的轻重没有区别。因此重要的是，音节重量是一个特征，而不同的语言可以有不同的情况。在语言中，它经常与词重音的规则相关联。例如，在许多语言中，如果有重音节和轻音节的区别，并且有词重音，那么词重音可能落在重音节上。如果一个词只有轻音节，那么词重音会落在其他某个地方，但重量可能与重音有关；在一种没有重音或者可能没有重音的语言中，例如常被提及的汉语，也许音节的轻重并不是一个重要的概念。但我认为，很难判断汉语中音节重量是否重要，如果重要，你如何定义它？

问题4：如果说词缀等音段可以作为形态标记，那么理论上，超音段也可以在形态学中发挥作用。那么，我们是否可以说，韵律不仅制约着形态，而且韵律本身也是一种构词过程？例如：形—名短语"小 / 工厂"是可以说的，但名—名复合词"金 / 工厂"通常不可以说。但有一些可以，取决于语义 / 语法关系，例如"金 / 项链"。

L：这里我重点关注的是韵律的音系本质。韵律在许多方面具有语法功能，有很多值得讨论的地方，需要考虑不同的理论因素。还有很多其他方面的因素，它们基本上是语法的、句法的、形态的，而不是音系的。我不认为韵律是一种形态过程，但我并没有真正思考过形态学，值得注意的是，在很多语言中，复合构词问题都与韵律有关。"金工厂"和"金项链"之间有所区别的这一事实也体现在英语中，例如"'steel warehouse"和"steel 'warehouse"。有很多类似这样的事实，但在我看来，这主要是一个语法问题，而不是一个音系问题。在英语中，这个复合词是强—弱还是弱—强？我认为这不在音系学的研究范围内。如果我们继续观察它的构词，我们可以说，如果它是强—弱，它很可能有某种语法关系；如果它是弱—强，它很可能有另一种语法关系。但是音系和语法问题之间的互动我还没有谈及过，也没有做过深入思考。当然，这是我们可以对整个问题进行讨论的一个方面。对语法和形态句法更感兴趣的人可能会朝这个方向发展。我对这些人想说的唯一一件事就是"请确保你们也掌握了音系学"。

问题5：我还是有点儿不明白重音和声调之间的关系。是否可以说重音（无论是词重音还是短语重音）是语调的一部分，但是语调和词汇声调在声调语言里是两回事？

L：每个人都对此感到困惑！我不同意"重音是语调的一部分，但语调和词汇声调在声调语言中是独立的东西"。我认为重要的是要明白语调指代句子层级的特征，重音和声调（在各自有重音和声调的语言中）指代词汇层级的特征。这里根本的理论问题是词与句子的关系，而不仅仅是韵律。在声调语言中，音高既具有区别词义的功能，又具有区别句子层级的功能。像英语这样的语言只有词重音，没有词汇声调，而重音同时在词汇层面和句子层面发挥作用。就像我说的，我更倾向于把语调看作句子层级的特征。换句话说，我不把语调和音高等同起来，因为区分二者可以让我们更好地区别句子层级特征和词汇层级特征。很明显，当你讨论类似复合词这样的现象时，任何一个理论都会涉及它是一个词还是短语这样的根本问题。

1.5　第五段答问环节

问题："他在煮饭？"中句尾"饭"的语调确实有轻微的上升，但是我不明白为什么"他在煮饭吗？"中的"在"上升得更高？

L：这是一个很好的问题。观察这类音高变化轨迹是一个很重要的视角。音高轨迹不一定与我们听到的相对应，特别是你可以看到在这两种句子类型中（"他在煮饭？"和"他在煮饭吗？"），第二个音节"在"的末尾部分对应"煮"的开始部分。需要注意的是，我们发音的时候能发出各种各样的阻塞音，就像音节"煮"开始部分的辅音，因此音高轨迹很可能是不可靠的，或者至少可以说，音高轨迹很可能与你通常听不到的东西相对应。重要的是要知道这些并不能证明音高的音系特征，它可能只是证明在这种情况下自动提取音高的难度。

1.6　第六段答问环节

问题1：我不知道罗马尼亚语的核心重音规则是什么，"我们可以／不可以到

你那里去吗？"的调形是基于陈述句"我们会去你那里"的核心重音调形吗？

L：不，事实并非如此。在希腊语、罗马尼亚语和俄语以及东欧的大量语言中，是非问句的核心重音在动词上；而在陈述句中，核心重音通常在句末。这实际上是具有语言学意义的不同。在我看来，谈论语调和重音时普遍有一种强烈的倾向，即假设语调有自然性和普遍性。这或许是正确的。当人们因为兴奋或者愤怒提高他们的声音时，可能会存在一些普遍现象。这可能是人类共性，但是我无法确切知道这如何运作或者这意味着什么。从语音学上来看，它可能因语言而异。一旦你遇到像焦点、疑问句和强调等内容，那么感觉上是普遍的事情往往最后会被证实并非如此。随着我们对未充分研究的语言观察得越多，就越会意识到语言的运作方式不尽相同，语调方面亦是如此。所以我认为这是一个很好的课题，有待你们去研究。我所介绍的研究语调的路径的一个优点是，我们可以允许具体语言的不同，而不去假设每个人用同样的方式做同样的事情。

问题 2：英语的不同变体可能有自己的不同的语调模式吗？

L：这是一个好问题。几乎可以肯定的是在大不列颠和爱尔兰北部，正常陈述语调的某些特征不同于其他地域变体。如果你观察一些语音细节，你会发现某一特定变体可能有轻微的语音细节上的不同。但一般而言，对英语语调进行总体概括还是合理的。和汉语相比，英语的变体肯定要少一些。仅仅因为"英语是这样""法语是这样"是不够的，语言在任何层面上都可以有变体。我想指出的是，仅仅因为英语以这种方式运作或者汉语以那种方式运作并不意味着所有语言的运作方式都是一样的。我希望这是足够清楚的。但确实存在某些语言变体，它们的语调模式可能会有所不同。

问题 3：在罗马尼亚语中，高调不一定会和焦点一起出现，这是真的吗？

L：是的，在疑问句中，高调不是焦点。

问题 4：我一直在研究汉语的重音，所以其他人所遇到的问题我们也遇到了。看起来每个人都知道轻音在哪里，但是当你谈论重音时，人们就犹豫了。所以如果我知道哪一个音是轻的，那么下一个音必然是重的；但是如果你问一个人哪一个是重音，他们就犹豫了。与之相应的观点认为，相对凸显的模式是韵律结构。因此如果你运用音系的方式，通过增强去实现相对凸显，或者通过其他手段（使得声音变得更长或者更强）去使得一个音节比另一个音节更加凸显，你就成功构建了韵律结构。在汉语中我们是怎样做的呢？我们不是用同样的方式，而是用另一种方式。我们减少一个音节的力量，使另一个音节与这个音节不同。我们不是在创造凸显的东西，而是在创造非凸显的东西，这个想法与罗马尼亚语焦点的例子完全一样。我们使用一种"低音策略"来实现韵律结构或韵律的组织。我想请您评论一下这种做法。

L：我对你说的这些很感兴趣。我认为，重要的是要认识到强—弱模式①或者弱—强模式是一种抽象的关系，它不一定意味着任何语音上的声学要素②。在英语和欧洲许多语言中，弱—强是无标记性的句子重音模式。弱—强可以是中和模式，可以体现在非常具体的强成分上。比如"five dollars"的重音模式既可以是中和的，也可以集中在强的成分上③。关键是在某种程度上，这两种都算作弱—强模式。而在Mark Liberman的研究中，"five dollars"总是特殊的、有标记的④。首先，这种实现方式的非对称性是很重要的。我想说的是，在汉语中有一个双音节的短语是很正常的。你会得到我所说的弱—强关系。这也意味着它们都得到了一个完整的声调。然而你在第二个成分上得到一个所谓的轻声，那就是"强—弱"模式。另外，我们发现在英语中同样存在这种不对称性。我认为重要的是要记住这种不对称性，而且这种不对称性在所有语言中的运作方式可能不一样。凸显的概念看似是一种中性的语音学描述，事实并非如此。值得注意的是，什么被视为凸显在很大程度上取决于语言的音系。因此，在罗马尼亚语或希腊语的疑问句中，一个具有低调的音节可以算作凸显。

问题5：我读过 **Myrberg** 和 **Riad** 在 2015 年发表的一篇关于瑞典语中韵律层级的论文⑤。他们在不同的范畴中分析了词重音和语调之间的相互作用：韵律词、韵律短语和语调短语。您如何看待这种方法？韵律层级是否可以通用于所有语言

① Liberman M. 1975. *The Intonational System of English*. Ph.D. dissertation, MIT.
　　Liberman M, Prince A. 1977. On stress and linguistic rhythm. *Linguistic Inquiry*, 8.2: 249-336.
② Ladd D R. 2008. *Intonational Phonology* (2nd ed.). Cambridge: Cambridge University Press.
　　Ladd D R. 2013. An integrated view of phonetics, phonology, and prosody. In: Arbib M A. *Language, Music, and the Brain: A Mysterious Relationship*. Cambridge: MIT Press.
③ Ladd D R. 2014. *Simultaneous Structure in Phonology*. Oxford: Oxford University Press.
④ Ladd D R. 1983. Even, focus, and normal stress. *Journal of Semantics*, 2.2: 157-170.
⑤ Myrberg S, Riad T. 2015. The prosodic hierarchy of Swedish. *Nordic Journal of Linguistics*, 38.2: 115-147.

（包括汉语）？

L：我认为韵律层级是另一种情况，人们采取了一种有趣的方法，并假定它必须是普遍的。我认为没有任何理由认为韵律层级是普遍的。韵律层级的概念似乎是相当有用的，但是我没有看到任何关于所有语言建立相同韵律层级的理由。至于瑞典语中的词重音，我自己的看法和 Bruce Morén-Duolljá 一样，他认为这根本就不是真正的声调重调，只是抽象的韵律结构的变化影响了声调的语调实现 [①]。这也是我没有谈论这个问题的部分原因，这本身就是一个完全独立的话题。我认为某种层级结构可能是普遍的，但我怀疑是否存在一个适用于所有语言的韵律层级结构。汉语中显然有这样的层级结构。比如"* 鞋工厂"和"皮鞋厂"（该例子为译者添加），可以是 [2+1] 结构，但不能是 [1+2] 结构。所有这些都涉及韵律结构以及与所讨论的语义和语用方面的互动。但是，存在一个普遍的层级结构的想法似乎是很可能的。如果层级结构的细节是相同的，我也不会感到惊讶。

2. Archangeli 教授答问集锦

2.1 第一段答问环节

问题 1：正如您之前提到的，人们所使用的语音并非离散的，而是连续的。那么您是否能举一个具体的例子来支持这一观点呢？

Archangeli（以下简称 A）：在我们说话的时候，如果我们看一下话语的语音方式，比如某个人正在发"memory（记忆）"这个词的音，我们会把"memory（记忆）"这个词看作 [m][e][m][ə][r][i]，所以这个词至少有六个音段。但是如果你看一下语音强度，会发现这些音段之间没有间歇。如果你看一下嘴部的发音动作，我们不会让 m 的发音动作自发地去到下一个发音位置，而是以一种连续的姿态在口腔中从一个特定的位置移动到下一个位置。所以这就是我认为的语音的连续属性类型。

---

① Morén-Duolljá B T. 2013. The prosody of Swedish underived nouns: no lexical tones required. *Nordlyd*, 40.1: 196-248.

问题 2：这种模型如何为语言变化留下空间？通过随机性吗？

A：哦，是的！如果大家熟悉 Juliette Blevins 的研究[①]，就会知道语言的变化很多时候是以演化音系的形式发生。作者的观点是，当人们听错或者分析错误时，就会发生语言的变化。因此，上一代人以一种方式分析，而下一代人则以另一种方式进行分析[②]。一个很好的例子是 Robert Kennedy 的研究[③]，他研究了多种语言中的重叠现象。研究表明，在不同的相关语言中，对重叠现象的形式分析是相当不同的。但当你考虑到重音系统和非重音词末尾元音中所发生的情况（末尾元音变得更加低沉，很多甚至完全消失）时，则将会发生如下情况：上一代人将某个元音分析为清音，而下一代人则会分析为不存在这个元音。在第一代人中得到一个重音，在第二代人中则会得到末尾重音，同时相应地进行了复制变化。因此，形式系统是相当不同的，当你观察语言变化的步骤时，很容易看出其中的规律。

我认为这个模型对人们学习多语的情况也处理得很好。因为在这个模型中，存在形态集合群：若一个形态集合被标记为英语，另一个形态集合则会被标记为普通话或者其他任何语言。我认为，有些人的语言学习实际上有那么一个阶段要同时面对母语和外语。我在学习其他语言时会遇到困难，因为我会将正在学习的语言和其他我之前学过的、但仅停留在使用一些词的水平的第三种语言相混淆（因为它不是英语，我也不知道我正在学习的语言中的这个词的意思），所以这个模型很完美地处理了双语（diglossia）以及第二语言、第三语言习得的情况〔因为它为说话者或学习者提供了一种可能性，使他们在一生中都有可能习得（其他语言），并简单地给事物贴上不同的标签，而不是试图建立完全独立的系统〕。

问题 3：我们如何对"both-ok"的情况进行定义或详细地解释？例如在哈萨克语中，"**Bala-lar**"和"**Bala-dar**（儿童，复数）"都可以。"**-lar**"和"**-dar**"在同一个形态集合中，出现的频率相似。我的意思是，我们如何更准确地阐述这

① Blevins, J. 2015. Evolutionary phonology: a holistic approach to sound change typology. In: Honeybone P, Salmons J. *Handbook of Historical Phonology*. Oxford: Oxford University Press, 485-500.

② Baker A, Archangeli D, Mielke J. 2011. Variability in American English s-retraction suggests a solution to the actuation problem. *Language Variation and Change*, 23: 347-374.

③ Kennedy R. 2008. Evidence for morphoprosodic alignment in reduplication. *Linguistic Inquiry*, 39.4: 589-614.

个问题？

A：在这种情况下，似乎会发生各种抽象的事情，而没有具体的数据可查。我认为，一个人使用词语的频率会根据他最近听到的东西而有所不同。因此，除非高频使用使形态发生改变，否则一个人不会更改最高频形态或最低频形态的使用规约。因为形态出现的频率会改变，所以如果由于某种原因多次输入"-lar"，那么你就更可能使用"-lar"而不是"-dar"。因为"-lar"的使用频率上升了。你也会遇到这样一种情况：由于你自己开始听到更多的"-dar"，你开始更多地使用"-dar"。如果两者的出现/使用频率都差不多，那么可能还有其他因素。有一个关于这类情况的研究，研究表明人们更有可能使用对话者正在使用的语法结构，所以这也可能会受到与之交谈的人的影响。

我认为这是一个非常好的话题，可以探索更多的事实，并在涌现模型（Emengency Model）下可以形成一篇论文。因为我认为这个模型具有发展前景，且可以为这种现象提供一个合理的解释。

问题 4：同样的表达在不同语言中有双语标签，有些标签是相互排斥的，若某人掌握不同的语言，标签的使用是否有等级（或先后）顺序？

A：我不太确定这个问题到底在问什么，我按照我的理解来回答。我们确实存在双语的情况，所以在第一语言和第二语言之间有一个（优先）等级。我想这是一个关于语码转换的重要问题。尽管我没有自己去做这方面的研究，但我认为这个模型确实可以用来处理语码转换。有一篇来自亚利桑那大学的论文，是 Essa Alfaifi 2020 年写的，标题是 *An Emergent Grammar Model for the Linguistic Notion of Diglossia in Arabic and Faifi*[①]，文中就谈到了这点。该文谈论的是两种相似但不同的语言，它们在不同的社会背景下使用，一种是在家里使用，另一种是在专业的工作场所中使用。所以有许多词都有两个标签。随着年龄的增长，你会变得更加熟练，就会知道在不同语境中使用哪一个标签更加高效。小孩子上学后有一个阶段习惯于在学校使用家里的语言。所以这就是关键的一点，即他们的选择有一个（优先）等级，小孩子更倾向于使用家里的语言，因为他们更熟悉这种语言，但是当他们逐渐适应正式的表达后，他们就能够更有效地运用这些正式表达了。

---

① Alfaifi E. 2020. *An Emergent Grammar Model for the Linguistic Notion of Diglossia in Arabic and Faifi*. Ph.D. dissertation, The University of Arizona.

我认为，这个问题中所描述的情况与语言语码转换有关，不同于我们提到的双语的使用情况。我在香港时有很多这样的经历：我可以在一个群体中听到不同成员在讲着普通话、粤语和英语，他们使用这些语言的熟练程度也不同，但是每个人似乎都能够听懂别人的话，并且每个人都在使用这三种语言来谈论他们所说的内容。这些不同的语言听起来有相当不同的变化。这很有趣，但遗憾的是我听不懂粤语和普通话，所以我无法参与对话。但是听到这些人在通过不同语言进行谈话时所做出的适应与调节，是十分有趣的。我认为这可能是存在某种（优先）等级，即倾向于用一种语言的术语而不是另一种语言的，即使你通常使用后者。

2.2　第二段答问环节

问题1：涌现理论（Emergency Theory）是由最简方案和优选论（OT）发展而来的吗？

A：有趣的是，当我在不同场合发表关于涌现理论的讲演时，我从听众那里得到两种普遍的反馈。第一种反馈是：涌现是基于最简方案的音系学。在某种程度上，我完全同意这点。而另一种反馈是：你现在跳到了功能主义，不再做关于生成（音系学）的内容了。在某种程度上，我也赞同。但是我认为我正在做的仍然是一个生成（音系学）的模型。只不过这种生成来自一个不同的领域，不同于优选论或者传统生成音系学。关于如何开始这样的研究是有一些历史缘故的，我们的首篇论文发表于2010年，已经有一段时间了。

问题2：请问您思考过双语的相关问题吗？我来自马来西亚，有时在分析或者解释这种情况时感到非常困难。因为在马来西亚，我们会说多种语言。我们接触不同的语言，学习和使用不同的语言。这个模型在构建时考虑过双语或者多语的情况吗？

A：是的，就像我说的，我只参与过一个研究双语的项目。那项研究给出的结论是，有些词项被标记为属于某种语言，比如来自马来西亚就会有英语、马来语和母语（每个人的母语不尽相同）三种语言。

我认为，当儿童正在学习这三种不同的语言并在其词库中输入这些词项时，当他们输入诸如"table"这样的词，"table"在英语中会有一个写着"[英语]"的小标签；在马来语中会有写着"[马来语]"的标签；母语中的"table"一词也会有一个标签，以此表示它在母语中是什么。学习者会发现这里有三种不同的语言，他们会将这些不同语言贴上不同的标签，这也是他们语言学习的一部分。

这可能不是完美的，他们可能弄错标签，或者有一些词项没有被贴上标签，所以他们可以在三种语言背景下或者类似的情况下使用这些词项。但我认为，他们是在特定背景下学习语言的，因此特定的词项被确定为与特定的语言相关。

现在，在某些情况下，可能没有必要把所有的东西都贴上某种语言的标签。比如你在处理一种有声调的语言，以及另一种有重音的语言，那么你在处理声调时的任何相关条件可能都与重音语言无关，反之亦然。因此，这些条件可能不需要总是贴上某种语言的标签，因为也许音系系统的属性可以帮助你区分哪些条件与哪些语言相关。我昨天提到的那篇论文① 讨论的是一种特殊类型的双语。在那篇论文中，两种语言之间有很多相似的词汇和语法，但是不完全重合。

问题 3：只有表层—实体的候选者（形态集合），没有 **UR**（底层表征），没有 **GEN**（生成器），这是很具体的，自由变体可以成为固定表达吗？

A：我想这个问题的意思是（但我不太确定）我们能否取消自由变体，使我们最终只有一种形式，而不是在多种形式之间变化。我认为，是的，这取决于频率。

自儿时起，英语中的"either"我只说 [iðɚ] 这种形式。那时我住在英国的殖民地，当时叫罗德西亚。然后我搬到赞比亚，那里刚刚独立。它也曾是英国的殖民地，那里的人说 [aɪðɚ]。为了和同学们打成一片，我在学校说 [aɪðɚ]，在家里说 [iðɚ]，很快我的兄弟姐妹们也开始说 [aɪðɚ]，因为他们在学校也这么说。很快，我们都在家里说 [aɪðɚ] 和 [iðɚ]。而现在在大多时候我又说 [iðɚ] 了。所以我的说话方式根据身边经常出现的情况而改变，由于某种表达经常出现在所处的环境中，我个人说话的语境也发生了变化，因此，我又改变了我的表达方式。我认为，变体可以成为固定的表达，这主要与谈话者在所处环境中经常接触的表达有关。

问题 4：涌现模型是否改变了您对词汇音系学的看法？例如，音系、形态和句法如何相互作用？

A：这是一个很好的问题。我一直在想这个问题，但是我至今没有答案。我目前的发现是，使用涌现模型分析音系更为简单。因此，在我看来，实际上具有

---

① Alfaifi E. 2020. *An Emergent Grammar Model for the Linguistic Notion of Diglossia in Arabic and Faifi*. Ph.D. dissertation, The University of Arizona.

仅限于某些形态的合格条件，或适用于某些形态类的形态集合关系，这些可能会代替词汇音系学中的层级，以此使得整个系统变得更加简单（仅需要合格条件与形态集合关系）。所以我想这已经改变了我的看法，但是我还没有发表论文去说明我研究至此的原因。

2.3　第三段答问环节

问题 1：请您再解释一下，为什么 [sɪt] 和 [sɪɾ] 在形式上能够与 [goʊ] 和 [wɛnt] 相提并论呢？

A：在时间上或在语法的发展上，这些形态集合，如 [sɪt] 和带有闪音的 [sɪɾ]、[goʊ] 和 [wɛnt] 是同一类型的东西，即在儿童或学习者还未在词尾 t 和词尾闪音之间建立系统联系之前的早期习得阶段。当学习者第一次学习这个时，必须能够识别出足够多的形态集合（如这两个词尾之间的联系），为此学习者才能明白他 / 她在这里获得了一个模型。所以一开始只是两种不相关的形式，就像 [goʊ] 和 [wɛnt] 一样是两种不相关的形式。然而，随着学习者年龄的增长，以及习得更多的内容，当 [sɪt] 中的"t"和 [sɪɾ] 中的闪音"ɾ"的关系被识别，就变成了一个不同类型的形式。这种观点得到了形态集合关系的支持[①]。在这个时间点上，"t"和闪音"ɾ"的底层表征关系被识别，而后所有闪音"ɾ"类的形态集合类型都会发生变化，但由于 go 类 {goʊ, wɛnt PAST} 与 knife 类 {nɑɪf, nɑɪv PLRAL} 中没有系统的联系，因此它们不会发生这种变化。

问题 2：我们是否需要引入一种新的约束来改变优选论（OT）中的和谐级别？

A：但这就变得复杂了，并且这与"和谐应该随着约束条件的增加而增加"的观点有些矛盾。我很同意这一点。我认为在操作、思考涌现理论和 OT 的最大的不同是：涌现理论关注表层形式是什么；而 OT 关注的是，我是否想到了 Gen（生成器）能做的或我需要做的一切，或者我能想到的一些数据是否会给我带来问题。

---

① Archangeli D. 2017. Assamese vowels: the role of the linguist. *ICU Working Papers in Linguistics*: 21-28.

　　Archangeli D, Pulleyblank D. 2018. Emergent phonology illustrated: Malagasy alternations. *McGill Working Papers in Linguistics*, 25.1: 1-10.

问题 3：我对您刚才提到的学习者或者语言习得的内容很感兴趣。那么是否有可能用涌现模型分析第二语言习得系统呢？当您谈到学习者时，我认为我得到了一个特别的学习模型，那么涌现模型是一种特别的学习模型吗？

A：你所关注的是第二语言习得，即我们能不能使用相似的模型来谈论第二语言习得。我认为是可以的。我认为它是一件非常有趣的事情，它提供了一种解释类似年龄效应的方式，即随着年龄的增长，学习另一种语言变得越来越难。部分原因是当我们学习一门新语言时，我们必须承受已经知道的所有语言的压力。如果你观察频率，你会发现第二语言习得过程中的操练频率可能远低于母语的使用频率。这将是使我们更难熟练掌握第二语言的原因之一。

问题 4：也许我可以用涌现理论去分析、解释第二语言习得的系统，因为有些人认为第二语言的学习是一个动态系统，这也是第二语言习得研究没有独立系统的原因。二语习得研究者总是说这可能是受到了第一语言或者其他方面的影响，但是有些人提到也许存在中介语系统或者其他的东西。你觉得是这样吗？

A：是的。所以我认为就涌现模型而言，这将是一个非常有趣的问题。因为即使对单语者而言，涌现模型也是一个动态系统。因为在你的一生中，你会接收越来越多的语言数据。现在你接收的语言数据越多，高频出现的词项就越多。因此，如果语言数据的输入越来越多，你拥有的词项数量也越来越多。但是，如果你开始输入第二语言，则学习者必须弄清楚如何将第一语言与第二语言分开以及如何发音。如果你一直学习的是一种语言，且你正在尝试学习其他语言，那么你已经学到的语言都会与你正在尝试学习的其他语言的新系统相抗衡。有证据表明，多语者在使用其他语言时的表现会更好，这可能是因为（在其所习得的语言中）没有一种语言的使用频率和其他语言一样高。我不太确信，这都是推测。但我认为它确实提供了一个模型，其中包括你提到的动态目标——语言如何在我们的生活中不断变化，无论是一种还是多种变化。

© 2022 北京语言大学出版社，社图号 22170

图书在版编目（CIP）数据

韵律语法研究．第九辑／冯胜利，马秋武主编．——
北京：北京语言大学出版社，2022.12
ISBN 978-7-5619-6224-4

Ⅰ．①韵… Ⅱ．①冯… ②马… Ⅲ．①汉语－韵律（语
言）－研究 Ⅳ．① H11

中国国家版本馆 CIP 数据核字（2023）第 014336 号

韵律语法研究·第九辑
YUNLÜ YUFA YANJIU · DI-JIU JI

排版制作：北京创艺涵文化发展有限公司
责任印制：周　燚

出版发行：北京语言大学出版社
社　　址：北京市海淀区学院路 15 号，100083
网　　址：www.blcup.com
电子信箱：service@blcup.com
电　　话：编 辑 部　8610-82300207
　　　　　国内发行　8610-82303650/3591/3648
　　　　　海外发行　8610-82303365/3080/3668
　　　　　北语书店　8610-82303653
　　　　　网购咨询　8610-82303908
印　　刷：北京鑫丰华彩印有限公司

版　　次：2022 年 12 月第 1 版　　印　　次：2022 年 12 月第 1 次印刷
开　　本：789 毫米 × 1092 毫米　1/16　　印　　张：14.5
字　　数：296 千字
定　　价：69.00 元

PRINTED IN CHINA

凡有印装质量问题，本社负责调换。售后 QQ 号 1367565611，电话 010-82303590